Yogini Magic

Some Other Titles from Falcon Press

Denny Sargent
Naga Magick: The Wisdom of the Serpent Lords

Christopher S. Hyatt, Ph.D.
Undoing Yourself with Energized Meditation and Other Devices
To Lie Is Human: Not Getting Caught Is Divine
Secrets of Western Tantra: The Sexuality of the Middle Path
Hard Zen, Soft Heart

Christopher S. Hyatt, Ph.D. with contributions by
   Wm. S. Burroughs, Timothy Leary, Robert Anton Wilson et al.
Rebels & Devils: The Psychology of Liberation

Christopher S. Hyatt, Ph.D. & Antero Alli
A Modern Shaman's Guide to a Pregnant Universe

S. Jason Black and Christopher S. Hyatt, Ph.D.
Pacts with the Devil: A Chronicle of Sex, Blasphemy & Liberation
Urban Voodoo: A Beginner's Guide to Afro-Caribbean Magic

Antero Alli
Angel Tech: A Modern Shaman's Guide to Reality Selection
Angel Tech Talk (audio)

Peter J. Carroll
The Chaos Magick Audios
PsyberMagick

Phil Hine
Condensed Chaos: An Introduction to Chaos Magic
Prime Chaos: Adventures in Chaos Magic
The Pseudonomicon

Joseph Lisiewski, Ph.D.
Ceremonial Magic and the Power of Evocation
Kabbalistic Cycles and the Mastery of Life
Kabbalistic Handbook for the Practicing Magician

Israel Regardie
The Complete Golden Dawn System of Magic
The Golden Dawn Audios
The World of Enochian Magic (audio)

Steven Heller
Monsters & Magical Sticks: There's No Such Thing As Hypnosis?

For up-to-the-minute information on prices and availability,
please visit our website at
http://originalfalcon.com

Yogini Magic

The Sorcery, Enchantment and Witchcraft of the Divine Feminine

by

Gregory Peters

Foreword by
Phil Hine

THE *Original* FALCON PRESS

TEMPE, ARIZONA, U.S.A.

International Standard Book Number: 978-1-61869-725-7
ISBN: 978-1-61869-726-4 (mobi)
ISBN: 978-1-61869-727-1 (ePub)
Library of Congress Control Number: 2022944708

First Edition 2022
First eBook Edition 2022

Cover by Kat Lunoe
Original Illustrations by Kat Lunoe
Photos by Gregory Peters and commons.wikimedia.org

The paper used in this publication meets the minimum requirements of the American National Standard for Permanence of Paper for Printed Library Materials Z39.48-1984

Address all inquiries to:
The Original Falcon Press
1753 East Broadway Road #101-277
Tempe, AZ 85282 U.S.A.

(or)
PO Box 3540
Silver Springs NV 89429 U.S.A.

website: http://www.originalfalcon.com
email: info@originalfalcon.com

Table of Contents

Dedication

To that Great Goddess Kalika
And to Her Yoginis
May this Offering be Accepted
And Spread your influence
in All the directions of Space!

Acknowledgements

Respect and gratitude to all of my teachers: past, present and future!

I want to express my deepest thanks to the great Dzogchen master Chogyal Namkhai Norbu, who brought me into the pristine clarity of the nature of mind, the radiance of non-dual Awareness. This book would not have been possible without the encouragement and help of many friends, family and colleagues. Special thanks to Phil Hine, who not only wrote the Foreword, but also read early drafts, providing essential feedback and suggestions, as well as additional research material. Many thanks to Michael Staley, who read through the typescript, offering his invaluable suggestions and depth of knowledge. Thank you to John Power, who has been a constant encouragement, and who has deep experience with pagan and tantric traditions. I also want to thank "Mad Mike" Magee, whose decades of work translating Hindu tantras has been an invaluable help over the years. Thank you to Charlotte Moore for reading early drafts and giving important suggestions, and to Suzanne Davenport, for providing helpful insights. Special mention to Chandana *(kapow!)* for encouraging me to reach into my heart, and write something other than a dry technical manual.

Many thanks to Nicholas Tharcher and the publishing team at The Original Falcon Press for enthusiastically embracing this project, tirelessly editing the manuscript, and somehow still managing to keep a keen sense of humor. Some of the first writings on spiritual transformation I ever read were published by these folks, leaving profound impressions on me—it is an honor to join their ranks!

There are several fantastic original illustrations in this book, and a truly stunning cover, all by the hand of the artist Kat Lunoe. Kat's ability to bring images to life is a magical gift; I hope to have many more opportunities to work with her in the future.

Living with a writer is not easy; living with *yours truly* is quite possibly the ultimate test of patience. Often a source of questionable entertainment or frequent irritation, with the odd and long hours of solitude, strange ritual habits (like blasting cacophonous music while drinking far too many cups of coffee for hours on end), ranting about Yoginis day and night, spontaneous laughing and weeping, wandering in forests, strange and seemingly random requests ("You want me to do *what?!")* all make for an endless and dizzying ride. With that in mind, I want to give special thanks to my beloved Natasha, *meri rani.* Your love, encouragement, and enthusiasm, especially during the last year of intense research, writing and editing, has been a blessing. That mischievous smile and firecracker energy are what keep me going. None of this would be possible without you.

Despite the suggestions and assistance from this distinguished group, its likely I have still managed to persist in writing errors, for which I am solely responsible.

Jai Bhavani!

Foreword
by Phil Hine

I am greatly honoured to present Gregory Peters' new book *Yogini Magic.* Here you will find a new world opening to you—the world of the *Yoginis,* the independent horde of female divinities worshipped, feared and honoured in the Tantric traditions of South Asia. Gregory draws on his own experience of long practice with the Yoginis, and has eloquently combined his down-to-earth advice and recommendations for how a modern practitioner might go about forming and nurturing a relationship with Yoginis—for enjoyment, magical abilities, knowledge and liberation.

Gregory has successfully tackled the difficult task of providing modern Western practitioners with a variety of avenues to understand and approach Yoginis, whilst retaining the spirit of the Tantric traditions out of which the magic of the Yoginis unfolded. He has assembled a wide variety of pathways for discovering the Yoginis—through dream, devotion, meditation and deepening our awareness of the everyday world. He has skillfully brought together the practical application of *mantra* recitation and *nyasa*—the installation of divine energies into various parts of the body, with more familiar techniques such as the creation of sigils. Gregory has also made use of a novel system of eight *chakras* from a tantric text—the *Kaulajnananirnaya* ("discussion of knowledge of the *Kaulas*")—which is focused on the placement and experience of the Yoginis within the body of the practitioner. Much of the Yogini practice Gregory has chosen is centred around the goddess Kali who is one of the most well-known and instantly recognisable of the pan-Indian deities. In the tantric traditions Kali is the supreme goddess—she not only creates the world, but she *is* the world, present everywhere, yet remaining unknown and secret. Kali is the supreme essence, residing in the heart of all living beings.

I particularly like the fact that Gregory has avoided the tendency—all too common in some approaches to magical practice—to be overly prescriptive. Instead, he encourages us to take the exercises and rituals as jumping-off points for our own experimentation. He also emphasizes the importance of rooting one's magic in the everyday world, and in seeking wonder and delight in nature and our day-to-day existence, which is a central concept in the non-dual schools of Tantra. Above all though, his deep love and respect for the Yoginis shines through on every page, as he enthusiastically invites us to join him in discovering the beauty and delight that the Yoginis represent, as divine powers within and around us.

Although the exact origins of Yoginis are obscure, it is generally agreed by scholars that their worship emerged out of the Saiva Tantric tradition, and from there spread into Tantric Buddhism, Vaishnavism, the Jain religion, and even Islamic mysticism. One of the features of the Saiva tradition that made it so successful was its inclusivity—many local deities were incorporated into Saiva ritual procedures, both secret and public. It was also open (at least in principle) to all, regardless of caste, gender or origin, demanding only devotion to Siva. The *Sivadharmasastra* says: "Even a foreigner *(mleccha),* in whom this eightfold devotion exists, is equal to the foremost of learned Brahmins, a glorious sage, an ascetic and a scholar."

The worship of Yoginis may have grown out of the incorporation of other female divine beings and spirits—the tree-dwelling *Yaksinis,* the celestial *apsaras,* the possession-inducing *grahas,* and in particular, groups of mother goddesses—into Saiva esoteric and public worship. There is considerable evidence, for example, for the worship of "mother goddesses" dating from the 1st century of the common era. By the 5th century, a group of seven goddesses emerge who are the female counterparts of principal male deities, bearing names such as Brahmi, Mahesvari, or Yami. The exception is the leader of the seven mothers—Camunda, a fierce, skeletal goddess who has no male counterpart. As the Saiva Tantric tradition grew in prominence and popularity, these seven mother goddesses became the leaders of clans of Yoginis, the latter considered emanations of the powers of the mothers, with an eighth goddess frequently added to the group.

Yoginis do not feature in the earliest texts of the Saiva Tradition, which date from around the 5th century, although these texts do mention the worship of mother goddesses and the *saktis* (powers of Siva personified as female). But as the tradition diversified, and became more goddess-oriented, Yoginis began to appear. By the 6th–8th centuries, Yoginis are depicted as fearsome, blood-drinking creatures, inhabiting wild places, demanding sacrifices of blood and flesh. Their ritual worship frequently required an array of magical objects fashioned from corpses, and a prolonged stay in a cremation ground— rituals that could be performed by only the most heroic practitioners (or at least those with a strong stomach). These rites were considered dangerous even to advanced practitioners. The *Brahmayamala* for example, warns that "If by mistake a *sadhaka* (practitioner) of weak spirit should tremble, the Yoginis, arrogant with their yoga, devour him that very moment."

The fierce, warlike nature of the Yoginis meant that they were frequently worshipped by royalty, and invoked to ensure success in warfare and protection of a kingdom. There is also some evidence suggesting that they were thought to follow warriors into battle, feasting on the bodies of the fallen and drinking the blood of the dying.

In the later *Kaula* traditions of the 10th century onwards, the sanguinary nature of the Yoginis softens somewhat, and they become identified with the body's capacities, as expressions of the senses, of delight and wonder, worshipped by offerings of the practitioners' own experiences, rather than his or her own flesh and blood. It is in these later traditions that the Yoginis come to reside in the body *chakras* as expressions of bliss and power. These later reconfigurations of Yoginis, in contrast to the rather bloodthirsty rites of their early worship, were a key factor in opening up their worship to ordinary householders, rather than ascetic practitioners.

To enter the world of the Yoginis means that we must embrace seeming contradictions and be ready for surprises. As Gregory says, it is unclear sometimes whether the Yoginis are human, supernatural or divine in nature. Their protean quality is in keeping with their powers of shape-shifting, enchantment and illusion.

With the exercises and rituals in this book, you will discover that Yoginis permeate and radiate throughout the entire cosmos; their forms emerging from trees and plants; wheeling across the sky as flocks of birds; a glimpse of mystery in a chance meeting or the smile of a stranger. You can make offerings to them in daily ritual or with your own sensory and sensuous experience. You may experience them in your body as the centres of the flaming energies of your *chakras*. You can feel their presence in those places which feel sacred to you, or close to your heart.

The Tantric texts tell us that the Yoginis are an innumerable horde—and whilst some Yoginis became immensely popular, achieving the status of goddesses in their own right, there are many others waiting to be discovered through ritual, dream or insight. Perhaps, as you try the exercises and rituals in *Yogini Magic,* you will discover your own Yoginis, unique to your own circumstances and needs.

Prologue: Wild Awareness

"He is always in a blissful state, conscious of his oneness with Bhairava and Shiva. It is very difficult for anyone to know his true nature. When alone he is like one mad, dumb, or paralysed and when in the society of men, he sometimes behaves like a good man, sometimes like a wicked one; and on occasions he behaves like a demon. But the Yogi is always pure whatever he may do and by his touch everything becomes pure. [...] There is for him no other worship, no vows and the like, as he is conscious that he is always complete in himself."
— *Kaulavalinirnaya Tantra*

Forests, wilderness, mountains. The wind and trees. Lightning, rain and thunder. Coyotes howling, owls hooting. The crunchy sound of the forest from the footsteps of the animals walking through the grass and fallen leaves. The sounds of water running over small rocks and twigs in bubbling brooks and rivers. Nature is magnificent, relentless and humbling. After a cold and dark night in the woods, those first glimpses of the sun rising above the horizon are a welcome sight, and the warmth makes you realize why the Sun and Moon have held such important roles in our lives, and those of our ancestors, for millennia.

The Goddess walks amongst us always. In every activity, in every sight. It is a hunt, a game, a rambling adventure. Our experience of nature is in many ways a reflection of the experience of our inner mind. Being lost in thought, like falling into the relentless current of a river, or being caught up in anxiety like a rip tide just off the shore. Being in the wilderness, in the elements unprepared, will have long-lasting and possibly devastating results; similarly, approaching the spirits of the forests and mountains may bring fortune or disaster.

This book is about finding glimpses of reality when not seated on the meditation cushion. About finding that wild, unbridled and unbound nature that is the truth of self, the core of reality that has no bounds, and from which the entire experience of reality comes—the

15

ever-birthing nature of the universe of which we are all conscious agents.

This is the path of the yogi magician, the *tantrika,* the tantrik practitioner of modern times, living in the cities and suburbs, moving hidden amidst the dreaming populations. With mind and heart open to the spirits, the voices of the elements are heard and felt even in the clamor of modern cities. This is a path of witchcraft, of sorcery and enchantment, where your awareness opens to the rich and populated world of spirits in the world.

This is my tale of tantrik awareness, the experience of several decades practice with tantra and Western esotericism. This is the experience of our daily life in the continuum of consciousness, the dance of *Lalita* ("She Who Plays") as she continuously eludes our direct perception. Yet with persistence and openness, out of the corner of your eye or in the glimpse of another's, there she will be smiling and laughing, untouched by creation and yet continuously creating our entire reality.

Central to this book are the *Yoginis,* often depicted as extremely beautiful, voluptuous female spirits, with both human and sometimes non-human heads. These shapeshifting beings are manifold, appearing throughout history and across cultures under many different guises. Many of the Yoginis are associated with the great goddesses of tantrik traditions, and are called by a variety of names and titles (for example, the 15 *Nityas* of Kali, the *Bhairavis* that are part of the retinue of Lalita Tripurasundari, or the Kriya Yoginis, also associated with Kali). There are countless classes of these beings in the tantrik texts of both Hindu and Buddhist traditions.

The Yoginis are associated with witchcraft, the vital magic of the crossroads, and the liminal space between worlds. These powerful, mighty beings bring great fortune to those that they favor, be it internal realizations or external worldly treasures. They are formidable, relentless and fiercely feminine in nature. These goddesses are at the very core of *shakti* (the divine feminine power of the Gods).

As powerful witches and sorceresses, the Yoginis are adepts of magic and non-dual realization. They initiate their chosen into their ancient lineages of sorcery, revealing the mysteries of their magic. They are the revealers of the science of Yoga, and increase the power and ability of human Yoginis. The Yoginis are treasure revealers, showing those that work with them the buried hoards that are hidden in plain sight, in consciousness itself. Through their magic, possession and dreams, the practitioner that approaches the Yoginis has an opportunity for countless benefits in the form of spiritual attainment and magical powers.

While the rewards of having contact with the Yoginis are plentiful, such interactions do come with a price. The responsibilities of entering into a relationship with them is not something to be taken lightly, as to cross a nature goddess or incite their jealousy has serious repercussions. In the same way that hiking into the wilderness without the right gear, some water, and directions can lead to disaster. Nature is wild and unpredictable, despite what the modern world may think about its false notion of "controlling" or "conquering" nature. Similarly, the Yoginis dance freely and wildly in the sky of our consciousness, the vast open skies of the mind. Nature and consciousness are their realms.

In this book I will discuss primarily the *Chausath* (Sixty-Four) *Yoginis,* and give detailed guidance on how to work with them directly. These goddesses are associated with sorcery, and the acquisition of *siddhis* (magical powers). Even more importantly, working with the Yoginis will open you to the non-dual experience of Reality —the very nature of pristine awareness.

My approach tends to have a strong element of *bhakti* (love and devotion), for these goddesses. This is not the norm for tantra, which more commonly is filled with details on strict ritual requirements and rules. Instead, most of my work tends to be based on a foundation that, if the Yoginis are approached with the respect, love and awe which naturally surrounds them, they respond in kind. This is certainly true of the Goddess herself, of which the Yoginis may be thought of as both emanations of, and attendants, too.

The Yoginis embody a wild awareness. Wild because the nature of our experience is wild, unpredictable, untamed. The minute you sit down to meditate you will notice that your mind is filled with discursive thoughts, lost in one day-dream to another. Trying to hold a thought, to concentrate on any one thing, quickly dissolves into a 20-minute reverie about what you had for breakfast, what you want to accomplish, what you are worried about, and so on. Not to mention thoughts like "Am I done yet?" "Am I meditating now?" "My back hurts," and more.

Wild is also the natural world. The forests, mountain wildernesses, the open sky, the wind blowing through your hair, rainfall. These are natural, energetic, unmanaged experiences of the world. Nature is both beautiful and dangerous, wild and unpredictable.

All of this is true of the Yoginis, perhaps more so. Wild describes the very nature of the Sky Dancers. These female goddesses are unpredictable, passionate and ecstatic. Approaching them can be like being dropped into the Lion's den of inner landscapes, where your very ego is the main course. Wild is also the landscape where the Yoginis temples were built in India, always in remote, difficult to reach locations, at the summit of some distant hill in a wilderness far from large cities.

Yoginis may reveal treasures, both inner and outer. Establishing a relationship with them has the potential to open up spiritual realization, profound states of mind and awareness. At the same time, more practical needs may be addressed. This is the work of magic and sorcery, where the Yoginis are petitioned to achieve various aims and the attainment of the *siddhis* (magical powers).

As with all relationships, there is give and take. Establishing a relationship with these fierce beings is nothing to take casually. Once a promise is made, or an offering given, that must be honored. With these transactional types of arrangements, it is usually best to define ahead of time what it is you want to achieve, and to approach with offerings and a clear request. If you are only willing to pay a specific price in the way of offerings for set period of time, be certain to bring this to the negotiations. Once accepted, do not back away or be in any way remiss with your promise. At the same time, these beings are very much alive, with personalities of their own. Each must be given the respect they are due, and you would be wise to get to know them and develop a relationship, rather than attempting to limit your interactions to a casual transaction! Depending on their mood and your approach, you might just end up on their dinner table.

For works of non-dual realization, as well as those of pure *bhakti,* you might find yourself approaching a Yogini out of pure love. In such cases it is enough to give offerings with love and an open heart, asking nothing in return. If you truly love someone, there is no sense of getting something back. The love comes naturally and flows out without thought. Why should it be any different if the object of that love is a spiritual being? In my experience, there is no difference. Love is the foundation of working with them.

Over the years I have come to appreciate nature more and more, and the desire to incorporate meditation and ritual work outside developed naturally as a result of this. Given the choice, I would much rather be hiking in a forest, trekking up a mountain, or exploring a jungle than being in a man-made temple, no matter how impressive said temple may be. Give me the open skies and alpine air rather than air conditioning and a roof. A lot of this preference has fed into my work with the Yoginis, and the development from rituals to a more creative, spontaneous approach.

The temples of the sixty-four Yoginis are expressions of wild, unpredictable nature. Circular stone temples in remote locations, with no ceiling. Unique among the structures of India, the Yogini temples are open to the sky. Like other circular ritual structures around the world, they demarcate a separate reality. To enter into the circle is to pass from the mundane into a sacred space, a liminal region where space and time may not be the same there as here. It is in these living mandalas that the Yoginis descend from the night sky to participate in their ritual circles.

In this book I will describe the ways that I have come to work with the Yoginis, and how to incorporate natural surroundings and dreamwork to help establish these connections. My experience is far from conventional, and may go against much of what you have heard or learned from other sources. While I draw inspiration from many traditions, the approach is solely a personal one incorporating my experience over the years. The non-dual view of Dzogchen has given the ground of all the work. My experience as a tantrika of several traditions, together with Kriya Yoga and a deep meditation practice, has provided a strong framework. With these decidedly Eastern traditions is woven a thread of Western esotericism and witchcraft, a pagan point of view that works with these incredible forces of the divine for spellcraft and illumination.

I would rather this book were some incredible piece of art—a set of paintings with rich colors and so many layers of texture that one could never tire of looking at it, and always find something new. Or a sculpture, the likes of which the great masters of Italy could only dream. Or a piece of music that you could listen to endlessly, never tiring of and always thrilling deep down in your bones when you hear it. Maybe this book should have been a long hike in the woods at twilight, or the slow progress up a mountain in Nepal or India, where the landscape is full of rich and diverse trees and flowers, fresh air, majestic snowcapped mountains and a sky all of stars. The repeated inner prompting from the Yoginis led me to write this book.

Words are truly inadequate, and I feel that even in the hands of a great writer, it would be challenging if not outright impossible to truly express what the inner truth of experiencing the Yoginis is. Still, my heart overflows at the very thought of them, and so I have tried to take down what I can and make it available to others.

For whatever reason, I am touched by them and find complete, utter devotion in working with them. My heart is filled with *bhakti*—pure love—for the Goddess and her retinue of Yoginis.

I readily defer to women on this subject. Real women in the world, in literature, in history. The physical embodiment of the Goddess, walking in flesh and blood on this earth. Throughout my life, it has been women that have given me the true instruction. Not necessarily by quoting tantras or scholarly studies, although women have absolutely contributed largely to these areas. Entire tantrik lineages have descended along female lines. I offer my deepest, heartfelt respect to the living breathing lineages of the Yoginis. Jai Devi! ("Victory to the Goddess!")

In my experience, it is the chance comment or look from a friend, family or strangers that has been received at the right place and time, feeding in to the ever-living and ongoing stream of initiation that has directed me. Maybe a book I needed to read would be mentioned. Maybe a friend would make an offhand comment about a guru figure or a teaching, that would unbeknown to her cut through layers of delusion in my mind and bring me right to the center. Maybe a chance smile or sidelong glance from the eyes of a stranger would be a sign at the right place and time. And often, just the sound of tree branches swaying in the breeze, or seeing cloud formations slowly drifting through the sky, or faces and figures in the trees, or the way the rain would fall, or the stars would radiate, and the sounds of the owls would carry on the wind.... We are surrounded, immersed, living in her. With every breath we take her in. With every sensation we experience her. She is everywhere.

A woman is, by her very nature, the living embodiment of the Goddess and her *shaktis* (powers). As the tantras state over and over again, women are sacred because they are the earthly embodiment of the Goddess:

Yoni Tantra:

> *"Women are divinity, women are life, women are truly jewels. Women are heaven; women are dharma, and women are the highest penance. Women are Buddha; women are the Sangha; and women are the perfection of Wisdom."*

Kaulajnananirnaya:

> *"Worship carefully a woman or maiden as she is Shakti, sheltered by the Kulas. One should never speak harshly to maidens or women. One who has taken shelter in the Kula should always worship women and maidens totally since they are Shakti."*

In India there is a long tradition of women manifesting the Goddess directly, either willfully or becoming possessed by the Goddess and her emanations. A woman working with the techniques outlined in this book may find that it helps to awaken that divine energy which is already embodied, but perhaps not fully conscious. Working with the Yoginis, she may awaken latent powers or realizations, even directly manifesting the power of the Yoginis.

What comes naturally to a woman working with the Yoginis, will be forever alien to me, or at least require a lot of work to get started. To the path of the embodied Yogini, I am but a spectator and a worshipper. I sincerely offer my approach, and my deepest respect and adoration to the many women who are attuned to the Yoginis on this earth. May they see fit to bless us all with their embodied wisdom. If anything, perhaps reading this book from a male devotee will inspire women to rise up and show us all the deepest truth of the Yoginis. May Shakti radiate and show us the way!

My work with the Yoginis can be broadly categorized into two major types of approach: one is worship—*bhakti* type devotion—the inviting of the Yogini to you. However, this is not the forceful evoca- tion of Western magic, but rather more an appeal, asking the Yogini to come and be present. With offerings of food, drink, light and scents, you invite them into your circle to partake and exchange energy.

The other approach is full integration—of inviting the Yogini to enter into your consciousness and body, to experience the world through your senses, and to let you experience through theirs. This is full-on possession, and should be treated carefully and with respect, as with all the practices.

Meditation, awareness of the environment and nature, intuition, dreamwork, inspiration—all of these are the most important tools in this work. In fact, I work with natural landscapes and the night sky far more than with Western forms of ceremonial or *puja* (formal ritual worship).

It is my hope that by sharing some of my own experience and prac- tices, you will be led to union with the Yoginis, develop your powers of intuition and sorcery, enchant your life with magical, dream-infused vibrancy, and ultimately, experience Self-Realization as you experience non-dual Awareness, awakening from the dream of separation. This world is alive, and it is Shakti.

The Yoginis are extremely responsive and powerful. While the *Kaulajnananirnaya* outlines methods of external worship, as Stella Dupuis states in her commentary to the text, "The main worship lies in the spiritual practice of going inwards, to the *chakras* where the *Yoginis* (energies) dwell. If one finds them, they are eager to bestow boons, i.e., to give the *siddhis*. 'One who meditates on them becomes immediately equal to them.' "[1]

> *To those eternal Yoginis by whose glory*
> *The three worlds have been established,*
> *To them I bow down, to them I pray.*
>
> — *Kularnava Tantra, 8:50*

— Gregory Peters
Sierra Nevada Foothills and Mojave Desert, 2021

---

[1] Stella Dupuis & Satkari Mukhopadyaya, *The Kaulajnananirnaya.*

Introduction

I love being outside. In my childhood, I was often alone outside in nature, listening to the rustle of leaves in the wind, or watching the clouds take on shapes and then disappear into the sky Whenever it would rain, I wanted to sit and listen to it and smell the difference in the air that it made. My favorite days were rain days. The world was enveloped in a quieter, more protected, dreamlike quality, and at the same time the atmosphere would feel charged such that anything could happen.

Grassy fields and tall trees were plentiful in the town I grew up in. There were plenty of oak and redwood trees lining the streets and parks. The schools had large fields of green grass, and often the perimeter of the fields was lined with oaks or large pines.

Something about being with nature always felt like really being home. I was more at home alone and wandering amidst the trees than I was with friends. At these times, I never really felt alone. There was always a welcoming, inviting presence.

When I was with friends or at school, I was always the one singled out as being the weird one; sitting alone at recess staring at the clouds and listening to the wind instead of playing or running around yelling. For me there was always a sense of mystery in the world—to which everyone else seemed oblivious.

Trees! What amazing things they are. I would stare at trees, feel their bark, smell their scent. Always fascinated by the sound of the wind rustling their leaves and making the branches creak and sway. They were alive and communicating! The trees and the air, the sunlight and scents, the clouds over head...all of nature was alive and constantly composing a symphony of the senses. As a child it seemed like I was the only one noticing any of this. My friends were too preoccupied with the usual activities, and the adults all seemed too busy or distracted to notice anything.

This feeling of the world being alive and present was not limited to just forests, groves and mountains. The ocean always held a powerful and majestic pull over me as well. For many years I lived near the ocean, enjoying the sound of the waves crashing, especially during rains. During big storms I would throw open the front door and just let the sound of the howling winds and rain blow in, with the constant and relentless roar of the waves. These were such intense, magical times with the atmosphere crackling with electricity and every cell of my body feeling invigorated and awake.

Later in life I would take up hiking and camping. The impulse to be alone and in nature has never left. I am most at home—and most awake—in the middle of a forest or hiking up a mountain pass, the wide skies open before me and the crisp air invigorating my body.

There is also something of an ordeal in being alone in the wild. Being caught out in the elements without the ability to make a fire, or have shelter that is fit for the environment, can quickly turn from being unpleasant to outright dangerous. You have to plan out your food, your clothing, your gear ahead of time.

At night is when things get very interesting. Yes, alone at night underneath that vast canopy of stars, with only the sounds of the trees and unidentified animals coming by, is an amazing, humbling experience. At the same time, it can be extremely terrifying! The mind can easily get carried away wondering what that sound was. Is it something big? Something dangerous? Human? For me, the most frightening sound out in the wilderness at night has always been the apparent sound of human footsteps.

It is during these solitary escapades in the wild that I am most able to relax and open up to the expanse of consciousness. During these times, the connection with the natural world is easy to experience, and the sense of self is more easily seen for what it is—an illusion. Nature is alive and vibrant, and consciousness remains, shining pristine and clear. In the wild, you are Awake. Outside in nature, it is easy to feel the divine.

This natural spirituality, a recognition of the divine when simply alone in nature, or underneath the stars and contemplating the vastness of space, arose spontaneously. It was never something I consciously tried to cultivate; it was just part of who I am and how I express myself.

In my 20's I was seeking answers. Being something of an outsider, while peers were going to bars and partying, I found myself wanting answers about the nature of reality. I dug into the subject of spirituality, reading everything I could find. Something that stood out in all of this material was the Eastern influence, which resonated deeply. Tantra, both Hindu and Buddhist, felt natural to me.

As the years went on, a lot of transformation that was brewing under the surface suddenly erupted outwards. With a lot of changes happening in my personal life, I knew I needed to take some time to reassess the direction of my life. A dear friend who shared my love of hiking and nature suggested that I take a solo trip to Nepal, to go trekking in the Himalayas. Not needing to be convinced, I bought a plane ticket to Kathmandu, packed my bags and took a month off from work. The sheer spontaneity of the decision was liberating, and the freedom in just flying off to this exotic destination with almost no planning was absolutely thrilling!

It was early September, just the tail end of the monsoon season. I was on my way to Everest Base Camp in the Himalayan mountain range. *Crunch, Crunch, Crunch.* The sound my boots were making as I slowly made my way through the thick forest path. The ground was covered with pine needles, small rocks, and of course, earth. Every step made that satisfying sound. At this altitude the air was crisp and full of the scents from the trees. The only sounds were of my boots on the ground, my breathing, and the wind blowing gently through the majestic trees. The first few days the landscape was lush with pine trees and waterfalls, dotted with Buddhist *stupas* (a type of oblong shrine, usually containing sacred relics) and the occasional *gompa* (Buddhist temple).

As the days go by and the altitude increases, the landscape begins to shift. At around 13,000 feet (4,000 meters) we are in rocky territory, surrounded by clouds. The forests of rhododendrons and magnolias have given way to rocks and sparse clusters of junipers, while in the distance are the sacred peaks of Lhotse, Nuptse, Ama Dablan, Kantega and Cho-Oyu. Far below runs the Dudh Koshi ("milk river"). In the small village of Macchermo, stories of the Yeti are still told, and I hear about the time in 1971 when three yaks were killed and partially eaten, and a young Sherpa girl was injured fighting off the hairy ape-like creature that terrorized the villagers, only to retreat once again into the mountains.

While hiking I took it upon myself to mentally perform *japa* (recitation) of a *mantra* of the Goddess Kali. By Kala Patthar ("Black Rock"), just north of the small village of Gorakshep, the altitude was over 18,000 feet (5500 meters). Trying to coordinate *mantra* with my (now labored) breathing, and the plodding of my feet up the mountain range paths, all while trying not to get knocked off the cliff by the occasional yak strolling down the mountains, made for protracted concentration and a flow state that persisted for hours at a time. It was here that *She* appeared.

Tunnel vision, as everything quickly became dark, then a sense of vertigo and stumbling, enveloped in redness and her face right in front of me, black hair flowing, dark eyes like the starry sky burning bright into my own, her blissful face smiling. I could see her lips moving, feel her breath, see and feel her long black hair flowing all around me. I could even *smell* her, the scent of flowers and incense. She took her left hand and reached into my skull, pulling closer and right in front of my face. Her voice in my head with her singsong sound *KRIM*. Then bright light and the mountains and sky and clouds all vivid and alive, pulsating with life. There was no difference between me and the mountains, or the clouds or sky. There was no me, there was only the world—no difference.

I quickly sat down on the side of the trail. My body erupted into a feeling of great bliss, not unlike the best orgasm you can imagine. Like warm, glowing honey dripping all over me, the cells awake and dancing in the sensations. It lasted perhaps a minute, and as I sat my brain reassembled quickly, with a headache. The dizziness was gone, although the tingling feeling inside my body continued, warmth flowing through my veins. The sound of the wind blowing through the mountain ranges seemed unusually loud, and the feeling on my skin was exquisite. My body felt good, alive. The rational mind kicked in and immediately started to justify it all as altitude sickness, hyperventilation, sleep deprivation. I rested for a few minutes, drank water and ate some trail mix before I felt steady enough to carry on.

That day, whenever I paused for a moment and closed my eyes, *Her* face and scent were there. Her black eyes, open to infinity, stared deep into my own, and her long, black hair flowed towards me. I felt an almost electric shock every time, and my body would have a spasm like the muscle movements after an intense, full-body orgasm. The feeling of my blood being transformed into a golden liquid would come, and I would feel blissful. This was the beginning of a continuous undercurrent of bliss that even now returns, underneath all experience.

After trekking for a few weeks, the descent back down to Kathmandu was fairly rapid. I spent a few days exploring around the city. The small shops were full of statues of Buddhas and Bodhisattvas, *malas* of various stones and beads, and of course, Tibetan singing bells and other ritual items. I walked into one shop and saw high up on a shelf a small brass statue of Kali. She almost looked like she was winking at me, and her face and entire composition was beautiful and blissful. I took her home and to this day she is the centerpiece of my altar.

It was the time of the Indra Jatra festival in Kathmandu, so all of the Bhairava (an esoteric and fierce form of the God Shiva) shrines were opened up, people were making offerings constantly, there were ritual dancers in the streets dressed up in costume, and the Kumari even made an appearance. All in all, a magical time, and throughout it all I felt like the Goddess was with me, especially any time I closed my eyes and looked inside. It felt like she had taken up residence inside my heart. From that day until the present, I have felt a strong relationship with Kali, something that is precious and to be nurtured.

Nepal is a truly magical place. In Kathmandu on the sacred banks of the Baghmati river you will find the great temple of Pashupatinath, a major Hindu temple dedicated to Shiva as the Lord of Beasts. This is also the site of many smaller shrines and sacred spots clustered around the temple.

There is a constant stream of sweet-smelling smoke surrounding the banks of the river and the temples, as the cremation *ghats* are located here. At the *ghats* are countless throngs of people, relatives coming to perform the last rites for their loved ones. As the bodies are burned, the ashes and any remains are poured into the river, a relentless stream of smoke, ash, bones and water. Within the precincts of the main temple grounds wealthier families are cremated, often on richly adorned biers, with the corpses dressed in fine clothing as they are sent off on the final great journey. Walking along the *ghats* outside of the main grounds, the poorer families are also having their funeral rites, although these are much humbler affairs.

Children, often orphans, are frequently seen playing in the water of the river, just a few feet from where the ashes are being poured into the water. They are playing, splashing each other, and searching in the mud along the banks for any treasures that may wash up. Women can be seen washing their laundry as well—life and death exist closely together here.

The Cremation Ghats of Pashupatinath
(Photo by the Author)

Also, along the *ghats,* close enough to be enveloped in the smoke of the burning bodies, are tantrikas. You can find them performing ablutions in the waters, or walking along the shore trying to find useful magical items, such as bone fragments or even a human skull from which to use as a *kapala* (tantrik bowl). I spent several days and nights meditating at the cremation *ghats,* the endless clouds of smoke from the burning bodies a constant reminder of the impermanence of life and the illusory nature of self. For hours I sat in contemplation while mentally reciting the *vidya* (feminine *mantras)* of Kali, trying to make sense of the experiences I had with her up in the mountains. I felt her immediately in the cremation *ghats,* dancing and smiling, always present. Here, in this place of ever-burning bodies, was such awful beauty and bliss.

Nearby on the southern banks of the river is the 17th century Guhyeswari Temple. This is a *Shakti Pitha,* devoted to Adi Shakti, also called Guhyekali. The root *guhya* means "hidden" or "secret", and this is a secret aspect of the Goddess that is also associated with the secret 16th *bija* of the *Sodashi mantra* in Sri Vidya. This temple is a very important site for tantrikas, as Adi Shakti is the primordial goddess. When Sati self-immolated, she was transformed into Adi Shakti, and this temple embodies her presence. Guhyeswari is mentioned in several tantric texts devoted to Kali and Shiva, and is considered a central power place, second perhaps only to Kamakhya in Assam where the *yoni* of Devi is enshrined.

Another important site is Dakshinikali Temple, about 14 miles (22.5 km) outside of Kathmandu near Pharping village This is a very active temple where regular sacrifices of goats and chickens are performed to the Goddess. In addition to Kali, her *Ashta Matrikas* (8 Mothers who are emanations of the Goddess) are also enshrined and worshipped. As the temple is in the south, the form of Kali enshrined here is *Dakshina* or southward facing Kali.

In Nepal, and especially Kathmandu, one finds shrines dedicated to both Hindu and Buddhist traditions, often mixed together and worshipped by the same people. There is a strong current of Hindu and Buddhist practice throughout this region. This is not entirely surprising considering the former associations Nepal has with tantra, even having the royal patronage of the Kings and Queens of Nepal practicing tantra.

Up in the mountains it becomes decidedly more Buddhist, with many Tibetan Buddhist monasteries and wandering monks. Countless natural standing stones are dotted around the mountains, often painted in rich colors and forming *mantras* such as "Om Mani Padme Hum" ("Om, the Jewel in the Lotus"). Prayer wheels as well are frequent, as are sacred threads tied around boulders and trees. The sacredness of the place is tangible. It is easy to see how the Himalayas have been considered sacred and central to so much of Buddhist and Hindu traditions. The natural landscape is alive, and the sense of sprits in the rocks, rivers, trees and animals is profound. Mount Everest herself is a goddess, her true name being Chomolungma, the "Mother Goddess of the World".

Through these travels and explorations, my own practice and experience has developed. Like what I experienced in Nepal and India, my spiritual life is a colorful, vibrant, living blend of intense love and devotion to the Goddess, the experience of non-dual awareness, tantrik Buddhism and Hinduism, and a rich undercurrent of paganism. This is the colorful manifestation of the Goddess in the Universe; or, to put it another way, the ornamentation of the Great Goddess herself.

If you are looking for a how-to manual with step-by-step instructions, you may have to search very deeply. Also, if you are expecting to find another dry and scholarly examination of the tantras and literature that mention Yoginis, with a critical analysis of translations and texts—well, no. While I enjoy reading such material, this book is *intentionally* not that. Neither will you find much *theory* in this book. I relish the *mystery* of the Yoginis, and enjoy the nocturnal dance of their ambiguity and uncertain natures. This work brings you into the shadows to feel and experience the Yoginis directly. Metaphysical speculation can be an entertaining pastime, but here I invite you to dive deeply into your experience and leave the intellectual analysis for another time.

This book is about colors and sounds, about the intermingling of elements, and the feeling of being alone and awake. This is breathing deeply and slowly and feeling the elements.

This is the moonlight shimmering on a quiet and lonely lake, with the distant sound of an owl deep in the forest, and the crackling of the fire as you sit alone in the campsite, your heartbeat suddenly jumping as you hear the crack of twigs just outside the circle of flickering flames and wonder what animal—or person—might be approaching.

This is traveling alone to a foreign country, with an old map and a notebook, and letting yourself get lost in the streets and sounds, the people and places, and relishing every taste, sound and emotion as it arises.

This is the warmth of lovers' bodies as they grope in the dark for each other, nothing but touch and taste and scent to guide them, while the small candle on the table by the window tries to mask them in dancing shadows and hints of light.

This is feeling the center fall out, subject and object collapsing into meaningless noise as concepts disintegrate into liquid dreamscapes of shadows, the clashing of symbols, the whisper of the wind in the trees, crying tears of rain that fill the earth with life, even as the seed of death is already present in every moment.

This is a Book of Shadows for working with the Yoginis.

The Yoginis are Queens of the Night, who bring with them gifts of sorcery and enchantment. You may come to them with a desire to achieve some aim, only to find that along the way they have completely enthralled you and enlivened you beyond what you came for. Mistresses of dreams and lonely places, relentless power and complete expressions of elemental forces, they will teach you to live in the present moment, and to go deep within to retrieve hidden treasures.

I invite you to enter into this world with me, to open your eyes and heart, to breathe deeply, sit at the crossroads, and listen for the call of the Yoginis.

A Note on All the Sanskrit

Throughout this book there will be references to words in Sanskrit, and Sanskrit *mantras* are used often in the rituals. To simplify reading I have tried to use English terms directly (for example, "skull-cup" instead of *kapala),* but there are some cases where it just made more sense to use the Sanskrit word. In such cases I have tried to make sure to also reference the English meaning so that it is clear. There is also a glossary at the back of the book to cover many of the terms that may be unfamiliar, or have a special context within this book. Many of the *mantras* used in this material do not have any literal meaning whatsoever; rather, they are the Goddess in vibrational form.

With apologies to my Sanskritist colleagues, I have opted to leave out diacriticals with the words. Sanskrit is a deeply rich language, and the subtleties of the different sounds and pronunciations are a lifetime journey in itself. With such variables as region, dialect and even the era, words and *mantras* may have different pronunciations. Different traditions and lineages may emphasize one way over another, even insisting that their pronunciation is the only correct one.

For the purposes of this book, I wanted to focus on the practical usage that is accessible without having to be a Sanskrit linguist. I am interested in exploring the rich sensual experience of being in a living, vital relationship with the Yoginis. This is beyond intellectual analysis—which certainly has its place, but not in the moment of direct experience. I come back to this example a lot: when you are in love, you experience it vitally, fully, in the moment. This instant presence of experience is vital, alive, and eclipses everything else. Rather than getting too hung up on proper pronunciation, I encourage you to feel your way through unfamiliar sounds and words, and let your intuition guide you more than your linguistic expertise. One of the benefits of our Internet era is that many of these once deeply secret *mantras* are easily accessible online, and you can search on YouTube, for example, to hear different pronunciations for the *bija mantras* and other words that may be unfamiliar. As your relationship with the Yoginis deepens, let *them* guide you on how *they* want you to sing to them their names.

This is Not a Book About Tantra

At least, probably not in the way that it is commonly thought of. In the West, "tantra" is a popular buzzword equated with exotic sexual practices that may have some distant yogic connection, held at expensive retreats for couples or singles. The tantra of Western retreats may more accurately be called "sacred sex." Contrast this with modern India, where the association of the word carries a more sinister tone, a sort of "black magic." Tantrikas are often feared, as mistreating or crossing one may result in your business being cursed, or your family ruined in a multitude of ways from malignant spells being cast.

Still, neither of these definitions really hits the mark. The topic of tantra is vast, and frankly there are still a lot of questions and ambiguities involved. Some of the earliest traditions seem to have grown out of village and rural practices, developing over time, and eventually being brought into more semi-formalized lineages. Historically there does not appear to have been any one "tantra"; rather there have been many schools, traditions, beliefs, gurus, all subsumed under the title of tantra. Aspects of alchemy, sexual rituals, and antinomian practices, have all been part of tantra in one form or another. Some were goddess-oriented cults, their rituals and practices collected into systems that worked with spirits and deities for sorcery, enchantment, magic and ultimately, Self-Realization.

The Yoginis have made frequent appearances in Indian tantrik texts, and have been associated with many of the tantrik schools such as the *Kaulas,* Goddess-worshipping "left-hand path" practitioners. Despite these associations, the enigma of the Yoginis and their strange circular temples, seems to predate any of the formal tantrik schools or traditions. It may be that there was an undercurrent of Yogini worship in the folk magic of the villages which had grown out of the worship of the *Matrikas* (Mother Goddesses). This was brought into nascent or already-existing tantrik lineages as a means of making their worship more formalized or accessible to a larger swath of society.[2]

This book works with the Yoginis outside of the context of any tantrik lineage. While aspects of tantrik ritual are used where it made sense, there is a synthesis of techniques that have been developed out of these older traditions. Aspects of witchcraft have wrapped around the practices, building it into a concise set of workings and framework for spiritual development and transformation, along with practical vehicles for spellcraft. In some cases, these practices have come through dreamwork and visions, as engaging with the Yoginis often moves things in strange and completely unexpected directions.

My own experience comes from several decades of working with several tantrik lineages, Kriya Yoga, Dzogchen, and Western occult traditions. Over the years I have leaned more towards a spontaneous, ecstatic approach to magic that relies heavily on being in the natural world, along with intuition, dreamwork and ritual that works with whatever circumstances may be present.

The blend of witchcraft and tantrik influences is both outwardly syncretic and, at least in my experience, feels strangely natural. In both we have traditions and lore that have grown out of folk belief and approaches to working with the natural world, spirits and elements, sorcery and enchantments, goddesses and gods—traditions that have usually been on the outside of society, on the periphery of what is considered acceptable or mainstream for religion or spirituality. These are traditions that, in the past, society has tried to ignore, or worse, to suppress. The relative freedom that many of us share now, to practice whatever religion and belief system(s) we may be drawn to, has opened the door to many new spiritual paths.

In my experience, the Yoginis stand outside of any formal lineages or traditions. They are a force of their own reckoning, answerable to no one. They make their own rules, and they wander the skies and the

---

[2] For a detailed historical discussion see *Yoginis: Sex, Death and Possession in Early Tantras* by Phil Hine (The Original Falcon Press, 2022).

earth as they desire. They can be powerful allies to those they choose to work with.

Part One:
Circles of Stone

64 Yogini Temple
(Photo courtesy of
commons.wikimedia.org/wiki/File:Chausath_Yogini_Temple_front.jpg)

1. Witch Goddesses

"...the most important Tantric deities in medieval India: the seductive yet dangerous Yoginis, reigning witch-like goddesses of Tantric Hinduism. [...] The Yoginis were shapeshifters who could metamorphose into women, birds, snakes, tigers or jackals as the mood took them. Their most famous ability was the power of flight. Initiated Tantrikas sought to access their siddhis (supernatural powers), from flight and immortality to control over others, by appeasing the Yoginis in nocturnal cremation-ground settings with 'impure' sacrificial offerings that were believed to nourish and energize them. These ritual offerings ranged from blood and alcohol to the Tantrikas' own sexual fluids released after ritual intercourse. If successful, the Yoginis would reveal themselves to the Tantrika, offering the powers he or she desired and granting exclusive admission to their 'clan.' If not (due to lack of initiation, experience or an offensive ritual mistake) the Tantrika could become the Yoginis' breakfast."

— *Tantra: Enlightenment to Revolution,* Imma Ramos

The Sanskrit word *Yogini* has a wide swath of meanings: female devotee of yoga, sorceress or witch, fairy, attendants of the Goddess Durga, and even a name of Durga. There are many references throughout the literature of these powerful females weaving magical spells. The yoginis are worshippers of Bhairava, the wrathful, esoteric aspect of the cosmic Lord Shiva. They are said to fly through the night sky naked, descending into their circles on full moon nights to feast on offerings and dispense the boons of magic. The connection to witchcraft and sorcery is paramount.

South Indian Temple Yogini
(Photo courtesy of
commons.wikimedia.org/wiki/File:Tamil_nadu,_epoca_cola,_yogini,_da_kan
cipuram,_890-1000_ca._02.JPG)

Within every person is the divine; yet Tantrik literature places exceptional importance upon women and their deep and natural expression of this divine nature. This is *shakti,* the very power of the Goddess. Every woman is a living, embodied presence of the Goddess. Some may be more aware of this presence than others, but this in no way changes the fundamental truth that women are divine and naturally adept at sorcery. The Yoginis are the ultimate expression of *shakti*. They are divine beings possessed of sacred wisdom and knowledge. It may be that at one time there were groups of female Yogini worshippers, tantrik adepts that worked with the Yoginis and were living embodiments of their teachings. These female practitioners were skilled in sorcery and yoga, and maintained their own lineages of teachings that were transmitted orally. They practiced their tantrik arts according to the guidance of the Yoginis, and were the beginning of the Yogini *Kaula*—a clan or family of initiates.

These are goddesses of the crossroads, those places where this world and the next commingle, intersecting between the mundane consciousness and the twilight consciousness of shadows and the unknown. Matter and sprit intermingle freely here, and there are no definitive boundaries. Offerings left at the crossroads for the Yoginis are quickly taken up.

They are goddesses of the Moon, in both the Full Moon nights when their worship in ancient temples was conducted, and the New Moon of sorcery, magick and enchantments.

They are also goddesses of the cremation grounds and cemeteries, and they are frequently associated with ghosts, vampires and other denizens of the shadow realms.

North Indian Yogini
(Photo courtesy of
commons.wikimedia.org/wiki/File:SAMA_Yogini.jpg)

Similarly, they are goddesses of sexuality, and the full flowering of it in woman. This is not the sexuality of male-centered satisfaction, where women are vessels of male desire. These goddesses are the very essence of desire, and sexuality flows naturally from them. They wield their voluptuousness openly, and are in full control, taking the fullness of their passions and desires when and how they see fit.

In more exoteric religions and society, a woman experiencing her menstrual cycle was considered to be ritually impure while the blood was shedding. To the Yoginis, the menstrual blood is a sacred and desirable flow of life, the essence of bliss-inducing nectar.

Sexual union with the Yoginis is an offering as well as the ultimate bliss. Through such encounters, the devotee may be swept up into non-dual realization, and ultimate flowering of Self-Realization. As an offering, the Yoginis are delighted in sexual play, and the combined male and female fluids are prized nectar. The fluids combined with the menstrual blood are the ultimate offering and gift of the Yoginis.

Finally, these powerful goddesses are the queens that reign over the realms of death. They hold the keys to life and death, and with it the greater death of the ego. With their sharp knives, scissors, scimitars and swords they will chop the devotee's ego into bits and swallow it all, drinking every drop of blood to the last.

Interacting with such messengers is not for the faint of heart. The physical manifestation of such unbridled energy can literally make the unprepared faint or piss their pants. However, if approached with respect and sincerity, they can accept the devotee, marking you as their own.

Three Yoginis from Hirapur
(Photo courtesy of
commons.wikimedia.org/wiki/File:Details_of_three_yoginis.jpg)

A Brief Historical Interlude

Scattered around India, always in remote locations atop desolate hill tops or difficult to reach locations, the *Sixty-Four Yogini Temples* continue to give up little of their secrets and ancient history.

The *Chausath* ("sixty-four") *yogini* temples share a design that is unique among Indian temples: a circular stone enclosure, open to the sky. Along the inside wall are sixty-four niches, which would contain the sculptures of the Yoginis, depicted as beautiful female forms, some with human, and many with non-human heads. In the center, a small structure devoted to Bhairava.

Most of the temples seem to have been built between the 9th–12th centuries, and are thought to have been active until about the 16th century, at which point they fell into apparent disuse—or so it would appear outwardly, as the state-sponsored traditions seem to have abandoned them.

64 Yogini Temple, Hirapur
(Photo courtesy of
commons.wikimedia.org/wiki/File:64YoginiTemple_Hirapur.JPG)

The villages near the Yogini temples have a very different story to tell. Outside the establishment, villages have local legends that the temples are places of black magic and witchcraft, dangerous to be anywhere near after sunset, and even during the day one is advised to be wary. There is considerable anecdotal evidence that despite outwardly falling into disuse, the temples continued to be secretly used by *siddhas* and tantrik groups. The folklore and local rumors of ominous nocturnal goings-on within these so-called abandoned temples may have been partly encouraged to keep non-initiates and the curious away, so the tantriks could conduct their rituals far from prying eyes.

Written literature tends to be scarce, which lends to the idea that the legends of these beings may have developed out of oral cult traditions. There is simply very little written about how the temples themselves were constructed, and what types of rites may have been conducted in them. When Yoginis *are* mentioned, the descriptions are awe-inspiring and full of warnings about how to approach and respect these powerful beings.

The oldest written references to Yoginis take the form of *namavali* (name lists). These have no introduction or explanation, only listing the names of the Yoginis, and sometimes ending with a verse warning that the Yoginis must be worshipped with great devotion. Adding to the mystery surrounding them, the names of the Yoginis vary among lists, and while there may be some points of correlation, for the most part each list is unique. These *namavali* were written on thin sheets of metal, or on paper, sometimes with *yantras* (magical diagrams) that depict their positioning in space.

There is mention of Yoginis in the 12th century *Lalita Sahasranama* ("Thousand Names of Lalita"), warning that the mere reading of the names to a non-initiate will result in being cursed by the Yoginis. One of her 1000 names is given as "She who is served by 64 *crores*[3] of Yoginis." Similarly, the *Jnananarva Tantra* mentions that anyone who would reveal the details of the tantra to a non-initiate will become "food for the Yoginis." From the start, they are surrounded by silence, secrecy and danger.

---

[3] A crore is 10 million. It is often used to denote incredibly large numbers of cosmic scale.

The Yogini also refers to the female participants of the *Bhairavi Puja,* the secretive rite of the *Kaula* tantrikas (also called the *Chakra Puja, chakra* meaning "circle" as well as the energy centers of the human body). In these ritual circles men and women would participate in the *panchamakara* or "Five M's" offerings, so called because each of the five elements of the ritual begins with the Sanskrit letter "m": *mamsa* (meat), *madya* (wine), *matsya* (fish), *mudra* (ritual gestures), and *maithuna* (sexual union). The male and female adepts would pair off in the circle to partake of the elements, and give the supreme bliss offerings of union.

Yoginis are seen as emanations of the Great Goddess herself. One of the names of the Goddess is *Maha Yogini,* the Great or Supreme Yogini. Another one of her names is *Kaula Yogini,* the Yogini of the tantrik family or tribe. The *Skanda Purana* has name lists that include many of the more well-known names of the Goddess: Durga, Gauri, Katyayani, Sivaduti, Chamunda, Mahamaya, Brahmani and others. It also indicates that while fighting the demon Mahisasura, the Goddess emanated from her own essence the Yoginis to battle the demon. The 15th century *Candali Purana* gives sixty-four yoginis as forming parts of the body of the Goddess, such as her forehead, cheeks, arms and feet, as well as such aspects as her voice and even her sweat. The *Devi Bhagavata Purana* says that each Yogini is a *kula,* (part), of the Great Goddess Bhuvanesvari (another name of Devi).

As attendants of the Goddess, the Yoginis are richly diverse. In the *Kaulajnananirnaya,* Shiva (the male aspect of divinity) tells Devi that Yoginis appear as doves, vultures, swans, owls, cranes, peacocks, jackals, goats, oxen, cats, tigers, elephants, horses, snakes and frogs. The *Phetkarini Tantra* describes the Goddess as Kalika, worshipped by a circle of Yoginis and Bhairava. The sixty-four yoginis are said to roam the earth disguised as animals, and one may seek their protection as well as other boons by propitiating them. The text also instructs that women must always be respected, as they are the embodiment of the Goddess.

The Yogini Hridaya ("Heart of the Yogini"), a text of the tantrik Sri Vidya school, gives an elaborate exploration of the very nature of consciousness and reality itself, where the Great Goddess and her attendants both manifest and participate in the universe. The origin of *mantra* is given as resulting from the love play of Shiva and Shakti, emanating throughout the universe as the Yoginis, who then radiate *mantra* into space and time

While all of these meanings bleed together, the Yoginis themselves continue to be mysterious, elusive figures that have a strong atmosphere of danger and wildness about them.

Buffalo-Headed Yogini
(Photo courtesy of
commons.wikimedia.org/wiki/File:Medieval_Yogini_Statue,_National_Museu
m,_New_Delhi.jpg)

What is certain and consistent is that the Yoginis have always been viewed with awe and dread, and are related to witchcraft and sorcery. They have always been shapeshifters, associated with the sky, and there are references to them descending from the sky as the sun sets to perform their various nocturnal revelries in the *chakra* or circle. The similarities to the Witches' Sabbath, with its nocturnal gathering of witches that fly in to attend, and with the Sabbatic Goat instead of Bhairava in the center of the circle, are striking.

"The danger and power of the yogini appear closely linked to engagement with impurity, particularly as expressed through association with death. [...] yoginis frequently bear skulls, bone ornaments, and skull-staves (khaṭvanga), as well as incorporate other elements of radical tantric iconography. Furthermore, yoginis have a strong association with crema-tion grounds: while a variety of liminal places are spoken of as their haunts, their primary locus is the charnal ground (smasana)[...] They epitomize a culture of ritual 'nondual-ism' (advaita) [...] Transactional encounters with yoginis often revolve around conventionally impure substances: practitioners offer wine or their own blood in lieu of the guest-water offering (argha), burn incense of neem oil and garlic, make offerings of flesh in fire sacrifice, or even offer mixed male-female sexual fluids. Conversely, a yogini might proffer impure food (caru) to the aspirant, the unhesitant acceptance and consumption of which becomes a medium for her bestowal of power."[4]

Visually, the images of the Yoginis are truly stunning. They are often depicted as beautiful, voluptuous human female figures with full, rounded breasts, slim waists and wide hips, often wearing a skirt low on the waist with a jeweled belt, and adorned with richly jeweled anklets, bracelets, armlets, necklaces, earrings, nose ring and orna-mented headdress. They often have beautiful female faces, but are just as likely to appear with fantastic animal faces such as the owl, horse, rabbit and snake. When they are depicted in human form, they usually have long luscious hair, free-flowing, braided or tied up. Large kohl-lined eyes, and often sharp fangs add to their overall awesome coun-tenance. Just as often they may appear as terrifying forms, with fangs

---

[4] "What is a Yogini? Towards a Polytheistic Definitiion." Shamon Hatley from "Yogini" in *South Asia: Interdisciplinary Approaches,* edited by István Keul, pp. 21–31 (Routledge, 2013).

and sharp claw-like nails, their stomachs caved in showing emaciated, skeletal figures with hollow, dark eye-sockets.

Overall their appearance is arresting, both inviting and fraught with danger. They are often depicted in dynamic poses, giving *mudra* (hand gestures) and in the act of dancing. The power of flight, magic, witchcraft, dance, yoga and art are all intertwined with the Yoginis.

Vidya Dehejia, in her work *Yogini Cult and Temples* gives a stunning passage from the Somadevasuri's *Yasastilaka* (sometime between 881–939 CE):

> *"As abruptly as darkness descends at nightfall, even so, without warning did the Mahayoginis appear out of the sky, the earth, the depths of the nether regions and the four corners of space. They traversed the skies at tremendous speed causing their locks of hair to come undone, and these flowing tresses swept across the sky, hampering and angering other denizens of the aerial regions. In their hands they held staffs topped with skulls and decorated with myriad of little bells which jingled furiously with the speed of their flight and sometimes shattered into hundreds of fragments. Their approach was heralded by this chiming, tinkling, pealing reverberation [...].*
>
> *The ornamental designs on their cheeks were painted with blood which was being lapped up by the many snakes adorning their ears. Hovering over the gruesome human skulls decorating their heads were vast numbers of giant vultures who obstructed the rays of the Sun. Sparks issuing from the third eye on their foreheads were fanned into flames by the gaspings of the helpless serpents ruthlessly enmeshed in the tangled masses of their hair; and these flames leapt forth so high as to singe the banners of the Sun's aerial chariot. The faces of these Yoginis were truly terrible to behold as they*

frowned with arrogance, uttering a tremendous and terrifying [...] sound.[5]

From the beginning, the word Yogini has had mixed meanings that could refer to embodied human women, or to a certain class of spiritual beings, or to the Goddess herself. The line is not clear; and it may be that there is no line when, in truth, all of these aspects intermingle. They embody the essence of the crossroads, the connection between the known and the unknown, in their very forms.

A Yogini Cult may have been extant around 700 CE, with its primary form of worship being with Yogini *chakras* and *yantras* drawn on cloth or etched on metal sheets. The worship of the Yoginis as their own distinct cult seems most likely to have developed out of the earlier cult of the *Matrikas* (Mothers), of which there is a strong relationship.

Associated with the secretive initiatory rites of the Kaula Shakta (Goddess worshipping) schools of Indian tantra, there are passages in the *Kularnava Tantra* that refer to the Yoginis. Perhaps one of the most significant references to them is in the *Kaulajnananirnaya* which may have been produced by a sub-sect of the Kaulas that identified as the Yogini Kaula (more on this below). It would seem that at least some of the Yoginis were associated with lineages of these Kaula schools, and acted as the creators of a lineage, and were the guardians of such traditions. There are also reference to the *astastaka puja,* an "eight by eight" manner of worshipping the Yoginis over sixty-four days. Some Kaula tantras also describe the Yogini circle as having Bhairava in the center, surrounded by the sixty-four yoginis.

The Yoginis, then, are deeply multifaceted and complex beings. Alluring and dangerous, they grant boons when approached with respect and devotion, and to the callous they will bring swift ruin. They are women, both of this earth, and of other dimensions. They are

---

[5] Vidya Dehejia. *Yogini Cult and Temples: A Tantric* Tradition. New Delhi: National Museum, 1986, pp. 26–27.

teachers of magic and occult powers, mistresses of yoga, the founders and protectors of lineages, and the gateway to liberation *(moksa),* and indeed are liberation itself. They are aspects of, attendants of, and in fact the Goddess herself, usually in her aspect of Kali or Durga. They are closely associated with the *Matrikas* or Mother Goddess—and in particular a grouping called the *Sahaja Mothers.* They are sorceresses and witches who celebrate their mysteries at night underneath the open skies. The more that we may think we know of them, the more elusive they become, as mystery is of their very nature. In this sense they are envoys of *Mahamaya*, an aspect of the goddess as illusion, the weaver of worlds and life itself.

Matsyendranath and the Kaulajnananirnaya

Female Ascetics (Yoginis)
(Photo courtesy of
commons.wikimedia.org/wiki/File:Female_Ascetics_(Yoginis)_LACMA_M.20
11.156.4_(1_of_2).jpg] Yoginis

Matsyendranath is a near legendary figure in tantra and in Eastern traditions overall. According to some sources he was born in Bengal around the 7th century; others give the dates in the 9th or 10th centuries. Revered by both Hindus and Buddhists, he is considered an avatar of Lord Shiva. In Abhinavagupta's *Tantraloka* (10th or 11th century), itself a commentary on the great *Kularnavatantra* of the *Kaulas,* he is referred to as a *Siddha* (enlightened being) and the "father of yoga." He and his disciple Goraksha are traditionally thought of as the founders of Hatha Yoga, as well as the Nath lineage.

His name means "Lord of Fish" in Sanskrit. Legends say that as a child he was born under inauspicious stars, and so he was thrown into the ocean where he was swallowed by a fish. For 12 years he survived inside the fish before finally emerging. According to the Natha tradition, the Ocean is *maya*—illusion—and Matsyendranath, by conquering the ocean, becomes the Lord of Knowledge. In conquering the oceanic depths of *maya,* he has liberated all beings from *samsara,* the illusion of the material world and the wheel of constant rebirth. In Nepal he is considered an avatar of the Bodhisattva of Compassion, Avalokiteshvara, and in Tibet he is called Lui-pa, "eater of fish guts." He is one of the 9 Nathas and one of the 84 *Maha Siddhas,* recognized in Hindu and Buddhist traditions alike.

Matsyendranath is credited with writing what is probably the central text of the Yogini cults: the *Kaulajnananirnaya* ("Knowledge of the Kaula tradition"). It is said that he wrote the text, and thus the first origin of the Yogini lineage, in Kamarupa (Assam), when in the "company of women and where each woman was a Yogini."[6] Narenda Nath Battacharya[7] suggests that these women were priestesses, possessed by the Yoginis, who worked with them regularly and built up a tantric cult around their worship. Matsyendranath came across this already well-established cult of Yoginis at Kamakhya, and after being

---

[6] *Sixty-Four Yoginis: Cult, Icons and Goddesses,* Anamika Roy.
[7] *History of the Sakta Religion,* Narendra Nath Battacharya, 1974.

welcomed and initiated by these priestesses, was authorized to transmit the teachings in the *Kaulajnananirnaya*. In this way the connection to Matsyendranath, the Kaula Yogini cult and the Natha cults are all intertwined.

But what of this idea of the Yogini *kaula* or cult? More recent research seems to show that this was an error in translation by Bagchi, an early editor of the *Kaulajnananirnaya*.[8] If this is correct, then the Yogini *kaula* takes an even deeper meaning, as a revealed wisdom that originates *from the Yoginis themselves*. The Yoginis are living embodiments of divine wisdom, with the ability to grant spiritual illumination, along with *siddhis* (magical powers) to their devotees. If there was a formal Yogini *Kaula,* that was likely the creation of men, quite possibly Matsyendranath, coming into contact with an already well-established and secretive group of women adepts that initiated him. "It is said that female adepts knowing yoga dwell at Kamakhya Pitha. If one joins with one of these, one obtains Yogini Siddhi."[9]

A passage from the 9th–10th century *Mrgendragama* says that the "Yoginis obtained scriptural wisdom that immediately makes the power of yoga manifest. For this reason, it is called yogini kaula." The Yoginis are said to possess eight different streams or categories of occult wisdom teachings—again, that number eight, which seems embedded into the mysteries of the Yoginis.

The *Kaulajnananirnaya* takes the form of an *agama,* in which Parvati questions Shiva about the knowledge of the *Kaulas.* It describes, in the so-called "twilight language" of tantra, the wisdom of the Yogini *Kaula.* The Goddess Parvati implores the God Shiva to lay out in clear language the doctrine, and Shiva describes the Self as eternal, uncreated—*Advaita,* non-dual. Emanating out of the Self through the interaction of the three *Shaktis* named *Iccha* (Will), *Jnana* (Knowledge), and *Kriya* (Action), all of creation is made manifest by

---

[8] See for example *The Brahmayamalatantra and the Early Saiva Cult of Yoginis,* by Shaman Hatley. University of Pennsylvania, 2007.

[9] *Kaulajnananirnaya,* Chapter 16 (trans. by Mike Magee).

the eternally uncreated, undivided Self. Shiva gives eight *mantras*; their permutations give rise to the Sixty-Four Yoginis.

The text of the *Kaulajnananirnaya* includes a description of the *chakra* system, and how to work with the energy for various means by changing the colors visualized. The text discusses the central place of the non-dual view. External worship is replaced by internal worship and realization of the nature of Self. An internal *linga* is visualized as being the essential interior worship, as favored over external types or practice.

Parvati goes on to describe herself a "flier in space" with the appearance of crystal. She wears white pearls and has a white *bindi* on her forehead. She is *Svecchacarini,* with the ability to go wherever she desires and do anything by the power of her self-arising will.

Candradvipa

At the end of every chapter of the text is mentioned the mystic island of the moon, *Candradvipa*. Matsyendranath reveals the Yogini knowledge from this mysterious Moon Island. This is a center of alchemical transformation, the magical Moon Island of the Yoginis. *Candradvipa* is also found within the body of the *sadhaka,* as the Yoginis materialize and take up residence as *shaktis* within the body of the practitioner. The island of the moon distills the *kalas* (emanations) of the Yoginis which will fill the practitioner's body and consciousness with *Siddhis*.

The moon island has similarities to other mystic lands: Shambhala, the nectar filled magical kingdom where Shiva resides in cosmic meditation; and Mount Kailash, the sacred mountain in the Himalayas which is the abode of Shiva and Shakti, whose continuous blissful love play maintains the very universe. In all of these cases, the outer symbol is also an indicator of a region within, a spiritual center to which the practitioner has access.

Through ritual and yoga, the *chakras* (energy centers) may be stimulated such that the body itself produces the elixirs which result in both changes in perception of consciousness, as well as outright magical powers. There is a great deal of lore associating the Yoginis with the *chakras*. To work with the serpent fire and the wheels of light is to work directly with the Yoginis.

La Danse du Sabbat (Dance of the Sabbath)
(Photo courtesy of
commons.wikimedia.org/wiki/File:La_Danse_du_Sabbat_(no_caption).jpg)

The moon itself has long been associated with sorcery and witch-craft. The full moon is central in the Witches' Sabbaths, and the lunar phases find importance in both paganism and tantra for the timings of rituals, meditation and other works of sorcery such as the producing of talismans and sigils.

The moon conjures up associations of shadows, illusions and dreams. The reflective quality of its light, as the full moon radiantly reflects the light of the sun, bleeds into the reflective quality of dreams. It will be found that when working with the Yoginis, deep communication may come by way of dreams, images, sounds and words. Meditation and reflection are keys to communicating and allowing their influence to penetrate within the core of being.

The role of the *Nityas* (eternities) and their association with the lunar phases relates directly to the Yoginis. Through the waxing and waning of the moon, the different aspects of the Goddess are invoked, given offerings and meditated upon. With the Yoginis this is further modified into a prismatic display of 64 different aspects, with the moon or *Chandra Bindu* at the center of the center of this circle of awareness. For a visual embodiment of this arrangement, see the illustration of the Yogini Yantra (Chapter 7, "East Meets West").

The Sahaja Matrikas

Eight Mothers (Ashta Matrikas)
(Photo courtesy of
commons.wikimedia.org/wiki/File:Ashta-Matrika.jpg)

The *Matrikas* (Mothers) are an ancient grouping of fierce, powerful goddesses. It seems probable that the *Matrikas* developed out of tribal cults in which they were worshipped in villages as the local goddesses to help with such needs as safe childbirth, the growing of crops, and protection against famines and illness. They eventually collected into well-known groups, moving from the periphery of society into central positions of worship in established temples. While you will often see a grouping of seven Mothers *(Sapta Matrikas)* in temples, another well-known grouping of the Mothers was eight *(Ashta Matrikas)*. Eight is a sacred number in Hinduism. In the usual groupings of Mothers, they are often depicted as beautiful and voluptuous women, with the exception of the leader who is the skeletal and terrifying Chamunda whose black eye-sockets show the universe burning within them. As with the Yoginis, these goddesses are both beautiful and frightening, requiring sacrifices and commanding respect. The Yoginis are intimately related to the *Matrikas,* often being said to have emanated from them, or being associated by tribe *(kula)* and partaking of the partial essences of the Mother Goddesses.[10]

In the *Kaulajnananirnaya*, the *Matrikas* are referred to as the *Sahaja Mothers. Sahaja* means "natural, free, spontaneous," and these forms of the Goddess arise naturally, of their own accord, when the Yoginis indwell the practitioner.

A secret tantric association of *sahaja* is the bliss of orgasm.[11] This bliss of union is beyond time, beyond boundaries and beyond any sense of separation—truly free, natural and spontaneous. The *Matrikas* and the Yoginis are intimately associated with spontaneity and bliss, and this is most easily approached through orgasm. Like the

---

[10] For a fascinating look at a contemporary Matrika practice, see *Ferocious: A Folk Tantric Manual on the Sapta Matrika Cult* by the Sephulcher Society, Theion Publishing, 2019.

[11] "When one meditates on the Shakti established in our own body and manifested as in sexual union, that is *sahaja*." *Kaulajnananirnaya,* Chapter 8.

sexual drive itself, which left unhindered is free, spontaneous and at times all-consuming, so too is the dynamic play of these goddesses that live entirely by their own will.

While the names of the Yoginis vary considerably, the association with the *Matrikas* and their names are fairly consistent. Described as beautiful and terrifying to behold, with radiant red skin and clothing, and wearing rich ornaments, it is said that "...the *Siddhas* and all beings worship the eight Mothers." *(Kaulajnananirnaya).*

Brahmi

Appearing with four and sometimes six arms, beautifully adorned with jewels, she holds a *mala* (rosary), noose, *kamandalu* (water pot), lotus stalk, book of sacred scripture, and a bell. She may be seen seated on a lotus with a swan nearby, or seated on the swan, her *vahana* (vehicle). Her crown is the *karanda mukuta,* a basket-shaped ornament.

Mahesvari

Adorned with rich jewels, serpent bracelets and serpents around her neck and showing three eyes, her skin is white like fresh snow (hence one of her other names is *Gauri,* meaning "white"). Seated on a bull, her four (or sometimes six) arms are holding the *trishula* (trident), *damaru* (drum), *aksha mala* (garland of *rudraksa* beads), *panapatra* (a cup), an axe, antelope, and a *kapala* (skull-cup). Her long hair is tied up in *jata mukuta* and adorned with the crescent moon and a serpent.

Kaumari

She is seen riding her mount, the peacock, and has four (sometimes twelve) arms where she holds a spear, an axe, silver coins and a bow. Richly adorned, she is crowned with the *kirita mukuta* (an ornamented cylindrical crown).

Vaisnavi

She appears with four and sometimes six arms, seated on her mount, the *Garuda.* Heavily ornamented with gold necklaces, bangles and earrings, she holds the *shankha* (conch shell), *chakra* (discus), mace, lotus, bow and sword. Sometimes she appears with two arms, in which case she is giving the *mudras* (signs) of *varada* (blessing) and *abhaya* (no fear). On her head she wears the *kirita mukuta.*

Varahi (Vajrahasta)

Often shown with a boar's head, or with a boar nearby as her mount, she appears holding a *danda* (rod used for punishment), a goad, a *vajra* (a thunderbolt) or a sword, and the *panapatra.* She is heavily ornamented and wears the *karanda mukuta.*

Indrani

She is seated on her mount, the elephant and appears with two, four or sometimes six arms, dark-skinned and heavily jeweled. She is armed with the *vajra,* a goad, a noose and a lotus stalk. She is crowned with the *kirita mukuta.*

Yogesvari

Richly adorned with jewels, inflamed with desire, and mistress of Yoga, she is said to have emerged from the flames of Shiva's mouth, making her unique amongst the *Matrikas* as being born of Shiva rather than the Goddess Durga.

Aghoresi (Chamunda)

Adorned in black, her skin is black like space, and around her neck she wears the *munda mala* (a garland of severed heads), and holds a *damaru* (a drum made from the craniums of a male and female child), *trishula* (the trident), a sword and the *panapatra*. She is mounted on a jackal, or sometimes the corpse of a man.

The *Sahaja* Mothers are said to be the *"protectors of the doors, who pervade the whole Cosmos."* These eight doors are the eight primary *chakras* of the human body, which are presided over by the Yoginis.

Each of these eight *Sahaja* Mother goddesses further emanates eight Yoginis, giving an 8×8 matrix of 64 goddesses. From this initial set, countless hundreds of thousands of Yoginis arise, each of their *chakras* forming unique name lists and groupings of energies.

Chamunda
(Photo courtesy of
commons.wikimedia.org/wiki/File:Chamunda_British_Museum.jpg)

But Really, Who Are the Yoginis?

As is fitting of their shape-shifting, unpredictable, nocturnal and erotic natures, there is no one answer:

• *Highly skilled female adepts of Yoga.*

• *Energy centered in the chakras, body goddesses that receive offerings of food and liquid that is consumed, appearing with theriomorphic forms that arise during meditation.*

• *Lascivious demonesses that lurk in graveyards, hang from trees and haunt cremation grounds and abandoned places, feasting on the souls of the unwary.*

• *Spirits manifesting in wind, trees, running streams and rivers, snow, starlight, moonlight and fire.*

• *Feminine spirits of the natural world that haunt forests, wilderness, wind-blasted heaths and mountain tops at night, and that may appear as animals such as crows, ravens, owls, foxes, coyotes, dogs, wolves and so on.*

• *Divine emissaries of the Great Goddess that hunt down evildoers and protect the true teachings of the gnosis.*

• *Star beings who descend to the earth at night to partake in sorcerous rites, feasting on the energy of the offerings of meat, alcohol and sex given in their name.*

• *Guardians and revealers of treasure and dream teachings.*

• *Embodied human sorceresses and magicians, and women possessed by such spirits and goddesses.*

The Yoginis aptly fit all of these descriptions, and many more. They are the embodiment and expression of the ultimate in feminine power—*Shakti.* And this power is highly adaptable and fluid. As the core of woman, it is both the center of creation and the source of destruction. It is happiness, sorrow, love, hate, nurturing, suffocating, grasping and giving; shy, bold, adventurous, timid, bashful, provocative, playful, vengeful, frivolous and deadly serious. The entire spectrum of femininity manifests through the Yoginis. From the regal appearance of celestial Empresses, to the earthy and tribal princesses, to the fiery and relentless warriors who take no prisoners. In any of her many forms and moods, she is a force to be respected and reckoned with.

The Yogini is the *Chaya Devi* or Shadow Goddess, who moves at night under the open stars. She comes forward in dreams to reveal hidden treasures or to give teachings. She reveals herself in the natural world, her voice the rustling of branches and leaves as the wind blows; the rushing and bubbling of water over rocks and twigs in remote rivers and streams; the feel of warmth from the fire; the sound of rainfall and the smell in the forest after the rain has stopped; she is the dazzling flash of lightning, and the powerful crash of thunder, as the dark storm clouds collect and darken the earth. She is the fantastical mirage of the rainbow as much as she is the alluring, Siren-like pull of the oceanic depths, and the cold and ancient silence of the stars beckoning from distant outposts.

The spirits and elementals of the natural world tend to come out in abundance when the Yoginis are present, as though drawn by their dynamic energies. There is also an otherworldly quality to the Yoginis, which is one of the distinguishing characteristics of their appearance, making them of a very different order than the spirits and elementals of a location. The Yoginis have an inherent regal quality, and a high intelligence far beyond anything human. Many of them also have an uncanny quality of playfulness, akin to how a lioness might play with its prey. They may charm and enchant, and at times even present an almost innocent naivety and curiosity. More often this is a sense of bewilderment on our part as we come into close contact with intelligences which are beyond what the human mind is accustomed to, and there is an automatic tendency of the human mind to try to categorize and label the unknown.

We find the Yoginis in dreams, landscapes of unbounded creativity. Regions composed seemingly of all shadows and muted lights that suddenly erupt into kaleidoscopic colors that defy the artist's touch. Approaching them in the night, in lonely and wild places, at the crossroads and on barren mountaintops during the blackest nights of the

New Moon, in the forests with coyotes prowling quietly nearby, and owls perched on tree branches observing the proceedings.

The more you are able to open up to the wild, spontaneous, unbound and creative parts of existence, the more they will be attracted to you and you might find them peeking at you from unexpected places. In the corner café while sipping on a cappuccino, you might catch their glance in passersby. In the boisterous noise of the pub, with pints flowing freely and conversations heated and passionate, and every sort of background and personality coming in and out, you might just catch a glimpse of one out of the corner of your eye, or seated at a table alone, deep in thought. It could be just a feeling or a hunch, an intuition to go left instead of right, the feeling of the evening breeze on your skin, or the long falling rain beating out a solid winter rhythm on a glass window pane. Maybe you are at a concert, the songs and dance swelling, moving bodies all around, and the energy synchronizing into one seeming organism, no boundaries between you or me or she or him, one beautiful and mad and passionate poetry in motion of sounds, sweat, song, dance and energy.

Nature and remote spaces are ideal. The solitude and ability to easily resonate with the natural world brings its own rewards, and is the holiest, most sacred temple of the universe in which the Yoginis play and dance and cast their enchantments far and wide. Alone in the wilderness, underneath a vast canopy of stars, call them forth to the circle! Revel with them in the wild, and drink deep of their magic.

Just don't think you are limited to these spaces. As you open up to their influence, as intuition increases, as you go deeper into the dream spaces and bring that back with you into the waking world, so too will you become more sensitive to what is around you already. The Yoginis are not confined to ancient circular temples in remote regions of India!

The Yoginis are in every place: on the edges of civilization, on the edge of light, around the hearth, at the crossroads, in the dream lands which permeate the forests, the mountains, the lakes, the suburbs and the cities. The night sky covers the entire world, no matter if you find yourself trudging through the streets of Maharashtra or in a café in

Paris; camping in Yosemite or running to the office on a Monday morning in Manhattan; exploring the catacombs before having an espresso in Rome; or at night at the pub after a day at the British Museum in London.

Throughout the entire world, one thing only remains—consciousness. And consciousness is the true Circle of the Yoginis. The circle has no beginning, no end. It is continuous, whole. While it may demarcate a space, it also encompasses all of space, with no apparent boundary besides the seeming limits of the technology being used to examine the frontiers, be it telescope or the lens of the mind.

It is from this Circle, standing as Awareness, that the Yoginis are entreated to come, to approach and commune with.

2. Commingling with Yoginis

I had originally written this chapter to outline only the traditional eight *siddhis* or "magical powers," and while I will still give an overview, I want to emphasize from the start that these are well-known powers that are associated with all types of mystical and magical development, but when standing as Awareness, they become little more than curiosities, ornaments in the great dreaming.

These classic *siddhis* have been laid out by Patanjali in the *Yoga Sutras,* and are frequently elaborated upon. All students of *Hatha Yoga* are probably aware of these at least in passing, and some may have worked at developing them intentionally.

The Yoginis, Mistresses of Yoga itself, may grant the boons of working with and mastering Yoga in its many forms, to include developing these powers along the way.

Portrait of a Yogini
(Photo courtesy of
commons.wikimedia.org/wiki/File:Portrait_of_Yogini,_c._1750-
1760,_Honolulu_Museum_of_Art.JPG)

1. *Anima:* The ability to shrink one's body to the atomic level or beyond, enabling one to see the complete workings of the world.

2. *Mahima:* The power to expand one's body, even to cosmic proportions, giving one power to see the universe.

3. *Garima:* To become extremely heavy such that one is immovable by anything.

4. *Laghima:* To become weightless at will, such that one can levitate and fly, as well as travel in the astral realms.

5. *Prakamya:* The power of an irresistible will and magnetism such that others are compelled to do as you say.

6. *Isitva:* "Lordliness", the power to have complete control over not only your own body and mind, but that of others.

7. *Vasitva:* All-conquering power over the five elements, such that you can control weather, and cause storms, high winds, lightning, earthquakes, floods and more.

8. *Kamavasayita:* Fulfillment of all that one desires.

In addition, there are further tantrik *siddhis,* traditionally associated with the Yoginis, that start to take on a decidedly sinister nature:

1. *Maranam:* To kill or cause death.

2. *Uccatanam:* To cause one to abandon home, family and work.

3. *Stambhanam:* To cause paralysis or strike one mentally catatonic.

4. *Jrmbhanam:* To cause unconsciousness.

5. *Plavanam:* To cause a sudden flood.

6. *Dravanam:* To cause a person to flee

7. *Ksobhanam:* To cause excessive agitation, panic.

8. *Parapurapravesa:* The ability to enter another's home.

9. *Kavittava manoharam:* The power to write bewitching or enchanting poetry.

10. *Vasyakarsanam:* The power of seduction.

11. Mohanam: The ability to delude and infatuate others.

12. Sphotanam saila vrksanam: The power to move rocks and trees.

Further powers include the ability to obtain the elixir of immortality, control over physical decay and death, to be loved by all, and more. Clearly, the Yoginis have a lot to offer. A final blessing—*Yogini Melakam*—is to be chosen by a Yogini to have union.

In addition to a literal interpretation of the *siddhis*, it is worth considering that there may be some nuanced ways that these could manifest or be applied. For example, paralysis may be directed inward to stop those tendencies in our personality that cause us to pause or falter (what if you could paralyze your sense of fear or inadequacy?). Subjugation might be applied towards those tendencies in your personality that block you from growing or achieving your goals. The power of killing might be applied to unwanted thoughts or even disease. Consider the *siddhis* carefully, and how they may apply in your own circumstances.

At the center of all of these is *empowerment.* By intermingling with the energies of these goddesses, you will increase your psychic abilities, intuition, and healing powers—all incredibly useful skills to develop for any aspect of life. In particular, those who are working in other pagan or traditions of witchcraft may find having these powerful allies deepens their practice significantly. For those who are practicing the science and art of Yoga, developing a relationship with the Yoginis will deepen your practice. The Yoginis are the empresses of Yoga after all, and by their enchantments is expertise in it mastered.

As their nature is wild and unpredictable, the Yoginis are closely associated with the unpredictable and relentless power of nature. Unlike the more well-known goddesses of Hindu tantra, or the clusters of goddesses such as the *Matrikas,* or the assortment of attendants to the goddess Lalita Tripurasundari of the *Sri Yantra,* the Yoginis are less well defined. It is perhaps because of this that they beckon us to come closer. When you work with them, you are encountering them directly. From this first-hand experience, you will then get to know in what areas they may be experts. One Yogini may be related with

Gnosis, or direct experience of reality. Another may excel at working with rain or wind. Yet another could be helpful with a project, such as finding a rare book or a better paying job. All are highly skilled in yoga, dance and the arts, and they will freely give such talents—and just as freely take them away if they are not petitioned sincerely, and approached with the respect due not only to any earthly woman, but to the Goddess herself. As the sky itself appears boundless, pure and self-luminous, so too are the Yoginis and their arts.

But let's step back a bit. Surely there has to be more going on here than just calling upon different goddesses to "acquire wealth and power," as one common example? We are talking about goddesses. While they are perfectly capable of granting material gains and other *siddhis* to those that they favour, is that really the best approach?

The Yoginis are closely associated with the Goddess Kali. She is the womb of consciousness itself, and the matrix of creation. In one hand she holds a severed head, around her neck she wears a garland of freshly severed heads, her skirt is made of severed arms, and she wears earrings made of the corpses of two small boys. In her other hands she holds a scimitar, a trident, and a skull-cup filled with fresh blood. She dances joyously in the cremation grounds, at midnight with the full moon shining down on the macabre scenery. Jackals, black dogs, crows and hyaenas all come around the burning corpses, and chew on leftover remains and bones.

Does this Goddess really sound like she has any interest whatso-ever as to your job status or income? The goddess will give you the ultimate experience, the realization of the nature of Self. All ego will be executed (decapitated). All false sense of self will be burnt up in the cremation fires. All transitory and material desires will be seen through for what they are—illusory in nature. Kali will bring you to complete realization—the Gnostic awareness of Truth. Your wants, desires, ego trips—She will let you see them as the frivolous and impermanent trinkets that they really are. Sure, play with them, enjoy them, but get possessed or obsessed and She will quickly chop away your illusions in a flash, leaving you with ashes so that you are able to experience the pristine clarity of non-dual realization.

What then of Kali's countless attendants, the Yoginis? These are each goddesses in their own right, sprung from the Goddess Kali herself and partaking of her nature. Each also has her own personality and expressions, her own interests and preferences. In the imagery of the Yoginis, there will often be seen a certain "family resemblance" to Kali, and yet each has her own distinct traits and expressions.

While the Yoginis are mistresses of sorcery and witchcraft, there are deeper *siddhi* that underlie all of this power—the path of devotion and the path of non-duality. Here will be found the deepest and truest expressions of the Yoginis and their direct relation to the goddess Kali.

Bhakti—The Path of Devotion

At its simplest, *bhakti* is approaching the divine from pure love. Rather than the rigors of ritual, *bhakti* is an approach that comes entirely from the heart of the practitioner. Rituals may be completely dispensed with, or they may continue but with a very different feeling—more of a love play or a dance that is done *with* the Yoginis, rather than to them or for them.

In many Western traditions it is said that *bhakti* can be developed, cultivated even. While this is true, I feel that the best *bhakti* is that which arises spontaneously, and truly is an expression of love. When you are in love, it does not need cultivation. Your entire being is overflowing with the emotion. Your every thought is of the beloved, every action is already devoted to them. There is no pretense, nothing is being done out of rote belief or in a formulaic way. Instead, you are filled with a true, palpable, visceral love for the person. Your thoughts go naturally to them—sometimes even obsessively! The heart overflows at the thought of them. Your every instinct is to be with them. You see them everywhere, and all the senses come alive in aching desire for the beloved. This may be sexual, but just as deep is the desire to simply see the beloved and drink in their vision, or to hear their voice and experience the thrill. Those sweet moments when you catch a glimpse of them or are so fortunate as to catch them looking

at you! The electric thrill of such moments drives you to more interactions. I am reminded of the great Troubadour traditions, where just
the thought of the beloved would inspire poetry and songs. There is
something truly sweet, and truly a source of power, in these interactions where there is no thought of "grounding" the emotions in actual
physical contact. Rather, it is all of the heart and mind, unleashing a
torrential stream of devotional love.

In the same way, the spontaneous arising of *bhakti* for the Yoginis
comes seemingly of its own accord. The Yoginis themselves may
grant *bhakti,* or it may arise unexpectedly during a meditation, a
glimpse of an image, a sound—and who is to say this spontaneous
arising is not from the Yoginis, as they are so deeply intertwined with
our experience.

Walking quietly through a forest, the sound of the wind in the trees,
a beam of sunlight shining down through the branches—and suddenly,
without warning, the heart overflows with love and tears form.

Waking up early to the sound of birds singing, as the first rays of
the sun start caressing the land. Are those birds, or is that the giggling
and singing of Yoginis on the breeze? The heart and mind flow naturally into these states.

The radiant full moon rising over hills, the clouds separating at the
sight of her so that she might shine more brightly over the land, while
the stars silently shine down their own light bathing the senses in
lustrous waves of radiance. The caress of the deep night, a majestic
cosmic ocean that flows over the body and into the eyes, filling the
body with a sense of wonder.

Dark rain clouds covering the sky, the feeling of electricity in the
air and the buildup of tension, before the thunderous rapture and the
downpour caressing the land. Listen to the sound of the rain and wind.
Let it take you into a quiet contemplation of the beloved.

The path of *bhakti* is open to everyone, regardless of creed, beliefs,
caste, race, age, sex and so forth. *Bhakti* is a unifying force, a relentless
torrent of devotion that knows no rules, no guidelines, no restrictions.
True love cannot be tamed, and does not answer to the rational mind.

You cannot really say "why" you love someone or something—it just *is*. This is one of the greatest mysteries, and a sacred blessing in life.

Love of this nature, true love that arises spontaneously, has no care for convention or society. The heart loves what it loves, and the expression of that love may take countless forms. This force is all consuming and absolutely relentless. It can be channeled into great works of art that span the course of time and across cultures, just as easily as it can be used as a force of destruction and war. Love, indeed, is the central fire of existence, the primal force of the universe, of the Goddess.

In the path of devotion, your entire being becomes a living temple dedicated to the Divine. Seeing the Goddess in everything brings a sweetness and luminous quality to life. Interactions with people will begin to change as your own luminosity shines through. Whatever in life that cultivates the sense of beauty, awe and wonder at being alive in the present moment, is suitable fuel to add to the pyre of passion that is devotion.

At the same time, love is an exposure of our innermost nakedness. It strips away all pretense, leaving us exposed to hurt, pain, betrayal. True love is a burning ground of emotions, and it's not a mistake that Kali asks us to turn our hearts into a cremation ground, for she loves to dance therein.

The beauty of human existence is in part because of its transience. The beauty of the flower will fade and die. We are born, live our lives and also die. There is nothing permanent in this world of illusions, and this is a cause to rejoice and truly feel love. Looking into the eyes of my beloved, I see the transience and the eternity of existence at the same time. This is a sacred, silent communion that needs no creeds, no traditions, no rituals or rules. The truth of the moment is right here, right now. The unveiling of the shrine is right in front of you, in every naked and natural moment of existence.

This love is everywhere, and can be felt at any time, in any situation.

You can help cultivate this with a sense of awe at the very nature of consciousness and the world. The very fact that you are here, right now reading these words, is a reason to rejoice. The truth is that in any moment, in any situation, the very fact that you are aware is a miracle. It's so obvious that the paradox is that most of us will miss it. We tend to think that a miracle or "spiritual awakening" must involve some sort of dramatic magical special effects. No! The truth is right here. Right at this very second, as you are reading these words, you have everything you could possibly need for Awakening *in this very instant.*

Should you find your sense of devotion suddenly arising, your love for the Yoginis—or even for a specific Yogini— developing, cherish this connection, as it will open the door to realms undreamed of.

Advaita: The Path of Non-Duality

In the eleventh chapter of the *Kaulajnananirnaya,* the Goddess asks Shiva about non-duality. He responds:

> *"Whoever is always identified with non-duality, will attain success. Whosoever acts in a dualistic way will be attracted to the Yogis who have been misguided from the right path and he will be an animal, O Devi, there is no doubt about it. Therefore, one should abandon thinking in the dualistic way and should identify oneself with the non-dualistic path."*

In this way the Yoginis and their blessings are closely associated with non-dual realization. What is this non-duality that they speak of?

Advaita is "not divided." This refers to the true condition of consciousness—of Awareness itself—which is non-dual in nature. Before thoughts and identification arise, before all conceptions, this pristine, non-dual consciousness *is.* In the non-dual path, the idea of *jivanmukti* (liberation and freedom while living) is paramount, which runs counter to the more traditional ideas that spiritual realization is only possible after death. Non-duality is more spiritual philosophy than religious belief system, with a wide influence that has permeated many other traditions. Its influence is found in both Hindu and Buddhist philosophies.

In the *Tantraloka* of Abhinavagupta there are many references to the non-dual qualities of the Yoginis:

> *"I am not, neither does another exist; energies alone exist. If he meditates on that thought, that place of repose, that true nature, even for a moment, then, having become a sky-traveler, he will enter the company of Yoginis.*
>
> *"I am not, neither does another exist; I am only energies. He should, in every circumstance, as a result simply of this recollection, maintain that attitude of mind.*
>
> *"No lunar day nor asterism, no fasting is prescribed. He who is engrossed in everyday life becomes a Perfected Being by means of continual recollection.*
>
> *"There is no succession of any sort in consciousness which consists of splendour. Consciousness is in no way absent. Therefore, the act of satiation is timeless.*
>
> *"The Self shines forth eternally.*
>
> *"His saktis are the whole universe and the one who possesses Sakti is Maheshvarah.*
>
> *"The fire that is born from uniting sun and moon is called 'The Pure.'*
>
> *"Or else, the circle of the goddess, which stands on consciousness alone, is to be satiated through an offering of consciousness which the wise man makes by utilizing every form of enjoyment."*

The circle of the goddess is said to "stand on consciousness alone." The circle is the *chakra,* the energy centers that are the nexus points between the material and the spiritual. The circle also represents the sky, and is reminiscent of the open-sky temple structures of the circular Yogini temples. The circle represents eternity, demarcating time and timelessness. The circle embodies the void, and is the womb of all creation. From it everything has its source, and to it everything returns. It is consciousness itself, and from this primal ground of consciousness, the base and foundation of all things, arise the Yoginis.

The Yoginis are "satiated through an offering of consciousness."
Awareness is the nectar that is offered to these celestial goddesses, an
awareness that is stimulated through the senses by "utilizing every
form of enjoyment." Tantra utilizes the body itself, and the senses, as
an offering. The natural result of such blissful union is non-dual
awareness.

The circle of the Yoginis is in the consciousness of the worshipper.
It is here, in your own mind and body, that you will experience the
pleasures of the worship, and the fruits. The desire that is cultivated
and experienced is given up to the Yoginis, who accept it and return
it a thousand-fold with the experience of union and bliss.

It is from this position, standing as Awareness, that the *sadhaka*
(practitioner) will rise up and approach the Yoginis. From this open
awareness, the experience and the experiencer do not exist. The Heart
of the Yogini and the heart and mind of the devotee are one.

As with *bhakti,* this realization can arise spontaneously, or it may
be cultivated. Sitting quietly in nature, thoughts stilled, the apparent
boundary between "self" and "other" dissolves into bliss. It is an ironic
twist to our human condition that to truly find yourself, you must lose
what you think your self is. A shift in perception occurs, a widening
of boundaries, and the sense of "I" drops away. This is not a loss, but
a great discovery. When the false sense of self is suddenly seen for
what it is, the entire universe is experienced as throbbing, vibrating,
pulsating awake awareness, boundless and endless, the source and
essence of every "thing."

At some moments I see that we are all ghosts in a sense. Personalities that think they are permanent and somehow "real", completely
severed from the wellspring of life itself, walking and talking heads
blindly hovering at the edge of the Infinite, thinking and doing as
though they are autonomous agents that are somehow outside of
nature and the cosmos. Our personalities fear the darkness and depths;
the abyss is a place to be avoided. At some level we know that our
sense of self is a lie, an illusion. Death is a stark reminder that this too
shall cease, and what will come of all the craving and pushing, the
fighting and planning and fears and hopes and desires, only to dissolve

into the great Black Hole at the end of Time? These fears and more the ego throws up in defense, to continually push us away from the truth.

The journey inward, whether from meditation alone or being taken along by the hand and thrown into the Void by the Yoginis, will dissolve this false illusory self and open awareness to the vast expanse of reality. The ego will scream and fight the entire way, kicking and yelling, crying and cajoling to make you stop. Be relentless, as relentless as the Goddess. You want Truth, and no substitute will suffice.

From the *Diamond Sutra* there is a phrase *"Dwelling nowhere, mind goes forth."* Take this into your heart. Every moment of experience arises from nothingness—from nowhere. Amazing! Whatever you are, you came from nowhere, and every single moment of your life has manifested out of this apparent paradox of nothingness. This nothing is, in fact, *everything*. Where were you, before even your parents were born? Where will you be when all of this is gone? Take these thoughts into contemplation, turning them over and over again, chewing on them, feeling them in every cell of your body.

It helps to contemplate these thoughts in nature, as the immediacy of the elements brings to light this natural clarity of reality. The pristine, open, naturalness of existence is directly accessible at every moment. This is not the false thoughts of nihilism, which is easy to fall into when simply rationalizing or thinking about spiritual concepts. Rather, the primal and visceral experience of the present moment opens and awakens the heart to the ever-creating, ever-radiant expanse of reality.

3. A Pathway into the Night

> *"O Supreme of the Kula, Iccha Yoginis are so called by the siddhas out of their divine will. Afterwards this knowledge was revealed by the Iccha Yoginis to the Khecaris (sky dwellers), and then again to the Mothers by the Kecharis. The Mothers revealed it to the Bucharis (earth dwellers).*
>
> *A person initiated in the Kula of the Yoginis [...] achieves great siddhis and becomes dear to the Yoginis."*
>
> — *Kaulajnananirnaya,* Chapter 8

A stumbling block that many, particularly in the West, encounter when trying to approach tantra is the often-cited requirement of needing to find a Guru and be initiated into a tradition. To many this is immediately off-putting, and the exploration of tantra ends there. To spiritual seekers that persist, it often becomes an endless journey of seeking a guru, as well as a relentless examination of lineages and their authenticity. Spiritual development gets bogged down and the mind is cluttered by pedigrees and intrigues rather than the clear light of Awakening.

It is true that the tantras express the importance of Guru and initiation, with grave warnings to those who would approach without such credentials. In this sense it is reminiscent of the very images of the Yoginis: often voluptuous goddesses dressed alluringly, with the promise of boons. As you come in closer, the beautiful form is seen to have fangs, a sword, blood dripping from her mouth and, instead of a bowl of food, you see she is holding a man's severed head as an eating vessel!

In my experience, tantra, and specifically the Yoginis, are open to everyone with a sincere heart and desire. No tradition or person holds the key; the gatekeepers are the Yoginis themselves. Initiation into their Mysteries will come directly from the Yoginis. If you can win their favor, *they* will initiate you.

This is not to disparage gurus and lineages. I myself have initiation in several traditions, and have had many gurus and teachers over the years. I value these connections and honor the work of these guides. The end goal of any guru who truly has their students' spiritual growth in mind, is to have the student learn to be their own guru. Ultimately, the role of the guru is to show you the *guru within.* They should encourage your growth and increased self-reliance, and not keep you subjugated and chasing after initiations or secrets. If you have an authentic guru, cherish this connection.

However, if you do not have a guru or initiation, do not let that be a bar to your progress. With courage, determination and sincerity, you will be able to establish relationships with the Yoginis. No institution, order or tradition has control over the Yoginis. They belong to no one, and roam the skies and the earth as they will. They grant their favors according to their own Will. As if to reinforce this point, the *Kaulajnananirnaya* lists several great *siddhas* as part of the lineage of the Yoginis, alongside the names of some Yoginis themselves. These are to be remembered along with the personal *gurus* with which one might have a relationship.[12]

In the tantras will be found elaborate descriptions for following the ritual injunctions in great detail, giving the *mantras* with the correct pronunciation, and perfect offerings will result in specific results that have been written down, encoded over time.

It will be found with real experience that what is written and what is experienced are often very different. Many of the tantras were written by men during the medieval periods of India's long history. The context in which they were written, and the very language, was typically coded in the "twilight language" or symbolic language of the specific lineages. The rules and regulations, the ritual practices, were all directed towards these particular schools and traditions. What was applicable in that time and context may not be applicable now. In particular, with the Yoginis where so much is not written but rather has been transmitted in more subtle ways—through dreams, ecstatic realizations, possession—written scriptures fall by the wayside.

---

[12] See the 10th chapter of the *Kaulajnananirnaya.*

To work with *mantra,* to give offerings and approach the Yoginis, to receive their boons—all of this is possible to those who sincerely approach with an open heart.

In her book *The Madness of the Saints: Ecstatic Religion in Bengal,* June McDaniel explores the two broad paths with an analysis of formal initiations and traditions alongside the ecstatic, spontaneous revelations of direct realization.

> *"The path of progression is associated with [a] gradual approach. It emphasizes order and harmony, and the divine is reached by self-control and obedience. The god is most present in the greatest purity—of self, of place, of statue. Such purity involved loyalty to lineage and tradition, acceptance of hierarchy and authority, and ritual worship and practice. Ecstasy is attained by faith and learning, by acceptance of dharma, and avoidance of siddhis (powers) and self-glorification. Such a path is yogic and devotional, and called in Bengal sastriya dharma, the path of scriptural injunctions.*

Contrast this formalized and well-structured approach with the following:

> *"The path of breakthrough is associated with [...] crisis, or abrupt change. It emphasizes chaos and passion, and the divine is reached by unpredictable visions and revelations. The presence of deity is not determined by ritual purity.*
>
> *"— the god may be found in pure situations, but also at the burning ground, at the toilet, in blood and sexuality, in possessions and ordeals. Initiation and lineage do not determine experience.*
>
> *"— often there is a "jumping" of gurus—where different gurus are followed at different times. The criterion of status is neither yogic knowledge nor ritual skill, but rather bhava, the ecstatic state that comes with experience of the divine. Such states are called sahaja (natural and spontaneous) or svabhavika (unique to particular individual). The path is*

*more generally called asastriya, or not according to the
scriptures."*

This, the path of *asastriya,* is the path of the Yogini. This is a
Dionysiac, ecstatic and spontaneous path. We will find that art and
creativity take us deeper into these relationships, opening us up to
sorcery and enchantments that are woven into the very fabric of daily
life. Emotions, devotion, spontaneity and earnestness will take you
across the ocean of ignorance that is the material world, and the false
separation of self and other. The guru is the Goddess herself, and she
is the one that can invite you in and initiate you into the path of the
Yogini.

Bhava is a Sanskrit word that roughly means "feeling" or
"emotion." This is very closely tied in with the practice of *bhakti,* the
pure love and devotion that is felt towards the Divine. In approaching
the Yoginis, the practitioner may experience many stages and flavors
of *bhava* as the Yoginis make themselves known. This is not a passing
feeling; *bhava* is an overwhelming tidal wave of emotion that arises
spontaneously. In this sense, the effect of *bhava* is associated with
possession. As the Yoginis enter into and possess the devotee, the
person becomes possessed of the qualities of that Yogini. This intoxicating, maddening love might appear as spontaneous crying, oracular
recitations, intense energy, and more. There are as many manifestations of *bhava* as there are stars in the sky (and Yoginis).

An important term associated with three modes of *bhava, bhakti*
and *sahaja* is the Sanskrit word *svecchacara* which means "acting as
one likes" or "living life according to one's own will." In his work
Sakti and Shakta, Sir John Woodroffe (Arthur Avalon) discusses this
doctrine in connection with the *Kaula* ritual of *Panchamakara,* the
"Five M's" offerings:

> *"[...] the illuminated knower of Brahman (Brahmajnani) is
> above both good (Dharma) and evil (Adharma) [...] Such a
> one is a Svecchacari whose way is Svecchacara or 'do as you
> will'."*

The *Svecchacari* is not bound by the rules and obligations imposed externally by society, culture, tradition and so on. One's Will is the sole rule and guide of life. Evil and good are seen as relative terms, where the Will reigns supreme. To such a person, the only law is that of *Sveccha*—one's own Will.

Woodroffe continues:

> *"Similar doctrines and practice in Europe are there called Antinomian. The doctrine is not peculiar to the Tantras. It is to be found in the* Upanishads, *and is in fact a very commonly held doctrine in India. Here again, as so stated and as understood outside India, it has the appearance of being worse than it really is. If Monistic views are accepted, then theoretically we must admit that Brahman is beyond good and evil, for these are terms of relativity applicable to beings in this world only. Good has no meaning except in relation to evil and vice versa. Brahman is beyond all dualities, and a Jnani who has become Brahman (Jivan-mukta) is also logically so[...] Svecchacarini is a name of the Devi, for She does what She pleases since She is the Lord of all."*

The path of *Svecchacara* appears in Hindu tantrik texts such as the *Mahanirvana Tantra,* prominent teachings of the *Kaula Shakta* traditions or "left hand path" worshippers of the Great Goddess. It is also very clearly expressed in the non-dual Yogini centric tantra of the *Kaulajnananirnaya.*

The Yoginis embody the principle of *Svecchacara,* and they are each *Svecchacarini.* Their spontaneous and energetic arising occurs of their own volition. It is to them that you are pledging any allegiances, and forging a *kula* (tribe) with the Yogini directly.

The Great Goddess manifests herself in three ways that are represented by her three primary *Shaktis* or powers:

Kriya: Action, Dynamic, Forceful Energy
Iccha: Will, Desire, Intent
Jnana: Knowledge, Gnosis

This dynamic combination gives rise to the action of *Svecchacara,* and the flow of divine energy throughout the universe. In working directly with the Yoginis, there is a vital intensity and immediacy to the experiences. No guidelines, no rules, no restrictions —this can be simultaneously incredibly liberating and terrifying. The Yoginis will expose the most hidden recesses of your Self, bringing light to shadowy regions that you may have only suspected in brief flashes during the darkest dreams.

Unlike formal lineages and rituals, the rigid structures which work more at controlling energy and experience, with the Yoginis we are invoking the wildness, the sensuous, the unexpected. The seeming randomness of the universe, the chaos of creation and destruction, and the illusory nature of the material world and self—all of this comes crashing into the forefront of consciousness in a blazing light of real-ization and awareness. The Yoginis will seize you by the hand and pull you up into the open night skies, where you must either quickly learn to fly, or come crashing back down in preparation to be the main course at their circle.

4. The Circle of Awareness

I sit down on the black cushion before the small altar made of wood, upon which is an image of Kali. I take a stick of incense, lighting it and setting it before the altar. Adjusting my posture, hands folded on my lap in the cosmic mudra, I take a moment to feel my core and base of spine like a strong tree trunk that reaches deep into the dark and cool earth, while my head feels gently pulled up, like the branches of the world tree reaching high into the sky.

Taking a deep breath, as I exhale I find the balance between relaxing the body and having just the right amount of tension to keep the mind awake and aware; breathe in and out. Eyes half closed, gazing easily through the incense smoke to the small statue of Kali, dancing her cosmic mudras of creation and dissolution.

She is a small bronze statue that found me many years ago in a small shop in Kathmandu. She smiled at me then as now, her tongue lolling out between her perfectly white and very sharp, wolf-like teeth. Her bright dark eyes, kohl-lined, all penetrating, like opening up to vast expanses of cosmic horizons, deep as far-flung galaxies, black holes that both absorb and emanate entire universes.

Her long black hair flows in thick rivulets, small tight braids along the strings interweaving with deep waves of flowing, thick energy and luminescence, down past her shoulders and back, a moving, vibrating, sinuously evoking forest of darkness. Her bare shoulders and neck peek out through the lush hair, warm wheat honey-colored skin, as though the light of the sun had been cast into her golden form, shining through smooth, creamy, flawless light.

Behind her head a glowing, radiating nimbus of black light, flowing forth continuously in deep circular patterns that modulate, creeping through the air itself, sound and light mixing even as a thunderstorm collecting the very air and electricity about itself as it gathers around cold grey mountains.

Her perfect face is dynamic bliss, her complexion perfectly radiant and glowing, her ears ornamented by golden, dangling earrings.

Her arms, all four of them, naked except for the armlets of golden jewel-encrusted bands of light that circle her upper arms and wrists.

In her upper right hand, she holds aloft a scimitar, golden starlight from a distant galaxy, blown across space from the explosions of ancient stars, projecting particles out across millennia, collecting on earth and forged into her mighty weapon.

Her lower right hand holds a trident, the handle composed of ancient hardwood from a sacred forest and encrusted with jewels. The head of the trident is composed of stellar platinum, glistening with dewy radiance.

In her lower left hand is a freshly severed human head—a male. She holds it aloft triumphantly, but so innocently and childlike, showing that the ego illusions that we take as such serious matters of life and death—even life and death itself—empire building endeavors, all just a game, a play, a menagerie for her to enjoy as she dances and twirls from one play to the next, always with that beautiful and innocent smile and playfulness.

In her lower left hand is a skull-cup, blazing red liquid light collected and glistening, the elixir of life itself, deep red as though collected from some fantastic primordial pomegranate, darkly spending blood of life, which she collects as her own, taking in every single drop and savoring it like she were tasting the most perfect and exquisite vintage, from grapes that the earth has never given birth to, a wine that intoxicates the entire being, all illusion and pretense vanishing such that reality in all of its nakedness and immediacy and presence shines forth, the wine of the Witches' Sabbath, a black mass of seeming outer horror, that reveals to those who will penetrate its outer gloom and see with their hearts burst open, eyes unclouded by delusion, that the seeming macabre scene is in truth the blazing, all-embracing, ever-present, all-creating void that is everything, and from which everything has its being. This, the sangraal of legend, contains the very elixir of immortality that will erase all illusions, revealing the visceral and primal glorious Truth of Self that is No Self, the All and None, the Alpha and Omega, beginning and end of all things, where time itself is caught up in the vast black holes of her eyes, where existence is rearranged into new patterns and structures by her hair; lives are born, live and die beneath her dancing feet, the sound of her anklets jingling echoes of the countless heartbeats across the manifestation of universes again and again that her dance weaves in and out of existence.

Her skirt of severed arms, flowing with her movements, is the rising and falling of entire civilizations and cultures, entire species coming and going out of existence, verdant fields turning after a season into dried and barren landscapes, only to cycle again to fertile and life-giving and illusory-making dreams of reality and experience.

Emanating from all of the waves, all the cycles, all the twists and turns, and arch of her waist, back, arms and legs, the flowing hair, the lava-like crimson flash of her tongue, the piercing, sharp white teeth—underlying it all, those eyes, always shimmering dark pools of luminesces, the portal of an immense, inconceivable darkness that is the source, being, heart of All, outside all concepts of time, beyond all conceptions, luminous, radiant darkness; a pulsating, wave after wave, undulating, serpent-like starlight coalesced into the circles of those beautiful eyes.

One thing that has been essential in my own work with Yoginis is meditation. I have had a solid practice for decades before coming to them, and this has only deepened since working with them.

My ability to tune in to the voice of the Yoginis and hear their songs, has been largely from having a solid meditation practice. The ability to still the mind and enter into a condition of quiet, awake awareness and contemplation opens you to receiving information from other realms. Importantly, you also become able to differentiate between your own thoughts, which are plentiful, and impressions or voices that you receive from the Yoginis.

You want to be able to hear the Yoginis, to see them in the world, and to feel their presence. You want to be able to receive their guidance and instruction, and be able to clearly differentiate between your own conflicted thoughts and feelings, and what the Yoginis are bringing.

The benefits of meditation are immense and plentiful. It is veritable cornucopia. For example, concentration increases, which is useful in everyday life as well as interactions with other people and beings. You become more in contact with your real self, and spontaneous with life and your interactions. Ironically (and rather unintuitively), after the initial stages of self-analysis, this true self begins to shine forth without the neurotic hindrances that are the hallmark of the unexamined mind. It is as though all of the introspection and self-analysis opens up into the universe, and the easy flow of energy shines forth in your everyday expressions and interactions.

There have been plenty of studies showing the physical benefits of meditation. Decreases in blood pressure, lower stress hormones, and the ability to deal with whatever life may throw at you without getting caught up in a loop of thoughts and emotions.

Why is meditation so important?

• Everything that you experience is your mind.

• Everything that you know, every thought, vision, sensation—all is your mind.

• The very sensation of your body, of having a head and looking out of it, of interacting with other people or things—all of this is mind stuff.

• No matter what the ultimate nature of reality may be, no matter what happens to be "out there," no matter what you may really be— your immediate, direct, personal experience is through your mind, whatever that is.

• Even your conceptualization of mind, perhaps as a brain sitting inside your skull with neurons firing off continuously, is a model that appears in the mind.

Where exactly this dividing line between self and other, inside and outside, may be laid out is irrelevant for our purposes. The point is that everything we experience, all of our awareness, is mind, or consciousness or Self. This Self is not the ephemeral ego and personality that you have built up, but rather something far grander, timeless and undying.

So while it may often be thrown around as an insult to say something is "all in your mind," the very literal fact of the matter is that you cannot escape your mind, and absolutely everything you know and experience is with it. Good or bad, painful or blissful, ego-bashing or world-building, has one point of experience. If you want to know what the state of your mind is right now, just look. No, literally, *look*. Everything you are seeing is mind stuff.

Examined closely, you will experience first-hand this mind stuff. It is everywhere, and everything! It will take some getting acquainted, as we are taught at a very early age to differentiate experience into subject and object, inner and outer. However, once the nature of mind is pointed out to you and experienced, the shift in perception—in Awareness itself—is life changing. This is true Initiation.

This realization is not something that most would just pick up from reading a book (although it can certainly happen, and there are instances of people reading a particular passage in some book that completely brings them to the direct experience). More often, it requires some work—ironic, as once "seen" it is the most obvious and direct experience there is. It has always been there, and will always be present. In fact, its very being is what allows any kind of "experience" at all.

To work with the Yoginis (or any beings, be they embodied or disembodied), it will be exceedingly helpful, therefore, to have some familiarity with the nature of your mind, or at least be able to sit still for a while without being lost in thought. This practice will also put you on the path towards being aware even in your sleep—lucid dreaming. As dreamwork is also an important part of working with the Yoginis, the benefits should be readily apparent.

There are countless types of meditation, and you won't necessarily be better off with one over another. The important thing is to have a regular practice, and some experience with both stilling the mind and concentrating it.

In addition to the benefits of opening your consciousness to clear communication with other realms, there is plenty of evidence showing that regular meditation can help with overall physical and mental well-being.

Going deeper, don't underestimate the depth of experience that you will develop and open up to from simple meditation practice. What we are accustomed to think we are, who we think we are, what we think our life is—all of that is a lie that we tell ourselves and each other. Through meditation, you will peer through this imagery that has been constructed and automatically taken for reality. You will begin to peer through it all and come to the pulsing, vibrating, juicy reality of the present moment. This is truly waking up. What we think of as our life is really a sort of dream, driven mostly unconsciously and controlled by biases, cravings and aversions, ego impulses and a false sense of being separate from everything and everyone.

Set aside at least 20 minutes every day to cultivate a meditation practice. It can be longer, but if you are just getting started, it's best to commit to something that you will be able to maintain. If you already have a strong meditation practice you can skip to the next chapter.

For those just starting, a few tricks help to make your experience easier and more conducive to keeping it going. Once you have a steady practice, some or all of this might be discarded; or, depending on what type of practice you are following, you might find that these instructions are a good basic foundation that you can keep in your toolkit.

First, find a place that you can dedicate to this work. Ideally you should have a room—or a corner of a room—set aside for your daily meditation and ritual work. I used to live in a small apartment with roommates, and used my closet as my space, with a small altar set up. Later, I was able to expand to a full, dedicated room. The point is, you do not need a lot of space. If you cannot dedicate a permanent space, or if you live with other people, let them know you need some private time each day to practice your meditation. If you have access to the outdoors, all the better! Find a place in nature where you can meditate. The thing about meditation is that, once you get past the initial learning stage, you can engage in it anywhere, in any circumstance. Eyes closed or eyes open; quiet or noisy; in a secluded room or on a busy commuter train—you always have it at your disposal. In fact, the goal (if something like meditation can be said to have one) is that eventually you will come to see that you can meditate and be aware in your daily life, beyond your formal sitting time. As Namkhai Norbu would often say, "Work with your circumstances." Any activity in any circumstance is suitable and perfect. But, let's not get ahead of ourselves! Start simple and with dedicated periods of time.

If inside, set up a small table to use as a shrine or altar. Have some incense and a candle. You can set up a shrine with anything that reminds you of the sacred: a Buddha statue, or a statue of a God or Goddess, a photo of a Guru, and so on. You might find that performing an opening ritual to cast your circle helps to differentiate this space from the mundane (see Chapter 7, "East Meets West" for more on this). Your shrine could have nothing more than a fresh flower on it— what is a more beautiful, obvious sign of life and mystery than that!

For sitting, the important thing is to be comfortable. This might be in a lotus position on the floor, or sitting upright in a chair—whatever your circumstances allow and where you can sit still without much discomfort or fidgeting around. Sit with your spine a little straighter than usual, but without causing strain. This is purely for practical reasons. We want to get on to the main act, and if you are constantly readjusting your position or if you are uncomfortable, it is going to be a distraction. Often meditation teachers will tell you not to lie down while meditating, for the very simple reason that most of us are used to sleeping in that position. That said, if you have back problems or otherwise find the need, it is perfectly fine to practice in any position that is comfortable.

Another, more subtle reason for having the back more erect is the flow of energy. At the beginning this is true, but it will become even more of a necessity as we progress into the ritual part of the workings, where the energy of the *chakras* is activated and the *kundalini* energy is stimulated to rise up the spine.

Sit comfortably before your shrine, light the candle and incense.

Breathe in deeply, and then relax and slowly breathe out. As you do so, imagine all of your thoughts about the day, any concerns or worries, flow out with the breath and into the earth.

Breathe in deeply again, and as you exhale, mentally decide to be fully present. Not dwelling on the past, or thinking about the future. Just here, now.

Breathe in deeply again, and as you inhale see yourself filling up with radiant white light. See it filling every cell of your body, filling you with healing, energetic light. As you exhale, relax and feel the calmness.

Now, just breathe normally. Do not try to force the breath into any pattern. Just pay attention to the breath, and observe it as though it were the first time you paid attention to breathing—it might be!

Find a spot where it seems easy to follow the breath, maybe the rising and falling of your chest, or the nose, or throat. Just pay attention to your breath.

It is often easier in the beginning to count the breaths, or mentally say on each inhale "in" and on the exhale mentally say "out."

Each time you find yourself lost in thought, just gently return to the breath. Do not criticize yourself or get frustrated, just return to the breath.

Do this for 20 minutes, every day, at the same time and place every day. This will help to build the habit, and will start to have an effect on the location where you sit, turning it truly into your shrine space.

The first few times you meditate, you might think you are some amazing prodigy, as you did not get distracted at all. Sorry in advance for bursting the bubble, but this is almost invariably a symptom of having such poor concentration that you do not even realize you are distracted. One of the biggest obstacles is thinking without knowing you are thinking. That 20 minutes flew by!

As you progress, it will start to become apparent that the mind is a never-ending, ceaseless chatterbox of noise. You will think you are a failure, and that you will never be able to meditate. When you reach this stage, congratulations! Your concentration is improving enough that you can now see how often you are thinking. This is good progress.

As this goes on, you will realize what seems at times to be a continuous, torrential undercurrent of thoughts, just barely perceptible. Just let them arise and pass away. Do not ascribe any importance to them. Just notice whatever thought arises, and notice it fading away.

Eventually you will reach a point of equipoise, where you are awake and aware. You will be able to watch the thoughts come and go without being moved or carried away by any of them. In the West this is often called the Watcher stage. You are actively conscious and aware, watching your thoughts—being aware of awareness. This is a powerful stage, where you clearly see that you are not identified with your thoughts. They come and go, forever changing and feeding upon one another. Meanwhile, watching it all silently, is this new point of view (not really new, but you may have never really noticed it before). Now, don't stop here.

You might switch from the breath, and instead start inquiring into the nature of your mind itself. If I am watching my thoughts, and watching myself watch my thoughts, then who or what is watching? Who watches the watcher? Keep going. Try to find where the source of the watcher is. Is it in your head? Behind your eyes? And by the way, while you are looking for this, who exactly is it that is aware of the watcher that is watching?

Pick one of your senses. Hearing is often an easy one to start with. With your eyes closed and sitting comfortably, just listen. Try to hear every sound. Don't grasp at them, just listen with as much attention as you can. Notice that they are all happening "right here." There is no concept of distance or proximity; if you hear the sound, it's in the same space as everything else—it is happening right here. Try to "widen" your sense of hearing. What is the most "distant" sound you can hear? Isn't even that sound happening right here? Where is "here" anyway?

Try feeling every sensation of your body. Remember not to judge or analyze; rather, just feel the sensations as intimately and exquisitely as you can. If there is a tingling in your fingers, for example, feel that as closely as possible. Feel the weight of your body sitting down.

Maybe you have the urge to scratch an itch on your nose; rather than immediately reaching up to your nose to scratch it, try to focus on the itching sensation. Pay attention to it as though it is the first time you have ever felt an itch. Get deep inside the sensation, so that all sense of shape and body parts vanishes; there is nothing but the sensation of an itch. What does this feel like?

Feel every sensation as though it is for the first time. Approach them with innocent curiosity. If you pay close enough attention, the shape of your body will dissolve into a purely sensory experience of temperatures, pressure, tingling, energy moving around and so on. Try to get really up close to this, really intimate with it.

Sight is another powerful sense to work with. You don't have to meditate with your eyes closed! Whether they are open or closed, everything that you see is an arising in consciousness. The same space where dreams arise is the space you see when your eyes are opened. Try to get a real sense of this by actively looking with your eyes alternately open and closed.

Get outside, day or night, and find a comfortable place where you can sit and gaze into the sky. If you can get out camping or into the wilderness, even better, but it's not required. You can step outside or even look out a window. Relax your body with some simple breathing, and then look into the sky. Soften your gaze, letting the peripheral vision come in. The sky is one of my favorite things to look at, an instant reminder of the expansiveness of consciousness. During the day you can dive in to the different shades of blue, white, grey that may be present. The yellow shades from the sun. Clouds drifting across the vast expanse, and how they change shapes. At night, the sky really opens up. On a clear night you might find yourself diving into the cosmos, an infinity of star-fields twinkling and shining in the depths of darkness, or the luminous Moon—what a gorgeous sight! Stare into the sky, day or night, and feel the expanse of consciousness.

Sunrise and sunset are very powerful times as well. While taking the obvious precautions (please don't stare directly into the sun), you can look near the sunrise or sunset gently, with soft focus, relaxing into the moment. After a few minutes turn your gaze up towards the sky, or close your eyes. In each case there may be an afterimage of the sun. Focus on this afterimage which is projecting into the sky or behind your closed eyes. Give it your concentration, and follow it closely, again with innocent curiosity. Watch how it changes shape, how colors evolve and change and rotate, how it moves across the sky. Can you make it change to a certain color? Or move it to the center of the sky? As you look closely at the image, does it start to take on a more definite form, resembling anything?

At night you can also try working with a candle flame, or a bonfire or fire pit. While meditating, gaze into the flame. Again, this should be a relaxed gaze. Widen your vision easily and don't strain. Just look easily at the flame. What sort of colors do you see in it? How does the top of the flame differ from the center, and the bottom of the flame?

Keep looking into the flame. An afterimage will start to form around it, adding some dark colors around the flames. Now, gently close your eyes. The afterimage will appear. Pay attention to this now, watching it closely. See how it moves around the interior landscape. Watch it carefully, seeing the colors shift, the size grow and shrink. The closer and longer you look, the more details you will see. Is there more than one color? Is it solid? Striped? Are there dots of color? Every few minutes take a moment to ask yourself, who is watching all of this?

Throughout all of these exercises, when you find yourself spacing out or daydreaming or otherwise distracted, notice the thought (become aware that you were spacing out, or daydreaming, or distracted), and focus again. This act of "coming back" to awareness is a powerful practice which will strengthen your concentration abilities. Try not to get caught up in more thoughts as you notice the one that distracted you. For example, I am quietly meditating and after some time has passed realize that I was actually *thinking about having some ice cream, and bills that I need to pay, and how cute my wife is, and a book I want to read, and how my back is hurting...* Suddenly I catch myself, and immediately am back to awareness. What you don't want to do is catch yourself, spend another few minutes judging yourself and thinking, "Dammit I just can't do this!" Oops, lost in thought again. Rather, notice it and refocus. The thought will drop away back into nothingness. No need for judgement or criticism or generating more thoughts. And remember, when you keep catching thoughts and coming back, this is a "good thing." Not that you need to judge your sessions of meditation, but it should encourage you to know that we all go through it, and it's normal.

Supporting Practice: Pranayama and Asana

This chapter has described the heart of meditation; if you keep to it diligently, a flood of benefits will come that will assist in every aspect of your life. As meditation is one of the branches of *yoga,* you can also take comfort in knowing that it brings you closer into communion with the Yoginis.

As additional support, we turn again to Patanjali's Eight limbs of Yoga and specifically *Pranayama* and *Asana*—the science of breath and of postures. There are entire schools dedicated just to these subjects; people can study them for years, and there are even Yoga certifications. The subjects are vast and interesting, and well worth the effort to learn. For our purposes as a supplement to your meditation practice, the emphasis is on a simple form of *pranayama* and *asana* that can be done for a few minutes before starting with meditation proper.

Sukha Pranayama

This very simple form of *pranayama* called *Sukha Pranayama* (*sukha* is a Sanskrit word for "easy"), will help get the mind and body into a relaxed state from which it will be easier to sit still calmly for meditation. There is a of lot mention in both traditional materials as well as more contemporary medical studies indicating that this type of controlled breathing may have some remarkable effects on improving overall health and emotional well-being. In Yoga, the breath is said to carry *prana,* which can be thought of as the life force. The manipulation of breath, therefore, has profound implications for quality of life.

As with meditation, sit comfortably, with the back a little straighter, and breathe normally. Now take in a relaxed breath, and with the right hand, close the right nostril with the thumb. Hold this position while breathing out through the left nostril. When the breath is fully exhaled, breathe in gently through the left nostril. Now release the right nostril, and with the ring and small fingers of the right hand close the left nostril. Breathe in gently through the right nostril, and then exhale through the right. This sequence is one round of *pranayama*. Continue this cycle of alternate nostril breathing for a few minutes, as the mind and body drop into a relaxed, calm state. It is important to not strain or try to control the breath; just breathe in a relaxed, normal way while directing the air through alternate nostrils in this way.

Surya Namascara Asana

Many people will already be familiar with this set of *asanas* which collectively form a practice called the "Sun Salutation" *(Surya* is Sun, and *Namascara* is "salutation", from which the familiar greeting *"Namaste"* comes).

1. Stand straight with your feet together. Place your palms together, touching your chest.
2. Now breathe in deeply while you raise your arms above your head and bend backwards gently from the waist.
3. Bend forward from your hips as you breathe out slowly. Knees should be slightly bent (you do not want any strain on your lower back). Hands are flat on the floor besides your feet. At this point your head should be near your shins.
4. Breathe in and stretch your right leg behind so that your foot is at right angles to your leg and resting on its toes. The left leg is vertical to the floor and your head is back, looking forward.
5. While you breathe, place your left foot back to match the right foot. Your body is now in a straight line, supported only by your toes and hands, which are in a vertical line.

6. Still holding your breath, lower your body and rest your toes, knees, chest, palms and forehead on the floor. Stomach and pelvis are off the floor with hands by your shoulders, elbows bent and arms by your sides.

7. Breathing out, lie flat on the ground.

8. Breathe in as you raise your head and then the upper part of your torso. Keep your pelvis flat on the ground and the head back.

9. Hold your breath and bring your feet flat onto the floor and raise your hips to form an inverted V shape.

10. Still holding your breath, bring the right foot forward so that it is vertical and the left leg is back (the complementary to Step #4).

11. Breathe out as you bring the left leg up, and place your feet together between your hands. Straighten your legs (with knees slightly bent) and place your head near your shins.

12. Breathe in as you straighten up from the hips. Bring your arms up, and stretch them backwards as you bend back gently from the waist.

13. Breathe out as you straighten your body. Now raise your arms over your head and back again as you bend your elbows to place your hands together at your chest.

This sequence completes one round of the Sun Salutation. I like to do three rounds, the first one slowly to warm up, the second round a little faster, and the last at a slightly faster pace. Try to maintain awareness of your body and breathe while doing the practice, as it is a meditation of movement.[13]

---

[13] It can be hard to follow the written instructions. If you find the instructions unclear, look online for videos. Even better, find a local Yoga studio and sign up for some classes. *Yoga Journal* has a good introductory article: www.yogajournal.com/yoga-101/surya-namaskar

Post-Mediation: Jyoti Mudra

When your meditation is complete, take a minute before opening your eyes to perform this *mudra*. *Jyoti* is a Sanskrit word that means "light", and this practice will give you direct experience of the ways light may manifest in the interior vision. This practice helps to sensitize your ability to perceive with the "inner eyes." The seemingly solid veil between "day" and "night" consciousness, or the "outer" and "inner" worlds, will begin to dissolve.

Close your eyes. Rub the palms of your hands together briskly to produce heat. Next, place both hands gently over the closed eyes, with the palms facing inwards (towards your face). Now just relax, breathe normally, while you gaze into the profound darkness that opens up to your closed eyes.

In this practice you may see vibrant colors, or spirals of light and coruscating geometric shapes radiating in space. The more you gaze, the more this vista will open up, expanding into what appears to be an endless view of space, color and light, all in a primordial energetic dance. These visions may begin to build and form the framework for the visionary work with the Yoginis.

Continue in this *mudra* for a few minutes, before gently opening the eyes. With some practice, you may notice that you can see the swirling images even after opening the eyes, almost as though they are superimposed on normal vision. This may be easier to notice first in a darkened room, as shadow images interact almost dreamlike in your vision, moving about the surroundings. With repeated exposure, this will become visible even in bright daylight.

As the incense stick burns down to just a small twig of light, I see her eyes brightly glowing in the collected darkness. The universe was torn down and burnt on the cosmic fire of the cremation grounds, and from the Great Darkness of the eternal Now comes forth something new.

Another breath, as she glows through the incense smoke that drifts through the air slowly, curling and slinking like the snakes of

Medusa's hair, weaving about the small statue. She smiles, a sidelong glance and shy smile.

> *And what rough beast, its hour come round at last,*
> *Slouches towards Bethlehem to be born?*
> — *The Second Coming,* William Butler Yates

5. Sorcery of Sound

The subject of *mantra* is really worthy of a book in itself (or several!), and many have been written. For our purposes, however, the emphasis is on *Shakti Bija Mantras,* feminine energy encoded into vibration of sound.

It is often said that any *mantras* are lifeless without being activated by a guru, and that no benefit can possibly arise from such *mantras* that are received without such blessings. Indeed, when you read the tantras, there are many dire warnings about using *mantras* without its first being transmitted by the guru. To this we can only reply that yes, *mantras* given from the mouth of the guru to the ear of the disciple are treasures and carry a power of their own, a power that is deeply seated with the specific teacher and lineage that they are representing.

What of *mantras* that arise spontaneously? Or those that are of the nature of the Goddess herself, and her attendants? Do they really need the intercession of a priest class to "empower" them? In my opinion, the Goddess probably laughs at such attempts to lock her into the chains of a largely patriarchal power play. If she chooses to convey her blessings, she will do it. End of story.

Many of the *bijas* were first heard by the *rishis,* highly tuned-in seers who experienced the powers directly and recorded the energy patterns as these seed syllables. Many of the *mantras* were encoded into the text of tantras and other writings, and through initiated lore had to be extracted from the Sanskrit verses. In Sir John Woodroffe's translation of the *Varnamala (The Garland of Letters),* the Goddess as Kundalini in her ascent gives rise to the cosmic pantheon of *Shaktis,* each vibrating and throbbing with a magical display of colors and sound that builds up the universe. Through ascending levels of sound and vibration, consciousness becomes light, which becomes matter and all of creation.

Again, sincerity and intent are paramount. If you approach the Yoginis with an open heart, asking for their guidance and initiation, they will enliven any *mantras* and bring their effects to fruition. In fact, as your relationship with them deepens, you may be given *mantras* directly. In my own relationships with the Yoginis, I have received some *mantras* that have proven to unlock deeply important and personal aspects of my initiation. These have usually been communicated by way of vivid dreams, or arising out of deep meditations.

It can be beneficial to take any *mantras* that you are working with, and offer them to the Yoginis, or even to the Goddess herself in her form of Durga. Reciting the 12th chapter of the *Chandi Path* (the full name is the *Devi Mahatmyam),* and then offering your *mantras,* will remove any obstacles or obscurations from them. This can also be done with your tantrik tools, such as the *mala* or the other weapons that are described later on. Offer them all to the Yoginis, and ask them to enchant them and remove any obscurations. In my own case, I enjoy doing this every year during *Durga Puja,* where, as part of the ceremonies, I offer up and rededicate all of my tools, *mantras* and even my own body and consciousness.

In this work, unique *mantras* can and do come in dreams. In such cases they are direct gifts from the Yoginis. If you find yourself receiving personal *mantras,* write them down and work with them. They will open doors and establish powers unique to you and your situation. This is a deep gift and one that should be cherished. In my own work I have received several *mantras* directly in dreams from the mouth of Yoginis, and these have gone on to be focuses of my work and opened doors to aspects of life in the "outer" or day consciousness world.

When doing *mantra* recitation, the best way is to do mental *japa.* This has a few benefits. For one, it aids concentration, which increases the accumulation of the current of energy associated with the *mantra.* In the tantrik tradition *mantras* are recited silently so that any people not initiated into the *mantra,* or nearby spirits that are attracted, do not overhear the *mantras.*

Shakti, as already mentioned, is a Sanskrit word that means "power"—and in particular, feminine power. *Bija* is a "seed". These *mantras* are seed syllables that embody the roots of specific powers of the Yoginis.

These seed syllables can be used alone or in different combinations with other *mantras* to produce powerful changes in consciousness. You might choose one and decide to work with it for some time before moving to another. Try to really experience the sound, how it resonates in your mind. Remember that these are highly charged sources of pure power—the Goddess herself. If you tune in your mind and have practiced sufficiently with the meditation exercises given earlier, just one sounding of a *bija* can alter your energy and mind. When I am deep in my practice, just saying the *bija* once has brought the needed result. Think of when you are in love, and just the sound of your lover's name gives you a thrill. Just thinking of them for a moment opens your heart and gets your blood pumping! When you are flooded with *bhava,* or a particular aspect of Shakti that you want to work with, it is the same. The very thrill of hearing their *bija* opens up the flow of energy and creativity.

Don't get discouraged if you do not experience this right at the beginning. For many reasons it may take some time to establish a relationship with the *bija,* for it to grow inside of you and to bear fruit. Try easing into the relationship, getting to know it and savor it with your concentration and senses. Here is a suggested start, and a way to help develop intuition and the finer senses at the same time:

1. Pick a *bija* to work with *by chance.* You can facilitate this in a lot of ways. Get creative! Since you are probably holding this book in your hands right now, one certain way is to turn to the list of *bijas* in the "Bija Mantras" section below, close your eyes, open your heart, feel your expansiveness and connection to the world, and then let your finger fall onto the page with all of the *bijas.* The one your finger lands on (or is closest to) is the one that is right for you at this point in time.

2. Go through the preliminary stilling exercises from Chapter 4, "The Circle of Awareness" (sit quietly, take a few deep breaths, relax). Make a mental commitment to focus right here, right now.

3. Say the *bija* quietly out loud. Try to really hear it while you are saying it. Feel the sound as it is made, how it feels on your lips, how your breath feels saying it.

4. Say the *bija,* again out loud, but a little quieter, almost a whisper. Again, focus on the sound, the way it moves in the air, the way it feels in your throat, your lips. Do you feel it in your head? Or in your heart? Or in your chest? *See* where you *feel* it.

5. If you had your eyes open, close them now. Say the *bija* even more quietly, but still with your lips. Again, try to sense it and feel it with your body as you do so.

6. Now, with your eyes closed, keep saying the *bija,* but mentally. Try to really focus on the "internal" sound. The speed of the repetition does not matter; in fact don't even try to control it. Just check that the *mantra* is there and listen to it mentally. Do you feel any different than when you were saying it out loud? Do you feel it in another part of your body? Pay attention to the sound and try to feel every aspect of it. Do you see any colors? Any sense of heat or cold? Any tingling or vibrating? Just continue to listen to the *mantra* while you observe with gentle curiosity.

Keep this going for 20 minutes as a good start. That's just enough time for most people to get into a rhythm and concentration with the play of the *bija.* When you are working specifically with a Yogini, this might extend much longer, or it may only be used once or twice in the space of a few seconds to "open" a space or level of consciousness once you have attuned to the vibration of the particular *mantra.* When you find that you have spaced out or are thinking about something besides the *mantra,* gently return your focus to it and continue.

When the practice deepens, extending beyond 20 minutes, there may be subtle mutations and changes to the *bija.* The sound may change, getting louder or quieter. It may sound as though someone else is saying it, or that it is coming from some place "outside." There may be more than one voice, like an entire chorus or multiple voices singing or chanting. It may start to sound as though it is an echo in a large cave, or it is being called out from a mountain top. Just observe all of these changes without trying to change anything yourself, or analyze anything (analysis and recording can come later). The *bija* itself might change into another *mantra,* or even another sound entirely (a high-pitched buzzing sound, like bees swarming, or rushing water, or wind through trees, or a deep and resonant humming sound, or whispering of many voices, or what sounds like many crystal bells clinking together are just some examples).

Unless you are on a retreat or working with a group that keeps to a schedule, it's a good idea to have some way to demarcate the time. This is a twofold advantage in that you will not only sit for 5 minutes thinking 20 have passed, but also you will not sit in *mantra* meditation for hours thinking only 5 minutes has passed! Setting a timer for 20 minutes is a simple solution. Most people seem to have their phones with them at all times, and most all of the smartphones have timers on them. So long as you can keep from scrolling through Facebook during your *sadhana* (spiritual practice) it should be all right.

Rather than a timer, another time-tested approach is to count with your *mala*. This has the distinct advantage of being a lot more esthetically pleasing, as well as at least a few thousand years of usage across multiple cultures and traditions. Experiment to see what works best for you, and how many rounds of the *mala* (100? 1000?) depending on your concentration and speed to get into the energy of the *mantra* in a session.

In the tantras, many of the *bijas* and longer *mantras* are said to have curses placed on them, keeping their benefits locked like a treasure chest. The key, in these cases, is in the hands of the guru. Having worked with *mantras* from gurus, as well as *mantras* extracted from tantras, and from *mantras* directly received in dreams from the Yoginis themselves, I cannot say that I have found any *mantras* locked in this way. The *mantras* are power, the Goddess herself in vibrational form. Again, approach with an open heart and sincerity. If you want to have a real relationship with the Goddess, why not talk to her from your heart? There are *mantras* in the forests and open wilderness; *mantras* in the sky and the stars; *mantras* that seep through into waking consciousness from dreams and intuitions. If you want to have a relationship with the Yoginis, the chances are they have already been right in front of you, waiting for you to wake up and see them.

Bija Mantras

Take a *bija* and silently repeat it to yourself, feeling it in your body. Try to "see" it. What color is it? What does it smell like? Does it have a taste? Do you feel it in any particular part of your body, as though it is centered there or comes to rest there? Or does it move around, maybe starting at your head and slowly undulating down your back, like warm honey filling your body? You might feel an almost liquid, fiery essence, while others might have a cool, soothing wateriness, as if the moon were melting into you and filling you with light. Still others could bring in the depth of the stars, or seemingly distant nebulae somehow commingling with your heart, filling your blood and cells, turning you into a cosmic vortex of energy. Others may make your head feel like it is a Black Hole, with the universe being expelled on each breath and forming anew.

Don't try to rush through all of them. You might have one that resonates, and you may decide to work with it continuously. Take it into every breath, every experience. Try to see the world through your *mantra*. Let it work its way into your dreams, expressing itself in shapes and colors, even figures that start out as willowy shadows and dancing fire at the periphery of awareness. As you become more intimate with it, the sound can become electrifying, making your skin tingle and your heart open with sensation. Don't try to fight with it, but do enter into a relationship with it. The *bijas* have personalities, and they are like magnets that bring the Yoginis closer in to you. Savor them, dive into the full sensory experience, and let it fill you, permeate you, enliven your body and mind.

Om—This is the energy of *prana,* the life force of the breath. *Om* is creative, all encompassing.

Hrim—Awakening, stimulating, commingling. The *Kaulajnana-nirnaya* says that this is dear to the Yoginis, granting an immediate connection to them. Sound it as an extended *"hreem"*.

Aim—Feminine energy *(shakti),* ascending energy. The sound is similar to a drawn out *"I'm"*.

Srim—Lunar energy that collects, unifies other powers. Cooling, liquid, watery, reflective. Sounds like *"sreem"*.

Krim—Dynamic, explosive energy, orgasm taken to the limit and finally exploding in ecstasy. Sounds like *"kreem"*.

Hum—The warmth and power of fire, of the heart, of collectivity.

Strim—Stabilizing energy, used to psychically nail or hold energy in place. Sounds like *"streem"*.

Klim—Magnetic, attracting, intoxicating, desire. Sounds like *"kleem"*.

Hlim—Grounding energy. The sound is *"hleem"*.

Svaha—This is a blessing, a conclusion, that seals and offers everything else. Sounds like *"swaha"*.

You might also try mixing some of them together. There are many well-known sequences of *bijas* with various associations in the tantras and other writings. I have found the best way to get to know them is to savor them slowly and intimately.

Kali Gayatri

The *gayatri* is a type of *mantra* with a specific meter. This is the *gayatri* of Kali, which is best given every night when seeing the moon in her different phases. Alternatively, you can chant this *gayatri* 108 times (at least) during your meditation practice.

Om Mahakalyai cha vidmahe,
shamshana vasinyai cha dhimahi,
tano Kali prachodayat

"Om, I meditate on the Great Goddess.
I contemplate She who resides in the cremation grounds.
May the Goddess grant increase."

Try it with both Sanskrit and English, and see what resonates with you. Sanskrit is an ancient language with a rhythmic flow to it, and when chanted or repeated in *mantras* can have very noticeable and immediate effects on consciousness. Sometimes though, saying the *mantra* in English (or whatever your native tongue may be), carries with it an additional emotional charge that opens doors. Some of my most inspiring moments have come from reading a translation from Sanskrit, Bengali or Chinese, for example. The way of the heart is a mystery, and what unlocks it for one might do nothing for another.

In all of this work, we are striving to connect with that part of you that is spontaneous, open and flowing energy. Yes, when necessary, follow technique and ritual. When needed, read through works that inspire you and give instructions. But never—*never*—surrender your spontaneity, your creativity, your emotion. This is the cauldron of magic fire from which you connect and create with the Yoginis.

The Heart Mantra of Kali

This is the great *mantra (mahavidhya)* of the Goddess Kali. It can be chanted on its own, or incorporated into other rituals and practices. This *mantra* conveys immense power, and if chanted alone should be done in a concentrated, worshipful manner. It combines two of the *bija mantras* (OM KRIM) with the name of the Goddess:

OM KRIM KALIKAYAI NAMAHAH
"Om Krim, I Bow to the Goddess Kali"

One approach is to light a candle and incense, offering this to the Goddess at your shrine. Then commence *japa* of the *mantra,* continuing until the incense has completely burnt out. Do not be fooled by the seeming simplicity of this *sadhana.* This act of continuous devotion will bring you deep into the realization of Self, and open you to the influence of the Yoginis. From something seemingly so simple, if taken deep inside and nurtured, will grow a seed; that seed if nurtured with attention, silence and love, will grow into a cosmic tree that spans from the depths of the earth into the infinite gulfs of space. And don't forget, the Yoginis love trees.

Magical Armor

A *kavacha* is a magical armor that may be used to attune to the energies of the Goddess and have her protection. There are many such magical armors constructed from the different *bija mantras* associated with the different aspects of the Goddess. These armors may be recited as part of a ritual, used on their own as protection, or even written down and carried as a talisman. The armor works exceptionally well if assumed in the morning after showering, while seated before your shrine.

The names in this rite are those of the Goddess Kali, and specifically are associated with her *Sahaja Mothers,* the eight great Mother Goddesses from which her Yoginis arise. These are derived from her powerful *Kali Kavacha.* This armor is built around the most fundamental seed sound of Kali, her very essence: **KRIM**. More than just a protective spell, the *kavacha* is a type of offering to the Goddess and the Yoginis, and forms a complete ritual in and of itself. It is said that by assuming this armor one can receive the boons of becoming a great poet and scholar as well as all the *siddhis.*

As you recite the verses, with your hands touch the part of your body indicated, as though you are placing the sounds into the different parts of your body.[14]

Kali Kavacha

Kalika protect my head with **Krim**.

Kali, carrying your sword, protect my forehead with **Krim Krim Krim**.

With **Hum Hum** protect my eyes and **Hrim Hrim** protect my ears.

---

[14] There are many *kavachas,* each one emphasizing different aspects and qualities of the goddess. The one presented here is an English adaptation of the *Kali Jaganmangala Kavacha* inspired by *Yogic Secrets of the Dark Goddess* by Shambhavi L. Chopra. Wisdom Publications, 2008. The book is dripping with *bhakti!*

Daksinia Kalika, protect my nose along with **Maheswari. Kali** protect my mouth and tongue with **Krim Krim Krim. Hum Hum** protect my cheeks. **Hrim Hrim Svaha** protect my face.

Kali protect my sides with **Krim Krim Krim Hum Hum Hrim Hrim Dakshine Kalike Krim Krim Krim Hum Hum Hrim Hrim Svaha.**

Kali with your sword and holding a severed head, protect all my limbs.

Krim Hum Hrim, Chamunda protect my heart, **Aim Hum Hum Aim,** protect my chest and **Hrim Phat Svaha** my shoulders.

Kali, protect my arms with **Krim Krim Hum Hum Hrim Hrim Svaha!**

Krim Krim Hum Hum Hrim Hrim, Kali protect my hands. **Krim Dakshine Kalike** protect my navel and torso.

Kalika with **Krim Svaha** protect my back, **Krim Dakshine Kalike Krim Svaha.**
Om Krim Kalikayai Namah, protect my hips, waist and genitals.
Hrim Hrim Dakshine Kalike Hum Hum protect my rear.

Kali protect my thighs, **Hrim Hrim Dakshine Kalike Hum Hum Svaha.**
Om Hrim Krim Me Svaha, Kali protect my knees.
Krim Hum Hrim Dakshine Kalike protect my ankles.

Kali protect me in all directions:
Kali, Kapalini, Kaula, Kurukulla, Virodhini, Viprachita, Ugra, Ugraprabha, Dipta, Ghanatvisha, Nila, Ghana, Valaka, Matra, Mudra and Mita! Together protect me in in all times and directions!

Brahmi before me
Varahi behind me
On my right side, **Aghoresi**
On my left side, **Kumari**
To the south-east, **Yogeshvari**

To the south-west, **Indrani**
To the north-west, **Vaishnavi**
To the north-east, **Mahesvari** —
Beautifully adorned goddesses, from the eight directions of space,
please protect me!

Vidya of the Sahaja Mothers

The *Kaulajnananirnaya* reveals the *vidya* (Goddess *mantra)* of the
Sahaja Mothers, and informs that they should be mixed in eight ways:
"divided and incorporated in the first octave. Similarly, like this, one
should know the order of the Yoginis. Multiplying eight by eight
equals sixty-four Yoginis."

As the specific way of performing these permutations was part of
the secrets transmitted from mouth to ear, only hints are given in the
text. Pronunciation also can only be intuited. More vibration and a
subtlety of sound arises, mixing with the breath and the pulse of your
heartbeat. The sounds come alive in a humming, buzzing, melodious
sensation.

Let your heart and creative inspiration guide you deeply with this
Vidya. Take it into the very fibre of your being, letting it warm and
invigorate you. Feel the Yoginis stimulating and awakening you, coming closer and deeper, intimately associating with you. Feel their
breath on your skin, the warmth of their touch, the piercing and direct
look of their eyes, their scent permeating the space. Watch the displays
of light with your eyes closed, the striations of color that dance and
exchange places, twirling and spiraling, in and out, above and below,
every breath warm liquid light of the stars. Commingling and giving
yourself entirely to them, let the Yoginis take you and fill you.

hrim a hrim

im hrim hrim

um hrim hrim

r hrim hrim

i hrim hrim aim

hrim hrim o hrim

hrim hrim hrim ah hrim

hrim ksah hrim lah

hrim hah hrim sah

hrim pah hrim sah

hrim va hrim ra

hrim kl

hrim

Over time the sound will start to reorganize itself. Don't try to control it; the vibrations are alive and will take whatever path they choose. At times quiet and slow, other times faster, almost yelling, screaming in between breaths. The sound of your blood pumping through your veins and your own breath echoing along with the breath and heartbeats of the Yoginis. You may begin to hear other voices along with your own chanting, singing melodiously the *mantra*. Teasing and playing as they come closer into the circle of fire that is consciousness itself, lighting a path in the astral night for the shadows and shapes, the strange colors that no painter has ever caught, the sounds that no musician has ever replicated. Deeper and deeper, breathing and sighing, as the stars ache with the melody, or it may be the boisterous cacophony of the Yoginis descending from the sky.

Allow the *vidya* to modify itself as it sinks into your being and infuses you with the energy of the Yoginis. Attend closely to every sensation, be it pleasurable or painful—these are all blessings, the magical display of the Goddesses.

Let the words mutate and change as they will. Let the order and speed shift and multiply, distant murmuring changing to raging thunder and lightning, before again slipping into a quiet stream flowing against the rocks, and the leaves rustling in the wind with a distant call of hawks, or the buzzing of insects and chirping and cicadas. The croak of toads and strange rustling in the bushes. Footsteps making their way through the forest, with the leaves crunching underneath each step. A brisk gust of wind that carries with it the scent of jasmine and honey. A taste of warmth and sweet saltiness, that invigorates every cell of being, arousing desire. Shy glances from dark eyes seen quickly out of the corner of the eye, only to vanish when turning the head to look directly. The soft touch, feather-like, on the cheek, as though a hand were caressing the skin. Soft whispers on the breath, trembling, anticipating.

Give up control, surrender to the moment, and let the Yoginis take you, possess you, fill you.

6. Wheels of Starlight

The *chakras* are subtle centers of energy within the body. There are countless maps of the *chakras* from different traditions, each showing energetic centers and pathways between them (*nadis* in Sanskrit). The *chakras* have made their way into Western paganism as well, and make important energy centers for any type of magical work.

From the *Kaulajnananirnaya,* a particular scheme of eight *chakras* is given. As has become apparent by now, the number eight is closely intertwined with the Yoginis and their practice.

To each of the eight *chakras* is associated a color, a *bija mantra*, and certain *siddhis*. Going deeper, there are associations with individual Yoginis themselves, as well as different Gods and Goddesses. In the world of tantra, your body is the Universe, and the Gods and Goddesses come to dwell within you.

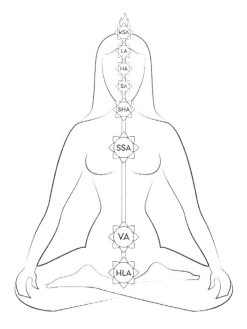

Chakra Diagram
(by Kat Lunoe)

#	Location	Appearance	Seed
1	Crown of head	Opalescent Crystal	KSA
2	Mid-forehead	Pure Flame	LA
3	Mid-eyebrow (third eye)	Diamond	HA
4	Inside top of palate	Pink	SA
5	Throat	Smoke	SHA[15]
6	Cardiac plexus (chest)	Liquid Gold	SSA[16]
7	Navel	White Full Moon	VA
8	Genitals	Reddish Gold	HLA

1. The first *chakra* is described as a lotus of eight petals, with an effulgence of pure opalescent crystal with flames shooting upwards. It has the qualities of non-duality. The power of being one with the Yoginis and achieving the eight *siddhis;* to know the past, present and future and to be free of the constraints of time; the ability to hear from a distance, to paralyze, seize and subjugate; to make one a conqueror of death and have the power of *vaca siddhi*—whatever one says comes to pass.

2. The second *chakra* is an eight-petalled lotus as bright as a beautiful flame. Ability to attract everyone, to subjugate, and take possession of another's will. Ability to assume manifold forms. Ability to do whatever one desires *(Svecchacara)*.

3. The third *chakra* is an eight-petalled lotus of diamond-like radiance. It grants the ability to enter into others' bodies, knowledge of the past and the future, and the ability to obtain what one desires. Other powers include being ageless, the ability to destroy all wrinkles and grey hair, see from a distance, pierce an object from a distance, and direct thoughts to one point.

4. The fourth *chakra* is also called the *santicakra* (*chakra* of peace). A pink-colored lotus of eight petals, it bestows happiness and

---

15 "sh" sound is similar to "shade".
16 "ss" sound is similar to "serpent".

any pleasures, enjoyment and liberation. Grants eloquence. Gives the ability to conquer disease. Also, the power to paralyze with a gesture, and to obtain the knowledge of languages that have been earlier heard or unheard.

5. The fifth *chakra* is described as a great lotus with eight petals with a smoky color. It gives the ability to control the wind with a word, to shake the three worlds,[17] to stall armies, and to silence anyone.

6. The sixth *chakra* is also called the King of Chakras, a lotus of eight petals bright as melted gold. It gives the power of *Iccha Siddhi*, bestowing whatever one desires. Perfect harmony between life and the laws of nature, material gains, fulfillment of desires, and spiritual illumination.

7. The seventh *chakra* is an eight-petalled lotus "as beautiful and auspicious as the Full Moon." It enables one to destroy old age and death, and to enter into other bodies. Freedom from bondage of birth and death, and the achievement of transcendental meditation.

8. The eighth *chakra* is an eight-petalled lotus of reddish-gold flame. It grants the fulfillment of one's own desires *(icchasiddhi),* power to conquer death *(marana),* material prosperity, and uprooting death. Additionally, the eighth *chakra* gives the power to paralyze, and to create delusion. One becomes a favorite of the *kula* (family of practitioners), and master of all the *siddhis.*

Serpentine Circulation of the Light

For activating the *chakras* and circulating their energy, starting from the first *chakra* (at the top of the head), see a beautiful, lustrous flame that moves downward, serpent-like, through each of the *chakras*

---

[17] The *triloka* or "three worlds": *swargaloka,* the divine realm; *mrityuloka,* the kingdom of death or the human dimension; and *pataloka,* the "underworld" or realm of *Asuras* ("demigods").

eight times, to complete a total of sixty-four circulations. In the *Kaula-jnananirnaya* it is said that this practice will make you the Lord of Breath and unite with the Devi herself.

During this circulation, reciting the *vidya* of the *Sahaja* Mothers will increase the flow of energy:

hrim a hrim im

hrim hrim um hrim

hrim r hrim hrim

l hrim hrim aim

hrim hrim o hrim hrim

hrim hrim ah hrim

hrim ksah hrim lah

hrim hah hrim sah

hrim pah hrim sah

hrim va hrim ra

hrim kl

hrim

After activating and circulating their energy, the *chakras* can all be changed to specific color spectrums. Visualize the aura around your body flooding with brilliant color:

Red: For works of subjugation and sorcery.

Yellow: Cause paralysis, stop negative speech/lies, victory in legal matters.

Black: To cause death or sickness.

Smoke-Coloured: Overthrow enemies, victory in battle.

White (like cow's milk): Conquer death, rejuvenation, youthfulness and vigor.

Pure Crystalline White: Self-Realization, spiritual illumination, realization of non-dual consciousness, union with the Yoginis.

As a daily practice, activate the Serpentine Circulation of the *chakras.* Bathing in the *pure crystalline white light,* meditating in this flood of liquid brilliance for 20 or more minutes twice a day (morning and evening) will quickly open consciousness to attune to the Yoginis.

Ascending Energy ("The Serpent's Kiss")

Another way to work with the *chakras* is from the bottom (Chakra 8) to the top (Chakra 1). This has the effect of quickly stimulating the energy of the body and invigorating the senses.

Seated in your meditation posture, move the concentration to the genitals. See the eight-petalled lotus of reddish-gold light open up with a single vibration of the *bija mantra* **HSA.**

Move awareness to the navel, seeing an eight-petalled lotus as bright as the Full Moon, and vibrate **VA.**

Coming up to the heart and the center of the chest, feel the warmth of the liquid golden sunlight with **SSA.**

Move up to the throat, see an eight-petalled lotus of smoky consistency. Vibrate **SHA.**

As awareness moves to the upper palate (inside the mouth), an eight-petalled lotus of pink radiance opens up with **SA.**

Bringing attention to the middle of the eyebrows, an eight-petalled lotus of diamond like brilliance opens up with **HA.**

Moving attention to the middle of the forehead, an eight-petalled lotus of pure flame opens up as you intone **LA.**

Finally, moving up to the very crown of the head, an opalescent, crystalline lotus of eight petals unfolds as you vibrate **KSA.**

With all of the elements awakened and acknowledged, both "inside" and "outside", you can then circulate them throughout consciousness. Feel the solid, nurturing ground and strength of the earth as your skeleton and muscles; the undulating waves, cleansing rainfall and flowing rivers as the water of life that makes up your body; the empowering, scorching flames and warmth of the sun as the blood in your veins and your heartbeat; the refreshing and invigorating power of the winds as you breathe; the vast openness and limitless nature of space itself as the very expansiveness of mind. All of this is present eternally now, in the only moment of space and time that there is, the present immediate moment.

Changing the color of all the *chakras* to Pure Crystalline White, and seeing your aura filled with this liquid radiance, you can now do the Serpentine Circulation of the Light as given above, along with the *vidya* of the *Sahaja* Mothers to seal in the energy. This will cleanse and open your psychic faculties, increase Awareness, and channel cosmic flows of power which can then be utilized for enchantments, sorcery and other magic workings.

Cultivating the Senses

To be awake and aware is not simply to quiet the mind. Tantra is not a denial of life, but rather an embracing of existence. A fundamental aspect of being alive is the body, and the senses are the gateway to the experience of the body. A deepening of sensory experience thus enriches life and goes a long way towards integrating your daily experience with your spiritual life. Really, there should be no difference.

During meditation, or throughout your day, become aware of the earth underneath your feet, the weight of your body that connects you to all the rocks, soil, earth, minerals and mountains of the earth.

Feel the water inside your body, and become aware of all of the lakes, rivers, storms, moisture on and in plants, the snowcapped mountains, the vast deep oceans. Feel this in the base of your spine.

In your stomach, become aware of the fire of digestion and of the life force pumping through your veins, resonating with all of the fire of the stars and cores of this and every other planet, the electrical lightning of storms, electricity in all of its manifestations, fire burning through forests, and light itself.

In your heart become aware of the feeling of the atmosphere, the winds, torrential hurricanes, gentle breezes, your breath as it flows in and out, the element of air in all of its manifestations.

Open up your awareness to the present moment, allowing yourself to be present to all of space, the vastness of consciousness, the deep space between stars and objects, the space between thoughts themselves, the space between one breath and the next.

Rest in this vast, open awareness.

See Chapter 13, "Day Magic" for some more exercises to incorporate sensory experience into Awareness.

7. East Meets West

In Hindu and Buddhist tantras, there are very precise rituals and rules to follow. Each lineage has its own interpretations and variations on these themes; however, it is exactly that—variations on a theme. Like a cook who takes an older recipe and changes it up with another spice or ingredient to make a fusion, or a musician covering an old blues classic, adding in their own interpretation, ritual can and does open up to the creative potential of the individual. My first book, the *Magickal Union of East and West,* explored a system for working with these themes of East meets West, and over the years has continued to develop and evolve, having a solid base of practitioners who recognize the creative impulse and energy, cultivating it and having it flow through them.

Unlike many systems that dictate "you must do this and nothing else," or that come across as the ultimate authority on the nature of reality and the universe, I prefer to keep a curious and exploratory approach. I create, experiment, explore and repeat this iteratively to see what works. I encourage you to do the same.

Over the years I have found a deep draw towards nature. My rituals may be more about walking mindfully through a quiet forest, and making a circle out of some found rocks and twigs, rather than wearing a robe and tracing figures in the air while in a Masonic Lodge. Formal ritual absolutely has its place, and ritual with implements and robes and well-defined spells certainly serves a purpose. As with everything, the real key is to be aware of what and why you are doing anything. Throughout this book I encourage you to look outside the box (or outside the "magical circle") and see how your experience— no matter how mundane or dull it might appear superficially—if looked at with awareness, is nothing less than the radiance of the serpentine power of the Yoginis, a continuous flow of presence that is creative, stunning and shocking, in every possible way.

In this chapter I give some ideas for ritual work of the more traditional "robe and wand" sense. These can be used directly as is. They

118

can also be modified to suit your own experiences or intuitions, and of course, your unique circumstances. You may end up discarding them entirely, choosing to work only with your Yogini Stones, for example, or even just a large crystal. There is no right answer, no real authoritative tradition—although I promise you that there are plenty of people who will tell you that what you are doing is wrong and you have to do it their way! My advice is to thank them politely, and then run in the other direction.

Give yourself permission to tap into your creativity. Be authentic to your Self, and do not be afraid to explore. To develop your own sense of authority and resilience is to express that aspect of *Sveccha-carini* that the Yoginis so clearly embody. This act, by itself, will do wonders.

The more you are willing to be open, to experiment, to dive deep into yourself, pulling up those creative instincts from within, the more you will also engage the influence and direct instruction of the Yoginis. Remember, they are deeply connected with the arts. You may find that stilling the mind and calling a Yogini by name three times, visualizing her in her human or animal form, opens creative doors that result in picking up a paintbrush or a sketchpad. You may explore them through poetry or other writings. You might feel them in your body with dance, singing, playing a musical instrument. Yoga is a powerful avenue of connecting with these goddesses, and as they are the true patrons and teachers of Yoga, what better inspiration?

Whatever makes you feel alive, connected with your body and nature, awake to your senses—this is ritual and worship with the Yoginis. Engage in those practices and attitudes that help you recollect that there is no distinction between the "inside" and "outside" of your skin. Cultivate such awareness; be aware of their influence. Feel their presence in your body, experiencing through you and with you.

At a minimum, the only tool required to work with the Yoginis is your consciousness! If your devotion is sincere, such energy feeds into your ritual work and there is nothing else required. Like the Yoginis, fly naked and free through the empyrean of consciousness, and invite the Yoginis into the laboratory of your body.

That said, for many it will be useful to have a ritual construct in which to work to help structure and channel the fierce and torrential energies that will be worked with. In this chapter we will discuss some of the magical tools and ritual processes that may help to support your work. In keeping with the Western approach, this will include decidedly pagan techniques that draw from Witchcraft.

Yogini Stones

These will be described in more detail in Chapter 9, "Initiation". They are a collection of small stones that become associated with the energy of the Yoginis. The Yogini Stones are used in the rites as both a meditative focus and an energetic link to have the Yoginis work with you. Over time, these become a communication device that can be used with the Yoginis to evoke their presence. You can add unique sigils of their names to each stone (see Chapter 14, "Night Magic").

Yogini Yantra

Yogini Yantra
(by Kat Lunoe)

The Yogini Yantra is a magical diagram that shows the entire circle of Awareness, with the 64 Yoginis, the 8 Sahaja Mothers, 3 primary Shaktis, and the Great Goddess. It is used as a meditative and ritual focus. The overall appearance is magnetizing, as though you are gazing at a vast cosmic flower that is opening up its many petals to the unbounded radiance of consciousness.

Make a circle, and divide it into 64 petals; one for each Yogini. Within the inner circle is an 8-petaled lotus, the *Sahaja Mothers.* Inside this, is an equilateral triangle with the single point facing down. The angles of the triangle are *Iccha Shakti, Jnana Shakti, and Kriya Shakti*; their combination makes a Kali *yantra.* Within is the *bindu,* representing the Goddess Kali. You might customize it by adding the sigils of the Yoginis to the petals (see Chapter 14, "Night Magic").You can activate the *yantra,* placing life into it, with the *Yogini Sadhana* (see Chapter 12, "The Feast of the Yoginis").

Shadow Circle

It is best to set aside a physical place for regular practice, be it a corner of a room or a completely dedicated temple space. If you are in a location where you can work outside in nature to cast your circles in private, all the better. This also has the added benefit of giving you more space to incorporate dancing and movement into your ritual work, as well as direct access to the elements and the open sky.

This space is your *Shadow Circle.* The center where you will sit is the *Dragon Seat,* a reference to the qualities of the heroine or hero who undertakes tantrik workings, as well as to the power of the Goddess Kundalini, snakelike and coiled about the base of the spine— a true seat of power, which a Dragon represents.

Over time your shadow circle will build up its own energy and even take on a personality of its own. When you sit to perform your rituals, it will have a magnetic effect on consciousness, drawing you in and changing the atmosphere of both your space and your mind.

In witchcraft traditions, we may be used to casting a circle as a sacred space to delineate between the normal wake-day world and the sacred. The circle has always been associated with ideas of the divine and the eternal. Sacred sites such as Stonehenge in England, and Gobekli Tepi in Turkey show that this instinct has a long history. The stone temples of the sixty-four Yoginis also show this symbolism, with their circular structures open to the sky. This is also seen in the *Yogini Yantra*.

If you have a dedicated space outside, you can create a permanent shadow circle. Like a large version of the Yogini Stones, arrange 64 large stones in a circular formation, optionally painting them with your unique Yogini sigils. All of your physical workings can be conducted from the center of this stone circle.

As well as the physical space, it will be good to have built up a strong astral temple that mirrors your physical in an ideal way. The more the physical and astral temples and circles are cast, the more powerful and energetic they will be, becoming a sacred space. This more subtle aspect is discussed in Chapter 15, "Dream Magic".

Altar

Your altar can be as simple or elaborate as you like. A small side table works well, as does a dedicated altar table. These days it is possible to find all kinds of altars at online stores dedicated to spiritual pursuits. If you have the skills, constructing your own altar would add strong personal energy to it, helping to consecrate it during its construction. Even with a pre-made altar or a repurposed table or shelf, you can personalize it and customize it to your liking. Ideally the altar should be easy to see and reach when you are seated for meditation, so take that into consideration. The surface should be large enough to comfortably hold your other items (although in a pinch they can all be gathered nearby). Ideally, the material should be wood, although other materials could work; however, it is best to stay away from plastics. If your circle is out in nature, a stone altar works well.

Have a statue of the Goddess in the center of the altar. This could be any of the Hindu goddesses (which are easy to find), or a Buddhist *yam-yum* image, Shiva-Shakti, and so on. There are many of these *murti* available; if you have the skills you might make your own. It is also perfectly fine to paint or draw an image and have that in a frame on your altar. A single *Shiva Lingam* is also a powerful item to have in the center. Anything that inspires you and the sense of connection to the Goddess is good. For some, this may be more abstract representations: perhaps a seashell or a rock or a crystal that was found in nature. If you feel drawn to any gurus or teacher figures, it's also good to have their images on the altar, to receive their blessings during your workings.

Mala

Mala
(Photo by the Author)

The *mala* is a string of beads (similar to a rosary) that can be used for *japa,* the recitation of *mantras* and counting the number of times a *mantra* is given. You should have one with 108 beads. *Malas* are easily obtained these days—check with any trader of Buddhist or

Hindu religious items. Custom *malas* can also be designed where you pick the materials. You can also make your own if you have the skills.

Malas come in a variety of materials and designs, and there is a good amount of traditional lore around what is best in different situations. *Rudraksa* beads are often used in tantrik rituals, and a *mala* made of *rudraksa* is a great choice. There are also *malas* made out of other seeds, bone, crystals, wood and coral. You may end up with several different *malas* over time, and use them for varying purposes or occasions. Or, you may settle on one *mala* and use that exclusively.

In my own case I have worked with many *malas* over the years, some found as is, some gifted, and some made. When I started working with the Yoginis, I had a custom *mala* built, and have been working with it ever since.

Cup

Kapala
(Photo by the Author)

The Cup, Chalice or Graal is used to hold the liquid offerings. It is also called a *patra,* and is symbolic of the element Water. A particularly tantrik cup is the *kapala* (skull-cup). This is made out of the cranium of a human skull. Sometimes they are adorned with silver or gold, and sometimes with intricate paintings. The Buddhist tantrik *kapalas* tend to be more ornamental, whereas the Hindu tantrik *kapalas* may literally be a skull fragment fresh from a cremation ground. While I advise against trying to make your own in this case(!), they can certainly be found from exotic import shops, or when traveling to locations where tantra is more widely practiced. The *kapala* has deep associations with tantrik rites, and often the images of the deities and Yoginis are seen holding the skull-cup aloft to eagerly drink the broth of blood from its contents. This blood is transformed into *amrita* (nectar), which brings bliss and magical powers.

If you choose to work with a *kapala,* it should be kept wrapped in silk when not in use, and treated with utmost respect. The energies associated with the deceased become a part of your workings. In Buddhist tantra the *kapala* is often made from wood or ceramics, thus bypassing the need to incorporate additional energies.

Plate

This is to hold smaller items such as a candle and incense. The size will be dependent somewhat on your altar and space, but usually around 8"–10" (20–25 cm) diameter works well. You can also have small food offerings placed on it. The plate can be of any material (though, as always, avoid plastic). Bronze, steel or silver plates called *thalis* can be found online or at many Indian grocery stores as this is a regular item in traditional *puja* (worship). This is also called the disk, paten, or pantacle, and represents Earth.

Dagger

Also called the Athame, the dagger or knife represents the element Air. Some tantrikas will use a *phurba* in its place, a ritualized and highly symbolic dagger used in specific rituals associated with tantrik rites.

Phurba (Tibetan Ritual Dagger)
(Photo courtesy of
commons.wikimedia.org/wiki/File:Tibetan_-_Ritual_Dagger_-
_Walters_52311.jpg)

Instead of a dagger, you might prefer a short sword, which works just as well. Another alternative is to have a *trishul,* the three-pronged spear-like instrument that is often seen being held by the God Shiva.

Damaru Trishul
(by Kat Lunoe)

Wand

The wand is representative of the element Fire. It can be made easily out of any material of your choosing such as wood, stone or crystal. It may be as simple or as adorned as you like, with gemstones or carvings. For wooden wands, almond is especially good to work with, as it becomes very smooth when the bark is removed, while retaining its solid feel; other common varieties are oak and ash. A traditional practice is to cut your wand from the branch of a tree on the morning of one of the special celestial days, such as an Equinox or Solstice. After removing the bark, sand down the wand until it is smooth. You can also rub in scented oils to make the wand aromatic.

Red Cord

This is the traditional Witch's Cord, also called the *cingulam*. It can be used to lay out a circle in your temple space, or out in the wilds when nature is your temple. Traditionally this is a 9-foot-long (3 meter) cord made from a natural material—preferably wool—that has been dyed red. The red color represents blood and passion, two essential ingredients for tantra and *bhakti*. Red is also a traditional color associated with the *Kaula Shakta* tantras, which are all Goddess-oriented. Red is the color of menstruation, the sacred blood of the Goddess, and a visual totem of feminine divine power *(shakti)*. It is favored by the Yoginis and the *Sahaja* Mothers, who often appear in red clothing or with red skin, and sometimes covered in blood, or holding a *kapala* filled with it.

Additional Items

In addition to the above, a supply of candles and incense of your choosing, and suitable holders will be helpful. These make up a part of the offerings, so you will want a good supply.

You may also want to have some *sindhoor*. This is the red powder that married Indian women place in the part of their hair to show their status. It is also used to adorn statues of the deities by placing some on their head during rituals. Tantrikas mark their foreheads, and sometimes other body parts with it. It is symbolic of blood, in particular menstrual blood. It is a sign of feminine divine power *(shakti),* and helps to mark one as a worshipper of the Goddess. In this sense, a single vertical line on the forehead in red *sindhoor* will act as a mark of recognition for the Yoginis.

Purification and Consecration of the Tools

To prepare the new tools, light your altar candle and incense. Fill the Chalice with wine or other spirit of choice. You can also use water that has some salt added to it. Sprinkle a few drops of the wine or salted water onto your tools, and then pass them through the smoke from the incense. Finally, hold them over the candle flame, feeling the warmth sink into the tool and consecrate it to your magic.

As an additional step, in particular for a new *mala,* after performing the consecration you can recite the 12th Chapter of the *Chandi Path* (see Chapter 5, "Sorcery of Sound"), asking the Goddess to empower your *mantra* or other tools, and dedicate them to this work.

The Yogini Stones may be initially purified using these techniques. For their full consecration and empowerment to the Yoginis, refer to Chapter 9, "Initiation".

Part Two:
A Fearful Symmetry

Court Ladies Meet a Yogini in the Forest
(Photo courtesy of

Whether fierce or gentle, terrible to behold, all powerful,
Residing in the sky, on earth or in the vastness of space,
May those Yoginis always be well-disposed towards me.
— *Kularnava Tantra, 7:13*

8. The Sixty-Four Yoginis

Yogini, 12th Century
(Photo courtesy of
commons.wikimedia.org/wiki/File:A_Yogini_at_a_12th_century_Hindu_temp
le,_Telangana.jpg

> *"Among devotees, ecstatic madness is believed to intoxicate*
> *the person so that he can perceive only the goddess. The body*
> *is suffused with sweetness, while the mind is confused and the*
> *heart melts. The Shakta states of divine madness are charac-*
> *terized by confusion, passion, and loss of self-control: trem-*
> *bling, laughing, weeping and crying out before the goddess,*
> *rolling on the ground. [...] the deity's name is invoked, but*
> *the behavior is too extreme even for devotion and may involve*
> *fear and other negative emotions [...]. Should the [practi-*
> *tioner] not conquer sexuality and death, but rather become*
> *subject to lust and dread, he is widely believed to be vulnera-*
> *ble to insanity and breakdowns."*
>
> — *The Madness of the Saints,* June McDaniel

At the center of the circle of Awareness from which the mystery of the Yoginis emerge, are the twin poles of Sex and Death. Throughout every aspect of working with the goddesses, these polarities will be stimulated, accentuated and dealt with directly. Entering into the circle means dealing with these profound subjects head on. Every person will face their own unique and different challenges. These obstacles must be faced bravely and honestly; to falter is to risk becoming a feast for the Yoginis, rather than to work with them. Enter into the shadow circle with your eyes open, ready to face some of the most secret, intimate and hidden aspects of your consciousness.

As discussed earlier, there are countless Yoginis. Some have been associated with specific tantras or other writings; some with places, temples and times; others are closely tied to the *Matrikas* (Mothers) in their different combinations, or the directions of space and the elements; still others are embedded with the *chakras*; and many have not been catalogued at all, and may even arise and go as circumstances dictate. As many stars as there are in the universe, there are even more Yoginis throughout the dimensions.

It may be that each village or tradition had their own groupings of Yoginis that were associated with a location—be it a mountain, forest, river, lake and so on. Over time, different *siddhas* would collect these into *namavali* based on their tradition, as the Great Goddess and her emanations manifest uniquely based on the needs and consciousness of those connecting with them.

The goddess Kali has been worshipped as her avatar Kamakhya (Goddess of Desire) for centuries in her temple at Assam, India. In this form she is also called Adi Shakti, the Supreme Goddess. The temple itself is one of 51 *Shakti Piths* (seat of the goddess), sacred sites scattered around the Indian sub-continent.

A tale from the *Puranas* relates how the *Shakti Piths* came to be. Sati was the first wife of the God Shiva. She came from a royal family, lived in palaces, and was accustomed to wearing rich clothing and jewels. Her father, Daksha, was the son of the god Brahma. Daksha had performed years of prayers and austerities so he would receive Adi Shakti as his daughter. When Sati was born, she was the embodiment of the Goddess.

Daksha never approved of Shiva, and certainly not of their marriage. Shiva was a yogi who spent most of his time in deep meditation, and wore his hair in dreadlocks. Not to mention he was always naked except for a lion pelt around his waist, was covered in ash from cremation grounds, and was always smoking *ganja*. Daksha felt his royal daughter could do a lot better!

Daksha decided he was going to perform a large *Yagna* (ritual sacrifice), and invited all of the Gods and Goddesses to attend—with the exception of Shiva. Sati was devastated and embarrassed by the actions of her father, pleading with him to invite her husband to the *Yagna*. He refused, instead heaping abuses upon both Shiva and his own divine daughter. Completely distraught, Sati used her yogic powers of inner heat and performed self-immolation in the middle of the ritual. Bursting into flames, she sacrificed herself at her father's *yagna*.

When Shiva heard what happened, his sorrow and rage completely devastated him, making him fall into a crazed trance. He came to the palace, picked up Sati's corpse and began a terrifying dance across the universe (the *tandav*). Everywhere he danced, destruction followed. To prevent the complete annihilation of the universe and get Shiva out of his trance of destruction, the God Krishna used his *Sudarshan*

Chakra (a divine spinning disc) to cut up Sati's body. As Shiva continued his dance of destruction, a piece of Sati's body would fall to the earth. Eventually she would be cut into 51 pieces, and as the last one fell to the earth Shiva woke from his rage. Every location where a part of the Goddess Sati's body fell to the earth became a *Shakti Pith*.

Kamakhya is associated with her *yoni,* and is a central and important place for tantra. In Kamakhya, the central shrine of Devi bleeds annually from her *yoni*. This sacred substance is collected and cherished by her devotees.

According to legend, Kamarupa-Kamakhya is said to be where Matsyendranath encountered highly advanced *shaktis,* tantrik practitioners who were devoted to the Goddess and embodied Yoginis themselves. They welcomed him and initiated him into their group, and it is from their grace and compassion in initiating him into the Yogini worship that he was able to write the *Kaulajnananirnaya* and spread the *Yogini Kaula* and the mysteries of the Yoginis.

The goddess Kali and her Yoginis are an energetic, dynamic expression of cosmic powers. The three primal *shaktis* that make up the trinity of *Iccha Shakti* (Will), *Jnana Shakti* (Knowledge), and *Kriya Shakti* (Will/Action) are closely associated with her. The Goddess Kali is, in a very visceral sense, the true Queen of the Witches, and her attendant Yoginis wield sorcery, enchantments and magical powers.

For over 12 years, I have been working with a grouping of Yoginis that immediately resonated with me energetically. The Goddesses respond quickly and directly, with a frequency and intensity that I had not experienced elsewhere. Even the first time I opened the circle and chanted their names, with little other ritual or preparation, I began to have energetic and visual responses that would reverberate through the rest of the day, leaving me in states of bliss and heightened sensitivity. Sounds were crisper and more vibrant. Vision seemed brighter, endowed with a deep potency. Smell was intensified, the fragrance of the incense being mixed up and confused with flowery scents that seemed to come from nowhere.

I once thought that this was the earliest grouping of Yoginis used at the Kamakhya Temple. Later I learned that it is associated with the Goddess Kali and Kriya Yoga. Learning of the connection with Kriya Yoga was a stunning and synchronistic coincidence for me, as I had been practicing it for years—long before I had ever encountered the Yoginis. The names were written down by Swami Ayyappa Giri, and it is said to have been received from the legendary guru Babaji, who asked that it be shared freely with the world.

Mahavatar Babaji Maharaj is an Indian saint and master of alchemy who is said to have been living in his cave hermitage in the Himalayas for well over 1000 years. An avatar of the god Shiva, he has practiced his yoga austerities as part of the older *Siddha* tradition. Like the Yoginis, his legends are shrouded in mystery. He is a master *siddha*, existing outside of time and space, who manifests in the world out of compassion when there is need. It is through his instruction that the lineages of Kriya Yoga originated, as Babaji divinely instructed his disciples. Many schools have grown out of these teachings, all tracing back ultimately to the divine inspiration and instruction of Babaji.

While many of these goddesses have names similar to those found with the Mahavidyas, the Nityas, Matrikas and the names of the *Lalita Sahasranama,* the Yoginis are not the same goddesses. Rather, the connection seems to be more of family lines, ancestral ties in a sense. There may be some similar appearances and qualities in these "tribes" that are recognizable as the more popular forms of the goddess, and these can be thought of as inherited family traits.

Each of the names is its own small Sanskrit *mantra.* There is a rich resonance in the names that can be felt tangibly. You may notice different parts of your body responding with a vibration of feeling of energy. There may be sensations of heat or cold, of feeling a breeze or a fire, as just a few examples. There may be seemingly auditory sounds or voices, snippets of language, the jingle of bells, the sound of rushing winds or thunder. Let the names be a meditation in itself, and feel how your mind and body respond. Pay attention to where in your body you feel the name vibrating. What is its temperature? What are the colors?

The English phrase under each name is loosely inspired by the Sanskrit words. Art, intuition and inspiration govern these more than literal meaning. The phrases are oftentimes provocative. There is an undercurrent of eroticism and sexual energy, and many conflicting symbols that can stimulate fear and yet be evocative. If you find yourself having an emotional or other reaction, try to observe it and see where it leads. How does it feel in your body? Which part of your body? Is there an increase of tension? Or do you feel an expansiveness, an openness as though your center has fallen out? Does it feel like fear? Aversion? Something else?

The descriptive visions of each of the Yoginis were received by me in working with them, images that came through trance and dream states. In some cases, I have added details about areas that a Yogini may specialize in, but again, these are more guidelines and not strict rules. Think of these as dream images that capture a certain vibration of the Yogini in this dimension. They are dreamlike reflections of the Yogini's essence.

The appearance of the Yoginis can be disturbing on a multitude of levels. The themes of Sex and Death are predominant. Often appearing as beautiful young women, this beauty can push the limits of what might be acceptable in society. It can feel uncomfortable, and may violate multiple societal and ingrained taboos. Pay close attention to these feelings, and see what it may mean for you personally. See what energy arises, and whether it feels liberating or binding. As you are coming closer to the Yoginis, you are encountering pure forms of *shakti,* unfiltered and unconstrained by anything in human consciousness. The mind, and even the physical body, do not know how to react to these encounters. On a purely instinctual level, the more animal instincts may take over—feelings of dread, abhorrence, fight or flight can all be intermingled with arousal, euphoric sensations and outright ecstasy.

Some of the imagery can be frightening and confusing. Severed heads, bloody corpses, and swords may appear alongside flowers, fruits and wine. Feel the fear as it arises, and make room for it, so that it transforms into something else. Instead of tightening up, try to breathe and open up, making space for anything and being present with whatever you encounter. There are references to mixed bodily fluids, including menstrual blood and semen. This, in combination with images of young women, violent weaponry and scenery, and an undercurrent of uneasy sexual desire, might offend the more conventional aspects of our personality. Again, try to be aware and make space for all of this as you encounter it.

The rational mind can become confused by the mix of imagery that is both strangely appealing and yet outwardly horrific. The feelings arising out of this confusion can be liberating if you stay with them. Make space for all the emotions and feelings that arise. If you have been meditating regularly, these vivid images can arise and wash over your experience like a cleansing, freeing wave for all of the senses.

The number 16 comes up frequently with the Yoginis. Sixteen is *Sodashi,* a name of the Goddess that literally means 16. While this is rendered in the form of a sixteen-year-old maiden, there is a deeper significance that is reflected in the phases of the Moon, in its bright and dark fortnights that are 15 nights each, with a secret 16th digit of the Moon that is the heart of the cycle and from which the magical dew or *kala* of the Goddess is emitted. In the images of the Yoginis, this may evoke feelings that are a confusing mix of mystique and allure that also gives rise to strong guilt and even disgust. Hold these contradictory feelings in the same space in the circle of Awareness. Allow them to arise and disappear, and see what remains underneath the outer imagery. Shakti weaves an endless menagerie of sensations and impressions. The Yoginis can be your liberation, or your downfall.

The best way to understand the Yoginis is to be with them, and to come into a sense of accord with them through frequent and regular interactions. This is true transmission. It stands outside of time, an immediate presence of Awareness—the root of all experience.

The 16th *kala* arises in the space between conflicting emotions, thoughts and feelings. Learn to sit with uncertainty, ambiguity, shadows; transforming moment by moment from swirling colors in the darkness, to beautiful and dangerous maidens, to theriomorphic and monstrous shapes with gaping skeletons and gore, to the arising awareness of non-duality. Through all of this, let the fluidity of the Yoginis wash over and through you. Let all experience arise from nothing and return to nothing, and pay attention to what is always present. What remains untouched, unmoved and always there? It is here that you will find the luminous petals of the 16th *kala* opening up.

As your relationship with the Yoginis deepen, you may find that their appearance changes; along with this, the type of communication and information that you get from them also mutates, or goes in new and unexpected directions. Expect the unexpected, and approach with openness. Use the information below as a map to get acquainted with the territory, to assist with tuning in to the right frequency, and to address any subconscious biases, cultural conditioning, and societal taboos that arise unexpectedly. Stay with all of the experiences, and let it mature and deepen in your heart, growing into something beautiful, vital and unique.

If you find that this particular grouping of Yoginis does not resonate with you, see the Appendix for additional name lists. You may find that you are drawn to a different association of Yoginis, or that you discover completely new ones. After establishing a strong connection, it is possible to receive unique names and transmissions which may result in entirely different combinations of Yoginis. In some of my work, I have received names that do not appear in any known literature. These have sometimes been for specific workings, to highlight a certain energy or place that needed attention. As many stars as there are in the universe, so there are Yoginis. Once you have the techniques down and have established communication, the possibilities for new discovery and creative application are truly endless.

The 64 Yoginis of Kali

Yoginis That Descend from the Tribe of Kali Nityas

1. Kali Nitya Siddhamata
Eternal Dark Goddess Mother of the Sorcerers

She appears out of a field of immense black radiance. Luminescent dark skin, piercing black eyes, and long black hair. Her short skirt is made of severed human arms, and around her neck is a garland of freshly severed heads. Her earrings are made of the corpses of two small boys. She may have a black crow or a black dog with her. Her smile and eyes are intoxicating and she bewitches with little more than a glance. She appears giving the signs of Bestowing Boons and Dispelling Fear.

2. Kapalini Nagalaksmi
Skull Bearing Serpent Queen of Wealth and Prosperity

She is clothed in a green and red *sari*, richly jeweled. She wears a garland of skulls. When her countenance is human, she has long, auburn hair tied into a single thick braid. She has serpent-like skin, and when she appears in her full *Naga* (serpent) form has the head of a cobra. She is the Queen of the *Nagas*, the female serpent spirits, and bestows wealth and prosperity on those she favors.

3. Kula Devi Svarnadeha
Illumined Tribal Goddess of Lustrous Golden Body

She wears animal skins, and is bejeweled with bones. She will often be seen holding a spear, and sometimes a *trishul* (trident). Her skin glows with lustrous golden light, and her eyes are fiercely passionate. She has a sweet, musky scent, and thick, rich hair often tied into braids. Her athletic form is that of a warrior goddess. She is protectress of the *Kula* (tribe or family).

4. Kurukulla Rasanatha
Mistress of Sorcery Offering a Skull-Cup of Nectar

She has lustrous crimson skin, and often appears draped in flames that caress her body. Her entire countenance is dynamic energy. She is the Queen of Sorcery and Mistress of Dark magic. She may be holding a bow and arrow made of crystalline flowers of light. She may also be armed with a trident, with a *naga* coiled about it. She reaches out with her left hand holding a *kapala* (large cup made from the cranium of a human skull). In the cup is nectar in the form of luminescent blood, which she may offer to you.

5. Virodhini Vilasini
Charming Mistress Who Dispels Opposition

Draped in yellow with flashes of purple, with large swelling breasts and a small waist, she has the appearance of a youthful woman in the prime of her sexuality. The sweet-smelling fragrance of jasmine permeates the atmosphere where she is present. She is often garlanded with a skull necklace and writhing snakes, and sometimes holds a trident or a noose that is made of the body of a serpent.

6. Vipracitta Raktapriya
Wise Goddess Who Loves Passion

She appears tall and slender, with blue skin, three eyes, long black hair, and large swelling breasts. She is often holding a skull-cup filled with nectar, which she may offer to you. She may be holding a freshly severed head. Her eyes are half closed, and her body sways in the throes of pleasure.

7. Ugra Rakta Bhoga Rupa
Enchantress of Terrifying Form
Who Enjoys Blood

She appears naked, black-skinned, with large fangs and blood dripping from her mouth. She wears a garland of human heads in various states of decay, some with the flesh still peeling off and blood dripping down. She often carries a skull and a sword, dripping with blood.

8. Ugraprabha Sukranatha
Wrathful Resplendent Goddess

She has deep, dark, blue skin, and is naked, with rising swelling breasts. Her face is peaceful and beautiful, with a relaxing, intoxicating smile. She wears a skirt of freshly severed arms, the blood dripping down her waist and legs. She rules over the seminal fluids, and delights in their release and consumption. Sometimes she appears with the head of a fox, in which case she may be holding a skull-cup and a large knife.

9. Dipa Mukti Rakta Deha
Whose Passionate Body is the
Lamp of Liberation

She appears with electrifying sapphire skin, as though composed all of space and lightning. She wears human-bone bracelets and armlets, a necklace of skulls, and a crown of human bones. From her right hand she emits a flame, and her left hand holds a skull-cup of blood. She emits lustful energy, her body dripping with pleasure.

10. Nila Bhukti Rakta Sparsa
Dusky Night Goddess
Who Enjoys Passionate Touch

She has dark blue skin, almost indigo, with a lustful body writhing with sensuality, her eyes and face intoxicated with desire. She is richly ornamented with both silver and platinum jewels, and garlanded with skulls. Sometimes she appears wearing a dress made of flayed human skin, with anklets and bangles of bone.

11. Ghana Maha Jagadambha
Auspicious Dark Goddess,
Great Mother of the World

She appears naked, with full swelling breasts and a passionate body, with radiant deep black skin, as black as the depths of deepest space. Her eyes are deep black pools of infinity, and her lips are colored with deepest black. Her thick, long black hair is free and wild. When clothed she may wear a garland of human skulls and a short skirt composed of the hands of corpses. Sometimes she is holding a long sword, dripping with fresh blood, and in her other hand a flashing bejeweled shield.

12. Balaka Kama Sevita
Youthful Lady Served Through Desire

She appears like an adolescent girl of sixteen, naked with skin glowing a deep, orange-red like the setting sun. Her eyes are half closed, she is intoxicated by desire, her breasts are full and swelling, and her slim waist is ornamented with a belt of bones. She wears a necklace of skulls, some human and some from other animals. She may be armed with a sword in one hand, and a freshly severed head in the other. Sometimes she will appear seated on a throne composed of human skulls.

13. Matra Devi Atmavidya
Mother Goddess Who Reveals Highest Truth

She is naked, her skin a bluish-black lustre, and she is smeared with blue lotus paste. Her three lovely eyes are sparkling with radiance, and her long flowing dark hair drops down, covering her shoulders and breasts. She may hold scissors or a sword in her right hand, and in her left a skull-cup full of menstrual blood.

14. Mudra Purna Rajatkripa
She Who is the Seal of Graceful Governance

She is naked, and her skin is the color of the blue sky. Her three eyes are yellowish-brown, feline-like. She wears a garland of freshly severed heads, and a skirt of severed arms with the fresh blood dripping down. Sometimes she appears cat-headed.

15. Mita Tantra Kaula Diksa
Tantrik Initiatrix Who Establishes the Kaula Path

She appears with electrifying dark blue skin, wearing a crimson red *sari,* with long thick black hair, slim waist and slender limbs, her back arched slightly from the weight of her large rising breasts. Her three eyes are piercing black pools of night, with an infinity of cosmic stars shining from them. Her entire form pulsates with the intoxication of lust and passion, and the sweet scent of red sandalwood permeates the atmosphere around her. She sometimes appears holding a sword dripping fresh blood, and a *kapala* filled with blood nectar.

16. Mahakali Siddhesvari
Radiant Dark Queen of the Shaman Magicians

She appears clothed in space, with luminous black skin like the darkest moonless night. Her long black hair flows freely. She wears a necklace of severed heads, and armbands, bangles and anklets of skulls. Sometimes she appears accompanied by a black jackal or hyaena, as well as black ravens. She may be carrying a large, curved sword and a skull-cup, and sometimes a trident. There is flashing, purplish auric light around her countenance.

Yoginis that Descend from the
Tribe of Lalita Tripurasundari Nityas

17. Kamesvari Sarvasakti
Empress of Sexual Desire and Power

She appears as a sixteen-year-old girl, with lustrous and flushed warm golden skin, smeared with red paste, fragrant long black hair, and dark eyes. Her scent is honey mixed with sandalwood and hibiscus flowers, and an underlying hint of feminine sexual fluids. Her eyes are half-closed in pleasure and desire, and her large swelling breasts move up and down gently with every breath. She is garlanded with red hibiscus and golden jewelry, and often holds a skull-cup that has been plated with gold. Sometimes she will appear in a field of lotuses, holding a sword, bow and arrows, all dipped with gold.

18. Bhagamalini Tarini
Saviouress Whose Yoni is Flowering

She is clothed in yellow with flashes of violet. She is richly jeweled with long, auburn hair tied into ringlets, and scented flowers tied into her hair. She wears a garland of flowers and the scent of jasmine, honeysuckle and hibiscus strongly permeates the atmosphere. Her kohl-lined eyes are a brilliant green, half-closed in the throes of desire. Sometimes she may appear naked, smeared with fresh blood, wearing a garland of flowers and skulls, holding a sword and bearing a skull-cup filled with menstrual blood and honey. She drinks deeply of the *kapala,* the nectar trickling down from her mouth and eyes aflame with passion, and may offer the cup to you to drink.

19. Nityaklinna Tantraprita
Eternally Wet Goddess Who
Takes Pleasure Through Tantra

She appears naked, wearing a necklace, armlets, bangles and anklets of bones and gemstones. Her red body glistens with the sweat of vigorous love play, and her *yoni* is moist and glistening, a golden glow from the nectar. Her thick, dark hair comes down around her shoulders and heaving, full breasts. She may hold a skull-cup filled with the *amrita* from her *yoni,* and offer this warm, golden honey-like liquid, bestowing powers of psychic manipulation and omens.

20. Bherunda Tattva Uttama
Terrible Goddess of Excellent Essence

She appears as a slim, youthful maiden, naked, with radiant warm golden skin and a dazzling, beautiful smiling face. She wears rich jewels around her neck, as well as bangles, anklets and armlets of gold and gemstones. She holds a silver sword and shield. A strong scent of jasmine emanates from her, and her *yoni* is wet with golden sunlight. She may appear with the face of a two-headed eagle, with a serpent in her beak. She bestows boons of magic powers and strength.

21. Vahnivasini Sasini
Fiery Mistress of the Crescent Moon

She appears out of a cloud of sparkling flames, a youthful maiden naked with a body composed of golden fire. She wears a necklace of skulls and ruby, and is adorned with ruby jewels. Her eyes are a silvery, white light like opalescent pearls, and her glance casts beams of liquid moon-fire. She may hold arrows composed of flowers, and a glistening red sword. She burns up the karmic accumulation of past deeds and bestows direction and clarity.

22. Mahavajresvari Rakta Devi
Great Thunderbolt Goddess of Passion

She has red skin like a setting sun, is dressed in a red *sari,* and her skin is smeared with red sandal paste. Bedecked with rubies and other jewels, she wears an ornate crown of a human skull with encrusted rubies. Her rich, black hair is tied up and dressed with red hibiscus flowers and golden lace. She may be holding a bow with pomegranate flower arrows, and a sword encrusted with rubies and gold. Sometimes she may be holding a human skull in her right hand, and a large curved sword, covered in fresh blood, in her left, while she floats on an ocean of blood. She is intoxicated with wine, and is swaying from the intense feelings of passion. She brings swift and lasting action, removing all obstacles or evil influences.

23. Sivaduti Adi Sakti
Highest Feminine Power, Messenger of Awareness

She has three eyes, a dark reddish skin and a dusky complexion, covered in blood. Her long, black hair is matted. She wears a skirt made of a tiger's skin, and holds a trident and a scimitar, both dripping blood. She is sometimes accompanied by a black jackal, or may appear with the head of a jackal. She gives strength, courage and steadfastness to her chosen, and brings one to the realization of power.

24. Tvarita Urdhvaretada
Swiftly Raises Energy Upwards in Ecstasy

She appears as a girl of sixteen, with three eyes, dark skin, and long, black hair piled up in coils on her head. She wears a crystalline crown with peacock feathers. Her face is beautiful and she smiles easily. She is wearing green banana leaves around her waist, and is adorned with a skull necklace and jewels. Her large, rising breasts are smeared with red sandal paste. Writhing over her body are eight serpents. She brings swift action to whatever is desired, and raises the *kundalini* energy, giving the ability to produce great acts of enchantment and sorcery.

25. Kulasundari Kamini
Most Beautiful Voluptuous Tribal Goddess

She has long, rich, black hair, and is naked with warm, glowing, golden-red skin, wide hips and large, swelling breasts. She is smeared with red sandal paste, and wears hibiscus and jasmine flowers in her hair. Her eyes are half closed in lust and ecstasy. She embodies desire itself, and the visceral, raw power of lust. She is mistress of the sorcery of desire and channeling of lust for works of enchantment and magic.

26. Nitya Jnana Svarupini
Eternal Goddess Whose Form is Gnosis

She appears with three lustrous eyes, and warm red skin like the sun at dawn, wearing a red *sari* and adorned with rubies. She also wears a necklace of skulls, and sometimes bangles, armlets and anklets of skulls and ruby. Her feet and hands are smeared with red paste. She may be holding a skull-cup, and often a large sword. She has a strong scent of honey and hibiscus flowers.

27. Nilapataka Siddhida
Auspicious Sapphire Goddess of Perfection

She is naked, three-eyed, with deep, sapphire-blue skin. Red paste is smeared on her breasts, upper arms, and stomach. She is wearing rich jewels and an ornate jeweled crown from which her long black hair drops down over her shoulders. She holds a skull-cup filled with nectar, and a sword. She may sometimes appear with the head of a sapphire cow. She grants boons of magical powers, and the ability to enchant objects and people.

28. Vijaya Devi Vasuda
Victorious Goddess Who is Giver of Wealth

She appears naked, with lustrous reddish-orange skin the color of the sun at dawn, and wears a garland of skulls and rich jewels. She bears a bright curved sword with fresh blood dripping from it, a shield, and may sometimes have a bow and arrow, or a *chakra*. Sometimes she may appear with the head of a tiger. She gives wealth of all kinds, and victory in all endeavors.

29. Sarvamangala Tantrada
All-Auspicious Giver of Tantra

She appears naked, her skin the warmth and color of golden sunlight. In her left eye is reflected the light of the moon and in the right the light of the sun. She has red sandalwood paste and *sindhoor* smeared over her body, is richly jeweled with gold, and wears a garland of skulls. She has the strong fragrance of marigold, sandalwood and jasmine. In her left hand she is holding a skull-cup filled with wine, honey, menstrual blood, and the combined male and female sexual fluids. Her right hand is giving the gesture of blessings.

30. Jvalamalini Nagini
Snake Goddess Wearing a Garland of Flames

She is naked, has warm and glistening golden skin that seems made all of sunlight, and wears a garland of flames, radiating heat and fire from her presence. Her eyes and face are intoxicated with lust, her rising breasts are smeared with red paste, and she is richly jeweled. Writhing about her body are many snakes, giving off rays and flashes of prismatic light as they move across her skin. At times she may appear with the head of a hyena. She teaches the arts of desire, as well as the magical channeling of such force for sorcery and enchantments.

31. Chitra Devi Raktapuja
Prismatic Goddess Whose Worship is Passion

She is naked, her skin radiating all colors in magnificent waves of light. Her blissful smile is all-conquering, and the honey scent from the nectar of her wet *yoni* is intoxicating. Her presence is energetic and stimulating, and she demands passion from those who would approach her. She gives victory in subjugation over others, including the subjugation of one's own thoughts, granting Self-Realization. She also gives gifts of sudden treasure and wealth (wealth may come in many forms).

32. Lalita Kanya Sukrada
Playful Maiden Who Gives Semen

She appears naked, as a sixteen-year-old maiden, seductive and overcome with lust. Her swelling breasts are smeared with *sindhoor* and she wears a small garland of skulls. Her long black hair is glistening with oil and tied into thick braids. Her large eyes are half-closed as her body sways gently with desire. She holds an empty skull-cup out to you, with the expectation that you will fill it and offer it back to her. At times she may appear with the head of a fox. She makes the barren fertile, gives virility, ripens crops and bears fruit, controls rain, and gives powers of enchantment and sorcery.

Yoginis of the Tribe of Serpents

33. Dakini Madasalini
Resplendent Sorceress Shining with Bliss

She appears in an ornate red *lehenga,* her skin the lustre of the rising Sun, with two crimson red eyes and a pleasant face that is intoxicated by bliss. She has a vermillion *bindi* in the form of Shiva's *trishul.* She wears a garland of skulls, and is richly ornamented with bangles, armlets and anklets made of *panchadatu* (magical metal composed of five alloys: mercury, silver, copper, zinc and iron). In her long black hair are marigold and jasmine flowers, the scent of which permeates the atmosphere. She holds a skull-cup of wine in her right hand, and in her left a *khatvanga* (large staff with a human skull). She teaches the art of spellcraft and enchantments.

34. Rakini Paparasini
Sensuous Enchantress of Witchcraft Who Destroys Sin

She is naked with radiant skin like a blue lotus, and has three eyes that sparkle with glittering, blue fire. Her long, black hair is tied into multiple braids, and coiled into a heavy mass which cascades down

her left shoulder. She wears a garland of skulls, and is richly ornamented. Her lithe body sways with passion, and she is intoxicated by
luminous wine which she drinks from the skull-cup in her left hand,
the red liquid dripping down the sides of her mouth and onto her
breasts and waist. Sometimes the liquid drops to the ground, where
blue lotuses spring up. In her right hand she holds a large spear
covered in fresh blood. Sometimes she will appear with the head of a
crocodile. If pleased she may help with conflicts and victory over
enemies, giving charms and spells to act as a shield against adversity.
She also gives clarity in complex matters, cutting to the root of the
matter to distinguish the real or essential from illusion.

35. Lakini Sarvatantresi
Desirable Enchantress of All Tantras

She is naked, with electric blue skin and three eyes as black as
night. On her upper arms and breasts is smeared vermillion paste. She
wears a garland of skulls, and is richly ornamented with various gems
and pearls for armlets, anklets and bangles. She has thick, dark, auburn
hair which has strings of pearls and gemstones woven into it and elaborately layered in back. Her rising breasts and stomach gently move
up and down with every breath as her body is filled with bliss, and her
eyes are half closed, her lips trembling as ecstasy flows through her.
She holds in her left hand a skull-cup filled with wine and combined
male and female sexual fluids, which she drinks and with which she
is intoxicated. In her right hand she holds a *vajra* (thunderbolt) that
emits crimson flames.

36. Kakini Naganartiki
Wanton Enchantress of Serpentine Dance

She has skin like warm, yellowish bronze, and is naked except for
a garland of skulls and a girdle of bones. Her hair is shining black. She
is adorned with jeweled bangles, armlets and anklets. A snake curls
around her shoulders. In her left hand she holds a skull-cup filled with
rice wine, and in her right hand a trident. She teaches the magic of

dance, the accumulation and projection of energy with rhythm and music.

37. Sakini Mitrarupini
Alluring Enchantress in Friendly Form

Her beautiful naked form is snow white, as though her body is composed of light itself. Her long hair is black, braided and tied into several loops that form a large bun to the left side of her head. She has jasmine flowers in her hair, and the scent permeates the atmosphere. She wears a garland of skulls, and is richly ornamented with gems and gold. Sometimes she appears with the head of a white hare. She gives knowledge of potions and aphrodisiacs for erotic play.

38. Hakini Manoharini
Sorceress Who Bewitches the Mind

She appears naked, her luminous skin beautiful like the full moon, with flashes of rainbow light. She has three eyes like pools of black ink. She wears a garland of skulls and roses. Her bracelets, armlets and anklets resemble serpents. Her long auburn hair is braided and plaited into layers that come down her back, and roses are interwoven in it. In her left hand she holds a skull-cup filled with wine, and her right hand may be holding a book, or sometimes a rosary of 108 gems. She helps one to know their true nature, and makes one's voice commanding such that what one wills manifests.

Yoginis of the Tribe of Great Wisdom

39. Tara Yoga Rakta Purna
She Who is Accomplished at Liberation Through Unification of Passion

Her skin is deep blue, with a beautiful face and lithe body. She wears a short skirt made of tiger skin. Her thick reddish-brown hair is matted and tied into a *jata* (top knot), and a snake is coiled around it.

She wears a garland of freshly severed human heads, and a crown made of five human skulls. She is richly jeweled. Her lips and mouth are smeared with fresh blood which drips down her neck and breasts. She holds a sword with fresh blood, and a severed head. Sometimes she will appear with flames and an aura around her, which are the fires of the cremation grounds, and holding a skull-cup filled with nectar. At such times address her as *Smasana Bhairavi* (terrible goddess of the cremation grounds). She gives swift results and teaches the arts of yoga and tantra to achieve Self-Realization.

40. Sodashi Latika Devi
Slender Creeper Goddess of Sixteen Desires

She appears as a ravishingly beautiful maiden, eternally sixteen years old, with warm, golden-pink skin like rays of the dawn sun. Her face is radiant and has a pleasant smile. She is clothed in a vermillion lehenga dress with flashes of green. She has thick, auburn hair braided into ringlets and adorned with jasmine, that cascades down her shoulders. She is richly ornamented with gold and ruby, and wears a golden crown set with rubies. In her left hand she holds a jewel-encrusted skull-cup filled with deep red wine. In her right hand she holds a red lotus flower; or sometimes a bow made from sugarcane, with arrows made of flowers.

41. Bhuvanesvari Mantrini
Queen of the World Who Gives Mantra

She is naked, appearing in bright, multi-colored lights that are reminiscent of peacock feathers. Her perfect coral-white skin is smeared with red saffron paste on her forearms, belly, hands and feet. Her long, dark hair is thick, falls over her left shoulder, with red hibiscus buds woven into it. Her lips are deep red, like pomegranate, and they may be moving as she quietly sings *mantras*. Her large dark eyes are luminous like the deepest, dark night, half closed in pleasure. She is richly adorned with jewels, and her scent carries the fragrance of honey and betel leaves. In her right hand she holds a *mala* of bones and ruby.

Sometimes she may appear as a voluptuous woman wearing a red silk *lehenga* with the head of a peacock. She breathes life into all *mantras,* and grants powers of sorcery and enchantment with the voice.

42. Chinnamasta Yonivega
Wanton Enchantress with Wet Yoni

She appears as a naked, dusky maiden, with a voluptuous body, rising breasts, and long black hair. She is richly jeweled with armlets, bangles and anklets, and a garland of skulls. A serpent writhes about her waist and between her breasts. She is in the midst of sexual ecstasy, and her body shakes from bliss. In her left hand she holds a skull-cup, and her right hands holds a large scimitar. Sometimes she may use the scimitar to chop off her own head, the blood gushing out in two thick streams from her neck, one stream going into the mouth of her freshly severed head, and the other filling the skull-cup. She may offer this to you to drink. She has mastery over the powers of sex and the mysteries of death.

43. Bhairavi Satya Sukrini
Terrifying Sorceress Whose Truth is Fertile

Naked, with dusky skin, three eyes, large rising breasts, small waist, beautiful limbs and long, dark, matted hair. She wears a garland of freshly severed heads, and is adorned with skull bangles, armlets and anklets. A serpent is wrapped around her left arm, and she wears a crown on her head with three serpents. She wears a girdle of severed arms that is strung with *rudraksa* beads. The scent of red sandalwood permeates her atmosphere. She holds a bright sword in her right hand, and in her left is a skull-cup filled with menstrual blood and semen.

44. Dhumavati Kundalini
Dark Smoky Goddess of Serpentine Fire

She appears naked, vibrant, with dark skin and long, black hair. Her lithe body sways with passion, and her eyes are half closed in desire. She wears a garland of skulls, and is adorned with snake brace-lets, armlets and anklets. She may appear in a cremation ground, or at the crossroads, and there are often black crows in her presence. Some-times she may first appear as dark smoke that swirls into her form. At times, she may appear with the head of a crow. In her left hand she holds a skull-cup, and in her right a spear. She wields illusion, teaches the use of sexual energy for sorcery, and gives control over sleep and dreams.

45. Bagalamukhi Guru Murti
Intoxicating Beauty in the Form of Teacher

She has warm, yellow skin, and her lithe form is wrapped in a bright yellow *sari*. She is garlanded with yellow flowers and richly jeweled with gold. She radiates beauty, and stuns the mind with her form. She is mistress of all magical powers. She is particularly pow-erful at stopping enemies in their tracks with paralysis, be it physical or mental. In her right hand she holds a club, and with her left she grabs the tongues of enemies which she smashes into paralysis so that they cannot speak ill of her chosen. Sometimes she may appear with the head of a crane, or there may be a crane with her.

46. Matangi Kanta Yuvati
Youthful Beauty Enhanced by Love

She appears as a young maiden of sixteen, with dark blue-green skin and beautiful long, auburn hair. Her eyes are intoxicating, and she will usually be seen in a dense forest. She holds a skull-cup in her left hand, and in her right is a sword. She favors those who worship her with polluted offerings, such as leftovers offered to her at the crossroads. She prefers those who approach her without bathing, and women to come to her during menstruation. She is sexually dominant, and will take from her devotees whatever she pleases. She teaches powers of sorcery, and in particular the ability to have control over others, and the power of attraction.

47. Kamala Sukla Samsthita
Arising as Radiance from the Lotus

She has radiant warm golden skin like sunbeams, wears a red silk *lehenga* and is richly adorned with gold jewels. Her eyes are half closed in pleasure, and her lips have a slight smile that is intoxicating and alluring. Her scent is of lotus flowers and honey. In her left hand she holds a lotus flower, and her right hand is free. She gives mental and emotional pleasure, as well as success and wealth.

48. Prakriti Brahmendri Devi
Nature Goddess of Supreme Reality

She appears with greenish blue skin and long black hair that flows freely down her back and over her shoulders. Her eyes are a luminous greenish fire, and her lips have a sweet smile. She wears armlets that are snakes, a golden crown, golden bangles, necklace and earrings. In her left hand she holds a skull-cup that is filled with golden nectar—this is the *amrita,* or elixir of life. Her right hand holds a trident. She rules over forests and is guardian to the wildlife.

49. Gayatri Nitya Citrini
*Brightly Ornamented Goddess of the
Eternal Sacred Song*

Wrapped in a silvery blue silk *sari,* her three eyes are deep, indigo blue. Her luscious black hair is piled high on her head and crowned with a silver diadem that is encrusted with deep sapphire gemstones. Her skin is a pure, luminous, coral white. She wears earrings, necklace, anklets, bangles and nose ring, all of bright silver as though made of moonlight. In her left hand she holds a skull-cup filled with bluish silver nectar, and her right hand is sometimes giving the *mudra* of *abhaya* (dispelling fear). If pleased, she may give gifts of art and creativity, musical talent, poetry and writing. She will sometimes appear with the head of a large, white swan.

50. Mohini Matta Yogini
Intoxicating Desirable Sorceress

Clothed in space *(digambara)*, her lovely body is luminous darkness. Her black eyes are penetrating and filled with desire, her thick, dark hair flows freely in rivulets down her back and across her shoulders to below her waist. She is bejeweled with onyx and gold necklaces, earrings, nose ring, armlets, bangles and anklets. She dances across the sky in a mind-stunning, alluring sensuality. The atmosphere around her smells of rich jasmine flowers and honey. Her left hand holds a skull-cup filled with wine, from which she drinks liberally, and continuously dances, swooning with desire and intoxication.

51. Sarasvati Svarga Devi
Eloquent Goddess of Heavenly Bliss

Appearing out of a cloud of crystalline white radiance, her entire form radiates beauty, but her smile alone is so dazzling that it hypnotizes and stuns the mind into bliss. She has long dark hair with red hibiscus flowers and ruby woven into the long strands. She wears a thin red silk *sari* with flashes of emerald and gold. Sidelong glances from her large, doe-like eyes send shudders of *kundalini* energy up the spine. Her voice is the essence of music, thrilling like warm honey. She may give gifts of eloquent speech and writing, musical talent, and creativity in every sense. She is the mistress of art and speech, and effortlessly wraps the practitioner into blissful, dreamlike states.

52. Annapurni Siva Samgi
Auspicious Goddess Who Nourishes All Beings

She has a youthful appearance, skin with a reddish golden hue, three beautiful eyes and large high breasts. Her hair is dark and long, cascading down past her shoulders. She wears a red and gold silk *sari*, and is richly jeweled. Her left hand holds a golden skull-cup filled with ambrosial nectar, and in her right is a vessel filled with fresh food. She will nourish with food and drink, as well as the deeper nourishment that comes from the non-dual realization of reality.

53. Narasimhi Vama Devi
Warrior Goddess of Tantrik Magic

A fierce warrior, her lithe body appears with dusky skin, a beautiful and powerful face with piercing black eyes and long, black hair tied into thick, braided knots that are bound together behind her head. She wears a black bodice and a black, stranded, short skirt with bones woven into it. She wears serpent armlets, bangles and anklets. Around her neck is a garland of skulls, and around her midsection a serpent is her sash. She may be riding a lion, or sometimes she may appear with the head of a lioness. Her left hand holds a skull-cup, and her right hand a trident. She may give boons of *mantras* for powerful magic, as well as protection to those she favors.

54. Ganga Yoni Svarupini
Sorceress of Beautiful Flowing Form

She appears in a white silk *sari* with flashes of silver and blue. Her skin is fair, and her eyes are large and peaceful. Her hair is dark and long, with white lilies placed along its length. Her entire form is voluptuous and sensuous, yet regal and refined. She is richly ornamented with nose ring, earrings, silver bangles and anklets, and wears a large silver crown encrusted with sapphires and opals. Her left hand holds a silver water jug *(kamandalu)* overflowing with glistening, silver liquid like starlight. Her right hand may hold a flute. She may appear with a large crocodile, or sometimes with the head of a crocodile. As with her namesake, the river Ganges, she gives protection, purification and cleanses all wrongdoings.

55. Aparajita Samaptidha
Bestowing Unconquerable Perfection

Her complexion is like early morning sunlight, with large sparkling eyes and long, dark hair braided and tied back. She wears armor composed of a bodice and a short skirt of adamantine, giving off sparks and flashes of light with its brilliance. She wears serpent armlets, and holds a bright, metallic spear in her right hand. Her left hand holds a skull-cup filled with wine. She is a powerful warrior, and gives success and strength in all battles, combat and confrontation.

56. Chamunda Pari Anganatha
Slayer and Ruler of Imbalance

Her appearance is fierce and that of a tribal warrior. She has long black hair piled on top of her head, plated with skulls and serpents. Her skin is ruddy, like dark storm clouds, with a tinge of crimson. She wears a garland of freshly severed heads, and is adorned with bones and serpents. Her eyes are dark orbs with blazing red flames. In her left hand she holds a skull-cup filled with blood, and in her right hand a *khatvanga* (short staff with a skull). She may appear in a cremation ground with fires, corpses, jackals and ghosts. Sometimes she will appear with the head of a jackal. She should only be approached late at night, at a crossroads, in the wilderness, or at other lonely, abandoned places, with offerings of meat and alcohol.

57. Varahi Satyekakini
Wild Enchantress of Truth

She has a beautiful body, with dark skin like the night, large swelling breasts and a slender waist. She wears an *amdrapali* dress of deep red. Her eyes are dark, and her long, dark hair flows freely, and is adorned with red hibiscus flowers. She is richly ornamented with jewels. In her left hand she holds a skull-cup of golden nectar; in her right hand, a sword. She may appear with a buffalo near her. Often, instead of her human face, she will appear with the head of a wild boar.

58. Kaumari Kriya Saktini
Young Goddess of Powerful Action

She appears as a beautiful maiden of sixteen years old, with warm, red skin like the sunset, wearing a red *sari.* Her forehead, arms, breasts and stomach are smeared with *sindoor,* and her large, dark eyes are half closed in passionate bliss. She is richly ornamented with gold and rubies, and has hibiscus flowers woven into her thick, pleated auburn hair. Her right hand is raised in the *abhaya mudra* (dispelling fear), and her left hand displays the *varada mudra* (granting boons). Waves of crimson light radiate from her. Often, she appears with a peacock.

59. Indrani Mukti Niyantrini
Lady of Heaven Who Gives
Liberation Through Restraint

Sensuous and warm, she has golden skin, and beautiful form with large, raised breasts and small waist. She is clothed in a blue silk *sari* with platinum necklace, armlets, anklets and earrings. Her long dark hair has fragrant jasmine flowers woven into the long plaits. Her two large, dark eyes are half closed in bliss, and her full lips tremble with subtle pleasure. Her voice is melodious and warm, and her scent is irresistibly enchanting. She may be holding a trident in her right hand, and a *damaru* in her left. Just as often she will appear with her hands in the *mudras* of dispelling fear and granting boons.

60. Brahmani Ananda Murti
Creative Enchantress Who is the
Embodiment of Bliss

Regal with warm, golden skin and a blissful expression, her long dark hair is collected into plaits that run down over her shoulders and back. She wears a white silk *sari* with red blouse and golden trim, and is richly adorned with gold jewels. Her beautiful face has large, brown eyes and perfect features, smiling slightly with an expression of deep bliss. In her right hand she holds a trident, and her left has a skull-cup. She may be attended by a white swan, or sometimes appears with the head of a swan.   .

61. Vaisnavi Satya Rupini
Goddess of Preservation
Whose Form is Truth

She appears as a beautiful young woman with blue skin, clothed in a blue *lehenga* with golden highlights. Her long black hair is thick and plaited, coming down her shoulders. Her three large eyes are like pools of black ink, sparkling with starlight. Her left hand holds a skull-cup filled with ambrosial nectar. Her right hand holds a large sword. At times she will appear with the head of an eagle, or she may have an eagle by her side. She may help those she favors with seeing the truth in matters that are obscured or in some way not clear, including the truth of Self. She is fond of ritual and responds easily to *puja* and *sadhana*.

62. Mahesvari Parasakti
Enchantress of the Highest Power

This powerful queen appears as a beautiful, youthful woman with fair skin and long, thick, auburn hair. She has three beautiful, intoxicating eyes filled with passion. She may be wearing a golden crown, or sometimes appears with a radiant crescent moon in her hair that is tied up into a top knot. She wears a red silk *lehenga* with green accents. A serpent twines around her neck, and she wears serpent armlets and a serpent belt. Her left hand holds a skull-cup filled with blood, and her right hand holds a large *trishula* with *damaru* (a large trident with a drum attached). With a sideways glance she may grant her exceptional powers to the devotee.

63. Lakshmi Manoramayoni
Goddess of Fortune
Whose Yoni Charms the Mind

She appears as a beautiful, youthful maiden, wearing a rich, red *sari,* with warm honey-golden skin, glistening as though the sweat from her skin emits sweet nectar. She has dark kohl-lined eyes, her breasts are full and rising, and a slim waist. Her long, auburn hair falls down her back in braided rivulets that are interwoven with small jasmine flowers and hibiscus. She is richly jeweled with gold and ruby. She radiates with youthful energy, fertility and desire. Her eyes are half closed in blissful intoxication, her lips quiver slightly with pleasure. Her left hand holds a clay pot that is filled with golden honey nectar. Her right hand gives the sign dispelling fear, or if seated, she may display *brumisparsha* (fingers extended touching the earth, extending blessings and fertility).

64. Durga Satchitananda
Invincible Warrior of
Truth, Consciousness and Bliss

Named after the supreme Goddess Herself in her form of the great warrior queen of the *Devi Mahatmyam* ("Glory of the Goddess"), this mighty enchantress is stunningly beautiful, wearing a bright, red *sari* and richly jeweled in gold. She has thick, long, auburn hair that runs down her back, and wears a golden crown. Her three eyes blaze with intensity and infinite beauty. Her perfect form is bliss itself. She may give the gestures of dispelling fear and granting boons. She will often appear riding a lion, or sometimes a tiger, and may have a *trishula* in her right hand. The embodiment of regal elegance and unstoppable feminine power, her presence stuns the mind and destroys all negative influences. All falsehoods collapse before her, and the radiance of the nature of reality blazes forth unhindered in non-dual realization.

9. Initiation

This ritual will begin your journey into the world of the Yoginis, and prepare you for being accepted into their lineage or tribe—the Yogini *Kaula*.

It will be best if you have access to an outside location where you can have privacy and seclusion. A grove of trees or a forest, a secluded beach, up in the mountains, or in the desert at night. Another option is a campground, which will usually have the added boon of a fire pit. Other good environments are a lonely, quiet crossroads (preferably in a rural location as the chance of having privacy is better). Graveyards at night are a powerful location, though if used, be respectful and maintain the dignity of the location. In India the *smashana* (cremation grounds) are preferred locations; they are numerous and have access at all hours. Perform the ritual alone, outside at night, underneath the open skies. Time the initiation for a Full Moon at midnight.

If you do not have access to a good outdoor location, don't let that stop you. While it's easier to feel the connection to the natural world by being in wild nature, you can manage this even inside a room in an apartment building, or really just about anywhere that you can have some seclusion and a little bit of space. In truth, inner and outer are all the illusory play of energy that makes up all of reality. You are just as connected inside a room as you are outside in the wilderness, staring up into the night sky. It may just take a little extra mental discipline or yoga to realize this and establish the connection. Eventually, all of your workings will be performed in an astral temple, your Shadow Circle, which you carry with you always in every circumstance. More on this in later chapters. For now, it helps to do the ritual physically.

For this initiation, have a few things ready ahead of time. First, collect your Yogini Stones. These are small stones that you find attractive or to which you have some draw. Try to keep them all about the same size. The color and material should be guided by your intuition. Each stone will represent one of the Yoginis, and their energy will be associated with it. You can also gather a collection of crystals, or even a combination of stones and crystals, allowing your intuition to guide you.

At most you need 64 stones—one for each of the Yoginis. You could also work with smaller amounts to represent clusters of Yoginis, for example 16 or 8 stones. Eight will connect with one of the most important numbers associated with the Yoginis, the eight *chakra* system that their energy flows through, the eight *Sahaja Mothers*, and the eight directions of space. Even a single, central stone or crystal that represents the entire circle of Yoginis can suffice. Let your intuition guide you, and try to open more to creativity and your artistic sense rather than the rational mind.

Take some time finding the right stones. You might be surprised when you start finding them on hikes in nature, or even by the side of the road. However, you can also easily find great selections of stones at stores that specialize in spiritual tools, like occult gems and so on; these days you can even find them online. The key is to take time to feel the energy and connect with the stones you are taking. You will not necessarily know which stone is associated with which Yogini, and that is fine. What you will know is the energy of the stone, and how it resonates with both you and this work. Later on, as you go deeper into the relationship with the Yoginis, you might realize that a specific goddess is associated with one particular stone, or a grouping of Yoginis may be attracted to one of them.

I will keep referring to these as Yogini Stones, but they may just as well be crystals, or a collection of berries, acorns, pinecones or even leaves. If you are at the beach, you might find a collection of seashells that can work. While these found items in nature may not have the durable qualities of rocks or crystals, they do have a special connection with the place that adds to the energetic ambiance. At times, even a collection of small twigs or fallen pieces of trees could work.

Before you use the stones, let some fresh water run over them (if you are working with leaves or other items that might easily disintegrate, add a few drops of water instead). A running stream in which you can hold the stones and let the cooling waters cleanse and vitalize them is a great option. Letting ocean waves cleanse them, as you hold them in the water, is another option. If nothing in nature is opening up, take a cup of water, and add a small pinch of salt to it. Use this to lustrate your stones and purify them by pouring the water over the stones. Then, light some incense and pass the stones through the scented smoke a few times. Finally, you can warm them briefly over the light of a candle. Now they are ready for your use. When not being used, keep them in a bag (silk is a great option), or if you have an altar set up, keep them there. It's usually best if you are the only one to handle them so the energy is kept clear and only associated with you and the Yoginis.

On the Full Moon night that you will perform the Initiation, have the Yogini Stones on hand. Also, it is good to have an image of the Goddess, in whatever form she speaks the most to you. However, if you are outside, you might notice that everything around you *is* the Goddess—and the image is not required. In such a case your central image might be a tree, a rock formation, a large crystal, or a fire pit.

Have a candle and incense, and for offerings, some fresh flowers and two or three fruits. Also have a glass of fresh water, beer, wine or other spirits on hand. If you are doing this outside, adjust accordingly. For example, instead of a candle you may be able to have a small campfire, or a lantern. The altar might be a large rock or a tree stump. If you can respectfully use what nature provides, this will add to your working.

It should go without mention, but always be respectful of the location you are in. If you bring items into a campsite or wilderness location, do not leave signs of your presence when you are done. Don't leave garbage, bottles and so on, and be sure to clean up any trace of your presence. Don't cut branches from trees or move rocks or part of the landscape. Try to work with fallen items and found nature as it presents itself to you.

Set up the stones in a circle that is large enough for you to sit inside. Set up the altar in the center, with all the items on it or nearby. If there is not enough room to delineate the circle with you inside of it, then set up as a smaller circle around the altar.

Light up your central fire, be it a campfire or a candle. Light the incense. Sit comfortably, taking in a few deep breaths, and exhale slowly, fully, relaxing the body and mind. Give a few minutes to get very relaxed, breathe regularly and allow all thoughts and concerns to flow out from your mind and body, into the earth. Feel yourself relaxed, with a sense of quiet expectation.

Now, starting at the first *chakra* (top of the head), visualize the *chakra* in brilliant, crystalline white light and vibrate the *mantra* **KSA**.

Move attention to the middle of the forehead, and vibrate **LA**.

Move attention to the third eye, with **HA**.

Move attention to the inside top of the palate, and vibrate **SA**.

Move attention to the throat, intoning **SHA**.

Move attention to the chest, with **SSA**.

Move attention to the navel, chanting **VA**.

Move attention to the genitals, saying **HLA**.

Pause to see all the wheels aflame with stellar fire, whirling and receiving vast amounts of cosmic energy.

Now, starting from the first *chakra,* see a beautiful, white, lustrous flame that moves into the *chakra,* circling through it eight times. The flame then moves down to the next *chakra,* again making eight passes before moving down to the next. This continues down through each *chakra,* so that when the flame has sunk down to the last one and rotated through it, it will have completed 64 passes through all of the energy centers on its descent. Now, the light reverses course and moves up through each of the *chakras,* again with serpentine swirling eight times through each of the *chakras* in succession as it moves up to the top of the head again, completing another 64 passes as it moved up.

Take your time. Feel the warm currents of light coruscating through your body, each circulation filling your entire being with bliss and energy. Do at least one cycle down and up in this manner, although you can complete as many full cycles as you like.

In the *Kaulajnananirnaya* it is said that this practice will make you the Lord of Breath and unite with the Devi herself. This unlocking of the *chakras* and circulating of the serpentine, flowing energy within produces divine nectar—the *amrita* of the Yoginis.

Now, continue to see yourself enveloped in this radiance, energy flowing and cascading throughout your body, and give the *mantra* of the *Sahaja* Mothers to open all of the lotuses and flood your psycho-spiritual body with a vast increase of cosmic energy:

hrim a hrim im

hrim hrim um hrim

hrim r hrim hrim

l hrim hrim aim

hrim hrim o hrim hrim

hrim hrim ah hrim

hrim ksah hrim lah

hrim hah hrim sah

hrim pah hrim sah

hrim va hrim ra

hrim kl hrim

Repeat the *mantra* 8, 16 or 64 times.

Now, slowly with every breath, inhale cool, watery starlight, feeling a *blue* flame ascend up your spine until it reaches the top of the head. Feel the coolness of the light as it moves up slowly, refreshing, rejuvenating and cleansing every cell of your body. With each exhalation, relax into the feeling of a warm, honey-like nectar of *red* light slowly dripping down your spine. As it descends with the breath, feel the warmth fill your body, feel the delicious honey-light filling every cell with health and vitality.

Become aware of your entire consciousness breathing, pulsating, throbbing in unison with all of nature and the elements; feel the pulsing heartbeat of the universe itself flowing through you. Repeat these circulations of upward-flowing, cool, blue flame, and slowly trickling down honey-red fire, for several cycles. The longer you go, the more you will feel the undulating, sensuous currents of coolness and warmth flowing through you. Your body and mind will begin to buzz or vibrate with this light and the feelings of bliss that envelope you, as the energy and tension build to a climax. Resist dissolving into the bliss; instead, let the tension build up slowly, luxuriously. Bask in sensations of pleasure that pulsate through your body with every breath.

After some time, or when the intensity builds up to the point where you can no longer resist, move awareness to about 6 inches (15 cm) about your head. Relax, and see a vibrant, pulsating lotus of pure crystalline light opening up above and showering nectar down on you. Allow your body to relax into bliss, alive with the sensations of life itself, as your body pulsates in symphony with the lotus, one ecstatic dance of pleasure.

Recall to mind your Gurus. If you are an initiate of an Order, or have taken initiation from tantrik lineages, then you likely already have a *parampara* (lineage) to which you can give thanks, and whose blessings and protection you now call upon.

Even without such a formal relationship, you no doubt have had people throughout your life who were in some way an inspiration or that you learned from. They may be gurus, alive or dead; authors from whom you have found inspiration; images of Gods or Goddesses with whom you feel a connection; friends and so on. Just take a moment to feel this chain of instruction and guidance that stretches back through your life, and even before this life. Feel the connection and give thanks, with sincerity.

Most essentially, the Guru is your own Self. Open and connect with that higher, most clear aspect of yourself.

As you make this connection, vibrate **OM**. Be present in the moment, experiencing the entirety of the universe in naked, blissful awareness, beyond all conceptual and temporal limits.

In this glow, call upon the *Sahaja Mothers,* inviting them to be present and to share in your energy. Request them to accept you into their lineage as one of their own, and to initiate you into the *Yogini Kaula.*

Here is a suggested oath, but as always, your own words and intentions, when spoken from the heart, are best. Feel free to adapt this to your own tastes.

> *Brahmi, Varahi, Agoresi, Kumari, Indrani, Vaishnavi,*
>   *Mahesvari*
> *Glorious Goddesses of the Yogini Kaula*
>
> *Mighty Reigning Queens of Space and Time,*
> *Primal Sorceresses of Nature*
> *I invite you to please be present and accept my Oath to you!*
>   *Please accept these offerings.*

Wave the incense towards the altar three times, then place it on the altar.

Move the candle around the altar in a circular motion three times, then set it on the altar.

Dip the flower into the water (or other liquid offering), and shake it gently towards the altar. Place the flower on the altar.

Offer the fruits by raising them up towards the altar, and then set them down gently.

Rub your hands together rapidly to generate heat, and then hold them outstretched toward the altar. Feel your energy going out towards the Yoginis, offering your very life-force to them.

Now say:

> *Mighty Yoginis of the Kaula Circle*
> *Open your dark lustrous eyes and look upon me with favor!*
> *A single glance from you bestows enlightenment!*
> *Cosmic Night is Awakening, and the celestial flowers are*
>   *opening their petals.*
> *The dark winds of your magic flow around me, embracing!*
> *Lotus hidden bees, having come out into the Night with the*
>   *raining stellar dew-laden petals, collect the dark rays from*
>   *your eyes.*

Let your flood of beauty wash over me! Let your nectar of Bliss rain down upon me.

With the next actions, touch the corresponding part of your body, marking it with horizontal line using the *sindhoor* and ash:

I consecrate my brow that I may know your Wisdom
I consecrate my heart to your love
I consecrate my navel to your embrace
I consecrate my genitals to your divine joy
I consecrate my feet to the path of the Yogini Kaula

Now raise both arms outward, with the head tilted up so that you are embracing the sky with eyes wide open, while saying:

Let my eyes be yours to see with!
Let my ears be yours to hear with!
Let my nose be yours to smell with!
Let my tongue be yours to taste and speak with!
Let my body be yours to enjoy with!
Let my heart be yours, a living shrine to indwell!

AIM KLIM SAUH!

Remain present in this awareness, relaxed yet awake and aware in the present moment, free of conditions. There is no past, no present, and no future—there is only the immediate awareness. Feel how awake you are with every breath, each movement of blood circulating through your body. All of nature is alive and radiating in harmony with your Self.

When you are ready to close the circle, thank the Yoginis for their presence.

Consume the remaining fruit and drink, or distribute it to the earth and the local spirits—it has been made sacred.

This ritual, though seemingly simple, is a treasure that will unlock the vast realms of these powerful goddesses.

If you are outdoors and ready to leave the site, be sure to carefully pack up your sacred belongings, and to clean up the site, leaving nature as you found it.

Pay attention to your emotions after this ritual. Try to be keenly present, aware of your surroundings. It is best if you can be alone and in a quiet place until the morning, so try to arrange circumstances such that you will have the space and time to really dive in and enjoy the sweetness and solitude of these few hours before dawn.

As you lie down to sleep, give a silent prayer or intention to the Yoginis that you want them to stay with you during sleep, and guide your dreams. Ask them to be with you and illuminate the landscape of your mind with their presence. It's helpful to have a notebook nearby so you can write down any dreams this first night after the initiation. Also, the act of writing down your dreams will reinforce the practice of dream recall, and over time, dreams will become more vivid and filled with personal symbolism.

At the same time, don't be discouraged if you do not remember your dreams, especially this first night. It will come with repeated intentions, and I encourage you to make this a nightly practice of turning your thoughts towards the Yoginis as you fall asleep.

After Initiation

A few days after this ritual, you can take your Yogini Stones and add the sigils of the Yoginis to them, associating each stone directly with one of the goddesses. This is done after the initiation ritual to first establish the connection directly with your consciousness, and open you up to the presence and influence of the Yoginis. Once you have been invited into their tribe, they will direct you—in either dreams or spontaneous inspirations—in the construction of the sigils of their names, and which stone is associated with which Yogini.

If you are very visual or artistic, you may see or feel colors associated with each of the Yoginis. These colors can be applied to the Yogini Stones to further personalize them, as well as the "petals" of the *Yogini Yantra*. See Chapter 14, "Night Magic" for more on this.

Whenever you see the moon in the sky, pause for a moment to say a silent invocation:

Hail Mistress of the Night,
Queen of Witchcraft,
Lady of Enchantments and Sorcery!

This is a general call to the powers of the Moon and the night, which will serve as a reminder of your initiation and your intent to work with and be attuned with the Yoginis.

Across many traditions, the moon is a reminder of the shadowy nature of reality. It functions as a gateway to dream states, including waking dream states, where the liminal qualities of reality are shifted in dimensions far outside of the typical materialistic viewpoint of the world.

As you begin to work with the Yoginis more directly, you might find that you enhance this call with the names of individual Yoginis, or a group of them with which you may be working with for a specific purpose.

On the first full moon after your initiation, prepare a small offering of your choosing (such as a flower, fresh water, and some fruit) and leave it at a crossroads at midnight. Open your heart and, using your own words, thank the Yoginis for accepting you into their tribe.

10. Meet Me at the Crossroads

> " 'I am not, neither does another exist; energies alone exist.'
> If he meditates on that thought, that place of repose, that true
> nature, even for a moment, then, having become a sky-
> traveler, he will enter the company of yoginis."
>
> — Tantraloka

After your initiation, make some time every day to reconnect consciously with the Yoginis. You have truly entered into the Crossroads, that place which bridges the rational mind and the supra-rational. Reality, as commonly thought of and experienced, is like a thin veneer, or a fragile layer of a frozen lake that is easily cracked, allowing the dark waters to rise. You have opened a door to the night aspects of consciousness and reality, and everything is not quite what it seems when looked at closely, or experienced with this fresh perspective.

This can be overwhelming to the "day" consciousness, which is used to the illusory world view of materialism. Again and again, the false personality will take over as has been its habit since it first started to collect into a sense of "self." Unless you have established your point of view firmly in Awareness itself (or maybe done a *lot* of hallucinogens), this materialistic view is bound to act as the main obstacle to overcome in commingling with Yoginis. This is another paradox, as your personality and ego are *not* villains to be annihilated. Often Westerners that embark on a spiritual path that has come from Eastern traditions mistake the goal, thinking they are supposed to be some sort of robot or zombie that has no emotions, no preferences, and, possibly, no personal hygiene. Don't mistake ideas of "detachment" with trying to turn yourself into little more than a cucumber. This is a common error that leads to becoming disassociated from the vibrant sensuous experience of life itself!

The personality, the ego—these are important evolutionary tools that continue to serve a vital purpose in daily life, allowing you to do some of the things necessary to function in this world, such as interact with other people in a civilized manner, pay the bills and hold down a job, take care of loved ones, brush your teeth, and so on. The goal is not to completely destroy the ego, but rather to put it in its place as a useful tool.

The medicine, once again, is Awareness. Again and again, make a conscious effort to shift your internal center of gravity to Awareness. Every exposure to the limitless ground of all being, of all reality, no matter how brief it may seem, is a reinforcement, a reminder.

This barrier breaks down at night during the dream cycles, or during periods of meditation. Learn to be vigilant with your wandering mind through daily practices of meditation to help see the intrinsic awareness that is always present—in fact, it is this awareness that is all there is.

The Yoginis will act as your guides if you appeal to them, bringing you ever closer to the non-dual truth of self. As every layer unfolds, a clearer experience is had, as though an old mirror covered in dust is being cleaned up, allowing the light to reflect clearly.

The Crossroads are found in every conjunction of apparent polarity. Thresholds serve this purpose well; every time you pass through one, consciousness changes. How often have you gotten up to do something in another room, only to find that as you enter the room you have forgotten what you came for? These are passageways through dimensions, where consciousness shifts from one mode or vibration to another. Try to maintain awareness when moving through these transitional spaces.

The Crossroads also appear in our actions. When moving from a seated to a standing position, this is a threshold where awareness can be glimpsed. Or when getting up from bed, or sitting down to eat. How often have you eaten a meal while watching television, only to realize later that you barely tasted the food, and that you missed half of the show you were watching? Where did you go? Or, rising from bed, instead of immediately reaching for your phone to mindlessly start scrolling through social media, pause a moment to acknowledge this transition from night consciousness to day. This is a good time to record your dreams if you have not done so already, before the concerns of the day take over. Rather than immediately jumping into the day, take a moment to open your perspective in awareness. Then, throughout the day, remind yourself to maintain awareness, and pay particular attention when doing any activities or transitioning from one state to another.

At the center of the Crossroads, the position between light and darkness, day and night, life and death, rational mind and creative dream expression—here is the still point of Awareness. This is the Heart of the Yogini, the nexus between the seeming "real" and "unreal", between the material and the spiritual, between time and timelessness. Again and again, become aware of this position that is always present, and take your stand there. From this position there is no subject, no object, no time, no boundaries…and yet awareness of all of experience is visible here. Like waves on the ocean, watch as emotions and thoughts arise from the depths, play out for a time, and then vanish back to where they came.

From this radiant darkness, witness the forms of the Yoginis approach and commingle with the elements, with nature, with the stars and with the *chakras*. At the center of the Crossroads, all of creation continuously manifests from out of the central black hole of the void—from nowhere—and expresses itself in lights and colors, sounds and sensations—a continuous moving, living, dynamic pageantry of experience in the present moment, the only moment that truly is.

Time is a deep meditation on non-duality. We are accustomed to thinking that we are a constant witness to the flow of time. There is the strong feeling that the past and the future are actual "things" somewhere in space, with tangibility. As with all aspects of the material world, when examined closely this illusion falls apart. What is the past but a memory, and memory is just another thought. As with all thoughts, they arise and disappear. The past is a dreamlike condition of thought, especially our personal pasts. Like everyone, our lives are a mix of highs and lows, good times and bad times, fond memories and even tragedies. I have fantastic, beautiful memories from childhood and growing up, and remembering them brings back the sensations and feelings as though it is all happening again "right now" in the present moment. Still, these are thoughts, ultimately no different from a daydream or fantasizing about the future.

And as for the future, those vivid fantasies where we imagine we are somehow controlling our destinies, or as is more often the case, blindly worrying about what will come to be—again, more thoughts. Everyone you see is lost in thought, either thinking about the past or worrying about the future. There is a third state, that of complete distraction and loss of awareness, which comes from mindlessly watching tv, social media feeds, and so on.

What underlies all of these reveries? Again, it is pristine Awareness, the visceral immediacy of the naked, present moment.

The crossroads are a liminal space, in between states. In the crossroads there is no distinction between waking consciousness, dream states, and deep, dreamless sleep. This is a place where day consciousness and dream states can meet freely, where the rational and irrational commingle and interact fluidly, one bleeding into the other and each affecting the other.

"At the crossroads at midnight" is a familiar aspect of American folklore. The blues guitarist, Robert Johnson, infamously popularized the idea from old folk songs of the Mississippi Delta. Taking his guitar to an empty crossroads at midnight, Johnson sat down to play. The Devil showed up, and for the price of Johnson's soul, made him a famous and talented musician. It seems to have worked, as Johnson went on to have a lucrative career, immortalizing his pact with the Devil in his song "Crossroads Blues" and many others.

The traditions seem to stem from old tales which indicate the crossroads as the meeting ground between the world with which we are familiar—the apparently materialistic world—and the world of the unseen, populated with spirits, demons, ghosts, all of which inhabit the crossroads.

In many ways midnight and the crossroads share similar qualities. The crossroads at midnight adds to the shadowy, otherworldly qualities of these spaces. Midnight is also a strange, transitional period between night and day, dreaming and waking, called the "Witching Hour" in Western folklore. Midnight is when the veils between worlds are thinned, and the nocturnal denizens of the shadow realms freely move between dimensions.

Looking at other traditions, this special category of space and time is found throughout history. The ancient Greeks, Romans and Persians all recognized the magical and shadowy significance of crossroads. The dark goddess Hecate is associated here, as the empress of night who guards the chthonic side of experience, and also ushers in the darkness, the unknown, the void.

India has deep associations with crossroads, space and time; these conjunctions are places where things are not quite as they may seem at first glance, and the otherworldly nature of reality bleeds through, transforming consciousness. Spirits of nature, such as the female *Yakshinis,* frequent these places, along with ghosts and other emissaries of the subtle realms. The Yoginis are queens of the crossroads. Many of the tantric *sadhanas* for the Goddess Kali indicate that a crossroads at midnight is ideal for her worship. The *Yogini Tantra* indicates that the crossroads are effective for *sadhana,* in addition to such abandoned locations as the desert, the cremation ground, or at the foot of a *bilva* tree. The *Devirahasya Tantra* similarly says that the *mantras* should be given near a fig tree, in the desert, a deserted house, the cremation ground, in the wilderness, or at a crossroads. The *Kulachudamani Tantra* mentions crossroads as the ideal location, along with other empty and barren places. There are many more examples throughout the tantric texts.

The twilight hour, when the sun is setting on the horizon, is another type of crossroads on a cosmic scale. It is at this time, as the shadows are lengthening and the light is fading into darkness, that Shiva and his troops of ghosts, ghouls, vampires, goblins and other denizens of the subtle realms freely roam the earth, causing mischief and spreading magic wherever they go.

These places and times are transitions from one state to another. To be in the center of the crossroads is to be the still point at the Center. This is standing as Awareness, boundless, present everywhere, the still silent point—Shiva—in the center of the chaos of creation and dissolution.

From the center, standing as Awareness, all of reality—in both its day and night phases of manifestation—is experienced directly, experienced as the depths of manifestation as well as the inscrutable heights of heavenly realms.

From the center, we arise firmly as the still point. We descend and arise freely, existing and non-existing simultaneously. Reality is malleable, fluid, and we can see through the illusory quality of so-called reality, and even of our self. The larger image breaks up into its component elements, such that the "I"-ness that entered freely into the crossroads now experiences that it too is a ghost—one of Shiva's *ghanas* (the troop of spirit companions)—another afterimage vibrating between the worlds of light and darkness, an ephemeral set of appearances, an apparition that is composed of a constant stream of impressions that arise out of nothing and return again to nothing. Seeing, hearing, feeling, tasting, smelling; all spontaneously throbbing, vibrating, snaking, radiating, and then vanishing again, ghosts or afterimages of awareness.

We enter into the crossroads confidently, blindly, as our "self"; we emerge from the experience as something "other." This new thing is Non-Self—the Void—clothed in a coat of many colors; the naked, immediate, raw and spontaneously arising luminous consciousness, richly bejeweled and ornamented like a god or goddess, all of the attributes and details of the waking dream a rich covering that for most people passes for reality.

Frequent these borderlands of place and time. Haunt the world, walking through it as a ghost. The inconceivably blazing radiance of Awareness will shine forth from the crossroads at midnight, a shimmering rainbow of black light in the darkness, an ultraviolet luminescence that seeps and crawls, trickling and dripping through shadow and matter alike, weaving dream states and shedding them snakelike throughout the waking state. Give yourself up freely to this place; open your heart to the cosmic darkness of the primal Night.

The New Moon Ritual

As a practical exercise, once a month on the night of the New Moon, visit a crossroads at midnight and leave a small offering. This can be a small portion of honey, milk and sugar; or, a few berries and nuts. Give a silent prayer to the Yoginis, and ask them for signs, and to grant boons. Then, as you go to sleep, enter the crossroads of consciousness, and meet the Yoginis in their circle.

11. Opening the Yogini Circle

This ritual is a suggested outline of how to work with the Yoginis and establish a strong relationship with them. As you have more experience, you may find yourself having intuitions or dreams with further guidance, or even specific instructions or requests.

To simplify matters somewhat, there are two approaches to take. First is the path of ritual, or *sadhana*. This should be worked with for weeks at a time, even longer, building up a strong momentum with the ritual. Make an intention to perform the ritual and stick to it. This is important! In Tantra your Will is the Way, and through commitment to a practice you will help to build up and strengthen this Will. An example might be to commit to performing the *sadhana* once a week, on the same day and time every week, for a period of 9 months. Once this commitment is made, *do not break it*. See it through to the end.

This may lead to a type of crisis or breakthrough. The psychological and emotional energy that builds up during a confined period of ritual work can be *intense*. This type of activity is unlike anything to which we are normally accustomed. The ego will feel threatened with the repeated dips into the deeper strata of consciousness and non-dual experiences. It will try to derail your efforts with a panoply of enticements and distractions. It might be experienced as sudden panic attacks or irrational fears, or even a gnawing sense of unease and paranoia. It can help to have an ongoing journal where you record your thoughts, impressions and anything else during the ritual (such as the phase of the moon, the temperature and other weather conditions, health, and so on). Others may be able to offset the pressure by painting, drawing, dance or music. Going for quiet and grounding walks in nature will also help to make space for these feelings, and to integrate them.

For this rite, a simple altar setup works well, although feel free to elaborate on it. These are suggestions to get you started. Have a small table on which you can fit a candle or tea light, incense, a cup of water or wine, a small plate with fruit, and some fresh flowers. Have the *Yogini Yantra* and *Yogini Stones.*

For this *sadhana,* choose one of the Yoginis and focus on her for the ritual. Use your intuition. You may already be drawn to one in particular; if not you can read through their descriptions to help select one, or leave it up to "chance."

I suggest practicing this opening physically before trying to establish a purely astral space. This way you will build layer upon layer, having a sure foundation from which to perform the work.

Sit before your altar, take a few deep breaths, and exhale fully to remove the stale breath and relax.

Energize by doing the **Eight Chakras** practice in Chapter 6, "Wheels of Starlight".

Perform a simple *pranayama* of 4/16/8: Close the right nostril, breathe in through the left to a count of 4; hold the breath for a count of 16; close the left nostril and breathe out through the right to a count of 8. Keep the left nostril closed, breathe in through the right for a count of 4; hold the breath for 16; close the right nostril and breathe out through the left for a count of 8. This completes one *pranayama.* Repeat the entire cycle three times.

Sprinkle the circle with the water or wine, and fume the incense around the circle three times counter-clockwise.

See a spark of deep, red light in the East, which becomes brighter, then in one swift flash extends counter-clockwise around you, forming a bright, flowing circle of crimson fire that pulsates with crackling, fiery energy.

In the East, South, West and Northern quarters, see glowing, swirling light that becomes brighter moment by moment. In the East yellow; South, red; West, blue; North, green. The lights swirl and thicken with movement reminiscent of serpents undulating slowly, almost sensuously.

Visualize the guardians of the directions. Each appears as a young, naked maiden, with long, disheveled hair, eyes half closed with desire and hungry with lust and passion, wearing a garland of human skulls, a rich assortment of jewels on their ears, wrists, hips and ankles. Each carries a sword and skull-cup, giving the *mudras* of fearlessness and granting boons.

Face the East where **Brahmi** arises, skin glistening warm, golden yellow, with a cool breeze seemingly coming down from the stars.

Turn to the right and face the South. **Narayani** rises out of the gloom, her skin radiant crimson, the passionate warmth of fire.

Turn to the right again and face the West. **Maheshvari** appears, majestic with deep, electric-blue skin, the dark waters of some ancient ocean behind her.

Turn again to the right and face North. See **Chamunda**, with deep, onyx skin that glows like space itself, with snowcapped mountains and a dark forest of trees behind her.

Turn again, returning to the East.

In the intermediate space, now see:

South-East: **Kaumari**, warm, golden-red skin like the Sun setting.

South-West: **Narasimhi**, heated, red skin with dark blue shadows flashing about her form.

North-West: **Aparajita**, with cool, greenish-blue skin and flashing white teeth.

North-East: **Varahi**, with deep, reddish skin and dark, green, shadowy flashes.

Now, see the 8-petalled lotus of Pure Crystalline White above your head. Each of the goddesses pours liquid from her skull-cup into the top of your head. Feel the warm, honey-like trickle descending slowly into your body, infusing your entire system with bliss. Remember all those from whom you have learned in your life—teachers, gurus, friends—and give thanks to them for instructing and helping you to grow in this tantrik knowledge. This is *parampara,* the living tradition which you are acknowledging and with which you are reconnecting.

In addition to any formal gurus or teachers you might have, you can bring to mind the people who have taught you, either formally or informally. Relationships can be teachers, for example, or parents, or friends. A guru may be someone you admire, even someone you do not know, or people who have passed. This is a recognition of the mutual interdependence that as humans we all have. This simple act of remembrance and gratitude opens the heart and the subtle channels of energy within.

Now call to the Yogini with whom you desire to work. I have found that a simple, spontaneous invocation works best. An example with Lalita Kanya (the 32nd of the 64 Yoginis):

> *Om Sri Lalita Kanya* svaha!
> *Om Sri Lalita Kanya* svaha!
> *Om Sri Lalita Kanya* svaha!

> *I welcome you, sweet Lalita Kanya! You are the maker of all that is auspicious, and all that is inauspicious. You are the giver of boons, and the taker of boons. I seek your refuge, and greet you! Please come and share in this feast!*

Hold up the plate of fruit in offering, circling it three times counterclockwise. Do the same with the water or wine, the candle and incense, and any other offerings. Rub your palms together to generate heat, and hold them out to offer your own essence.

Sit for some time in contemplation. Feel the energy, and see how the presence of the Yogini affects your senses. A point will come where there is a sense of accord with the Yogini, as though there is a synchronization of consciousness. There may be a feeling of a charged atmosphere, or dreaminess, or some other sensations that somehow feel "different."

Now make your requests or prayers, asking for specific boons or help as required. This is also the time to engage with the Shadow Goddess and Sigil work, which is discussed in Chapter 14, "Night Magic".

When the communion is complete, give thanks to the Yogini and gratitude for her blessings. Also give thanks for the Guardians of the quarters, and see them all dissolving into light. Any remaining offerings can then be eaten, or distributed to the spirits of the earth.

12. The Feast of the Yoginis

"Oh Goddess, may all my speech, howsoever idle, be recitation of Mantra; may all the actions with my hand be the making of ritual gesture; may all my walking be the pacing around Thy image in worship; may all my eating and other functions be Homa rites; may the act of my lying down be prostration before Thee; may all my pleasures be an offering to the great self. Whatsoever I do may it be counted for the worship of Thee."

— *Anandalahari, v.28*

The simplicity of this rite conceals a deep power. Equivalent to the Witches' Sabbath in Western traditions, in this ritual you will enter into the Shadow Circle with the Yoginis. Regular practice strengthens the bond between you and the Yoginis, and revitalizes the body and mind, unleashing the depths of magic, creativity and power that these goddesses embody. The ritual opens up the Yogini Yantra and the cosmic palace of which it is a diagram.

The Feast is best given regularly on the Full or New moon. The Yoginis will become accustomed to sharing in this energy, and it's best to honor the connection regularly.

Have your Yogini Stones with you, and lay them out in a circle.

You may also choose to have an image of the *Yogini Yantra* before you.

Have a plate with a small candle, incense, water and fruit. Optionally you might also have alcohol (beer, wine, heavy spirits) and cooked meat. The offerings are placed in the center of the circle where you will be seated.

Perform the **Chakra Activation** and **Circulation** exercises from Chapter 6, "Wheels of Starlight".

Perform the complete **Opening Rite** from Chapter 11, "Opening the Circle".

Now your Shadow Circle is established.

185

Sing, chant or say each of the following names with an open heart. The recitation may be spoken out loud, softly muttered, or recited entirely mentally. Over time you may find that the recitation turns into a singsong pattern on its own. Let it flow without judgement.

The recitations can be greatly enhanced with music and dance, and this also helps to build up the energy in the circle. A repetitive drumming has a trancelike effect on consciousness that will deepen the rite. Bring your creativity to this feast, offering it all at the feet of the Yoginis. Having the accompaniment of some musical instruments lends another layer of magical atmosphere to the ritual, a tradition that goes back through the mists of time and across cultures. Drums, flutes—these are just a few instruments that may lend their energy to the rites.

Along with music and singing comes dance and movement. These can also play large roles in rituals. The combination of sound and movement helps to break through psychological and other barriers that may prevent the free flow of energy and spontaneity. Does it feel awkward to dance and move around the circle? Good! Channel that awkwardness into movement and dance. Bring your circle alive, and feel the energy start to flow, moving in spontaneous and unexpected ways.

Each of the names is preceded by the formula *Om Sri*. *Om* is a famous *bija,* also called the *pranava.* It represents the entire cycle of creation, preservation and destruction of the universe in a cyclic fashion. *Sri* is an honorific title, given as a form of the highest respect. It is also one of the names of the Goddess herself, perhaps most well known as the heart of the *Sri Vidya* (the highest knowledge of the goddess). *Sri* has the connotation of "holy" or "sacred" as well. At the end of every name is the Sanskrit word *Svaha*. This word is used with offerings, having the meaning of auspiciousness. Putting this all together, for each of the Yoginis they will be called and invited to be present and accept worship with *"Om* respected sacred Goddess <name>, *I call you and ask you to accept this offering!"*

1. Om Sri Kali Nitya Siddhamata svaha
2. Om Sri Kapalini Nagalaksmi svaha
3. Om Sri Kula Devi Svarnadeha svaha
4. Om Sri Kurukulla Rasanatha svaha
5. Om Sri Virodhini Vilasini svaha
6. Om Sri Vipracitta Raktapriya svaha
7. Om Sri Ugra Rakta Bhoga Rupa svaha
8. Om Sri Ugraprabha Sukranatha svaha
9. Om Sri Dipa Muktih Rakta Deha svaha
10. Om Sri Nila Bhukti Rakta Sparsa svaha
11. Om Sri Ghana Maha Jagadambha svaha
12. Om Sri Balaka Kama Sevita svaha
13. Om Sri Matra Devi Atmavidya svaha
14. Om Sri Mudra Purna Rajatkripa svaha
15. Om Sri Mita Tantra Kaula Diksa svaha
16. Om Sri Mahakali Siddhesvari svaha
17. Om Sri Kamesvari Sarvasakti svaha
18. Om Sri Bhagamalini Tarini svaha
19. Om Sri Nityaklinna Tantraprita svaha
20. Om Sri Bherunda Tattva Uttama svaha
21. Om Sri Vahnivasini Sasini svaha
22. Om Sri Mahavajresvari Rakta Devi svaha
23. Om Sri Sivaduti Adi Sakti svaha
24. Om Sri Tvarita Urdhvaretada svaha
25. Om Sri Kulasundari Kamini svaha
26. Om Sri Nitya Jnana Svarupini svaha
27. Om Sri Nilapataka Siddhida svaha
28. Om Sri Vijaya Devi Vasuda svaha
29. Om Sri Sarvamangala Tantrada svaha
30. Om Sri Jvalamalini Nagini svaha
31. Om Sri Chitra Devi Raktapuja svaha
32. Om Sri Lalita Kanya Sukrada svaha
33. Om Sri Dakini Madasalini svaha

34. Om Sri Rakini Paparasini svaha
35. Om Sri Lakini Sarvatantresi svaha
36. Om Sri Kakini Naganartiki svaha
37. Om Sri Sakini Mitrarupini svaha
38. Om Sri Hakini Manoharini svaha
39. Om Sri Tara Yoga Rakta Purna svaha
40. Om Sri Sodashi Latika Devi svaha
41. Om Sri Bhuvanesvari Mantrini svaha
42. Om Sri Chinnamasta Yonivega svaha
43. Om Sri Bhairavi Satya Sukrini svaha
44. Om Sri Dhumavati Kundalini svaha
45. Om Sri Bagalamukhi Guru Murti svaha
46. Om Sri Matangi Kanta Yuvati svaha
47. Om Sri Kamala Sukla Samsthita svaha
48. Om Sri Prakriti Brahmendri Devi svaha
49. Om Sri Gayatri Nityacitrinni svaha
50. Om Sri Mohini Mata Yogini svaha
51. Om Sri Sarasvati Svargadevi svaha
52. Om Sri Annapurni Sivasangi svaha
53. Om Sri Narasimhi Vamadevi svaha
54. Om Sri Ganga Yoni Svarupini svaha
55. Om Sri Aparajita Samaptidha svaha
56. Om Sri Chamunda Pari Anganatha svaha
57. Om Sri Varahi Satyekakini svaha
58. Om Sri Kaumari Kriya Saktini svaha
59. Om Sri Indrani Mukti Niyantrini svaha
60. Om Sri Brahmani Ananda Murti svaha
61. Om Sri Vaisnavi Satya Rupini svaha
62. Om Sri Mahesvari Parasakti svaha
63. Om Sri Lakshmi Manoramayoni svaha
64. Om Sri Durga Satchitananda svaha

Now, hold the plate of offerings at heart level, with arms stretched out towards the altar. Say:

> *Queens of Witchcraft, Mighty Sorceresses of the Night! Yoginis of the 64 Dimensions, please accept this offering of food!*

Look at the plate of food, eating it up with your eyes. Smell the scent of the offerings. Take a bite of the food, relishing every taste sensation. Let the Yoginis enjoy the offering through your body and senses. Place the plate back down.

Hold up the liquid offerings, saying:

> *Sky Dancers, Powerful Enchantresses of the Void! Yoginis of the 64 Dimensions, please accept this offering of drink!*

Take a sip of the drink. Relish it, feel it with all of your senses. Taste the drink like you have never tasted it before. Again, let the Yoginis experience the offering through you.

Hold up the candle, offering its light and warmth to the Yoginis.

Hold up the incense, offering its scent.

Offer your body completely to them, and let them experience through your senses. Continue with dance and music around the circle as the spirit moves you.

Feel the presence of the Yoginis around the circle. This may be a tangible feeling, or it may come through as intuitions or inspirations that come later, after the ritual is complete. Meditation will help to tune open consciousness to receive clearly any communications. Pay attention to your dreams as this is a primary contact point between the realms and one that is favored by the Yoginis.

Often, what seems like a dreamlike quality will overcome consciousness, almost as though you are witnessing yourself from outside of your body. Movements take on a fluid motion, and colors are heightened in the presence of the Yoginis. Voices, sounds, shadows out of the corner of the eye—all of this and more might be experienced. You may feel tangible presences around you. The sensations appear of others breathing near you, smelling you, moving through the air. You might hear sounds like the buzzing of bees, bells, or deep vibration and snippets of language or full conversations. Shadows moving and slithering, undulating in serpentine waves.

It is possible you might experience intense *bhava* (emotion), which seems to have no source. Bouts of laughter, crying, anger, and so on are common. If these come up, do not fight them. Try to relax into the experience and allow it to flow through you. Savor this contact. This intoxication of the divine may lead to possession, a welcome blessing and visitation from the Yoginis. Allow them to experience your body and sensations, and you share in their experience of energy.

The feeling of love and even attraction may arise. This is entirely natural and indicates flow of force from the *chakras*. This energy can be cultivated, heightened and stimulated. Offer it all to the Yoginis.

You may feel drawn to one or more Yoginis, in which case turn your attention toward her. You can add additional recitations of their name, give them special offerings, and ask for boons or information.

It can be helpful to have a notepad nearby in your circle, so any impressions can be written down, or artwork drawn, and so on. If you play, having a musical instrument is also a good way to channel the energy.

Dance is one of the many ways they will express themselves, and you may find yourself moving spontaneously. Let your body and mind dive into this flow of creative energy and express itself.

Even if at first you do not sense any presence, it is important that you behave and act *as though your circle is filled with the presence of the Yoginis*. Always maintain respect and gratitude towards them, and always enter your circle with a sense of quiet expectancy.

An advanced form of this Feast is to recite the offering words and to take a bite and a drink after each of the 64 names. Follow the same pattern, but after each individual name, pause to give the offerings of food, drink and senses. Move on to the next Yogini and repeat until you have completed the entire circle.

After some time, give thanks to the Yoginis and close your circle, saying:

To the Goddesses who are rays of light vibrating in Darkness—
Illuminators of Consciousness!
I bow to you again and again in worship!

See the Yoginis merging into the luminous darkness, swirling back into the circle of stones, the earth, the trees, the dark sky and stars, the moon. See the guardians of the circle shimmering into spectral light that merges with the quarters and cross-quarters, slowly fading with a pulsing ambient light.

The remaining offerings of food and drink can be given to the local spirits of the place where you are located.

13. Day Magic

The Yoginis are goddesses of the night, cavorting wildly in circles of darkness during the new moon, or dancing in the shadows just outside the limits of peripheral vision. As with the shadows that pass outside the light from the circle of a campfire, the Yoginis stride easily between the known and the unknown, flitting between the light of our day consciousness and holding court in the realms of the subconscious. The Yoginis are *other* to normal consciousness, always beyond the limits of intellect and rational mind. Like their circular temples that are on the outskirts of civilization, the Yoginis are just outside of normal perception. The materialistic worldview does not acknowledge their presence, choosing to ignore the hints of otherworldliness that have occasion to seep in to day consciousness. This does not mean, however, that during the bright day the Yoginis are inaccessible, or worse yet, forgotten while we go about our days filled with the mundane cares of daily life. Their voices can be heard even in the noisiest of city streets, and their influence and presence are strong even in the brightest of summer days. The exercises throughout this book will help to open up your awareness to their presence. In particular, the Day Magic practices will open the gateways of consciousness to experience the enchantment of every moment of life.

The work of self-enchantment is to regularly experience the world through the eyes of this witchcraft. In so doing, the world seems to respond and transform in kind. The experience can be extremely psychedelic, with the world appearing to behave like a living entity that is interacting directly with you (which is not far from the truth). This type of experience may come through in many ways, but by far the most common way is an increase in synchronicities. You may find yourself wanting to start a new endeavor, but are not sure how to get started. Then, seemingly out of the blue, a random opportunity will appear which fulfills the requirements. For example, you might come across a book on the exact subject you were thinking about. A class that just happens to teach a skill or provide a piece of information that you needed suddenly becomes available. You meet someone on a bus or in a coffee shop, and strike up a conversation which just happens to answer the question that has been perplexing you.

Consciously make intentions with the Yoginis, and these intentions begin to appear. As your relationship becomes deeply established with one or more of the Yoginis, it will become uncannily common for what you desire to come to pass in one form or another. A strange sense of *déjà vu* increases throughout the day, and the weird coincidences that start to pile up can become almost comical. The world seems more fluid and dream-like, and you may find that you have to check yourself throughout the day and see if you are really "awake" or in a dream. (This practice also helps to develop Lucid Dreaming, a useful technique for all of this work.)

As discussed in Chapter 4, "The Circle of Awareness", the practice of meditation will greatly help in cultivating this added sensitivity and awareness of the more malleable aspects of reality. To take this practice deeper, meditating on the names and images of the Yoginis will open your awareness to subtle realms of perception that lie just outside the apparent boundary of "normal" or "day" consciousness. Cracks in the material world view will become more common.

With all of this luminosity penetrating and seeping through what may have previously appeared to be a mundane world or daily drudge, it can be easy to fall prey to the illusion of believing you are in some special condition or set of circumstances. Remember that in all circumstances, your primary tool—your instrumentation to experience what is happening—is your own consciousness. If you have been diligent with a meditation practice, you should have a good foundation for experiencing these dreamlike states without falling prey to ego aggrandizement. Remember, it's a very fine line between communicating with the Yoginis and tricking yourself into thinking you suddenly have a special direct line of insight into reality. If you start to feel or perceive ideas that somehow seem a little too good to be true, or are outwardly dangerous to yourself or others, it's definitely time to take a break and refocus on basic meditation before going deeper.

Outside of formal meditation, ritual work, and spellcraft, you can also incorporate enchantments during every hour of the day. Being in nature as much as possible will add to this. Hikes in a forest, a walk on a secluded trail, strolling through a field, sitting on a beach and listening to the ocean waves—all of these are great options for deepening the connection to the natural world, which in turn sensitizes and increases your overall connection with the Yoginis. If nature is not readily available, maybe there is a park nearby, or a tree-lined street to walk down. Even in cities there is usually some token of nature, and in some cases there are large parks or wooded areas. Do you have access to the sky? Watch clouds, stare into the sky, and breathe. This can be done almost anywhere. Seek these places out and frequent them. Open up to nature, get outdoors, underneath the sky.

If you are not in a location where you can get out into nature, it may take a little effort, but it is still readily accessible. Use your Shadow Temple, and have it built up in a richly detailed landscape of forests. As you enter it, try to bring all of your senses with you—smelling the fresh air and wild flowers, hearing the sound of the breeze rustling in the leaves of the trees, feeling the sunlight and wind on your face, and even tasting fruits or fresh honey. Use your imagination and develop the Shadow Temple in as much detail as you can. This mental *yoga* discipline becomes easier with practice.

As you encounter animals, greet them silently as signs or messengers of the Yoginis. Many synchronicities will start to come up with these sightings. On my hikes, I encounter coyotes, owls, deer, vultures, hawks and even the occasional tarantula. Living in a semi-rural area, these chance encounters may not seem incredible at first glance. With an open mind, the way an animal appears, showing up at just the right moment, is always an amazing experience filled with wonder. Consider every chance encounter as a sign or reminder of your connection to the Yoginis. If you act *as though* an emissary of the Yoginis has presented herself to you, *the world appears to respond in kind.* This is the secret to enchanting your world.

Women are direct manifestations of *Shakti*. As part of your practice, when you encounter women you might give a silent salute to the Yoginis—especially when you encounter women wearing red clothing, as that color has a strong affinity with the Yoginis. Watch with awe as the world appears to restructure itself according to your new orientation. It may be unsettling at first, maybe even disorienting, to realize from firsthand experience that what was thought of as static or external and materialistic is really dream stuff. Your experience of the world relies far more on how you approach it and what expectations you have than may be realized at first glance.

Pay attention to the weather and the elements. How is the wind blowing? Is it faint, barely perceptible? Or is it strong and gusty? How does it sound? Can you hear it blowing through trees, or maybe rattling the windows of buildings?

What are the clouds doing? Take some time to look at the sky, and drink in its vastness with your eyes.

Look—really look—wherever you are. Just the simple act of looking with awareness will go a long way towards enhancing your sensitivity to the subtle realms, and being able to sense and pick up the communications from the Yoginis.

Walk around during the day with an awareness of just how magical it is to be incarnate in the world, to be experiencing the universe through your senses. Be aware of your body, how it feels to be alive—the feel of the blood pulsing through your veins, the tactile sensations from interacting with and touching the world. Pay close attention to all of your senses, and how there is a constant stream of sounds, sights, tastes, touches and smells. See how they make impressions on your mind, and how your body responds to the different sensory stimuli throughout the day.

Make all of this a daily offering to the Yoginis. You might consciously dedicate your day, or an aspect of it, to them. Make a silent entreaty to the Yoginis before eating a meal, dedicating it to them and asking them to enjoy the tastes and experience using your body and senses. Expand this to other aspects of your day. This is also a powerful dedication to make during sex, giving the entire act to the Yoginis and inviting them to experience it with your body.

Go through your day with a sense of quiet expectation, and you will find the signs and symbols, meaningful patterns and inspirations, increasing and deepening.

This practice of enchanting your own life will also open you to more influence from the Yoginis during the night practices and dream yoga. The day and night practices work together, and you will find that there is little distinction between them.

Rather than making a hard line between formal periods of meditation and sorcery and the mundane world, strive to be awake and aware throughout the day. See the possibility of being open to enchantment in daily life, letting every moment and every act be one of magic and possibility.

The key in all of this—and as you go deeper it will become blazingly apparent—is that there is no difference between any of the experiences that arise. Calling to a Yogini, seeing a coyote, or performing a ritual—in fact, all acts, all expressions—are of the nature of consciousness. How these events *arise as consciousness* is part of the continuous unfolding that will give access to your own spells, your own omens and signs, your own direct and vital relationship with the Yoginis.

Here is a suggested set of practices to help with producing a more open, sensorily aware, and enchanted life. The Yoginis are found closely in our senses; to focus on them with awareness brings an openness and sensitivity to the subtle actions of the Yoginis that will add to your experience during formal rituals, meditations and life overall. Each group of practices is done during the day for 7 days.[18]

Week 1: Sight

Focus on what you are seeing. Look for a certain color each day. For example, if you selected red for the day, try to find it wherever you are. While out walking, look for red. Inside the house or office, look for red. When you find it, see how many different shades there are. Look closely and see if you can perceive subtle variations in the

---

[18] This regimen was inspired by the Academy of the Senses in *Tantra Magic* by Mike Magee.

color red. Even when your eyes are closed, see if you can find red. The next day, select a different color and go through the same process.

Week 2: Sound

Focus on hearing. Try to widen your experience of sound throughout the day. What is the most distant sound you can hear? Can you hear the wind? An airplane? Birds? And the closest sound? Can you hear the sound of your own body? Your heartbeat or breathing? How many sounds can you hear at the same time? Think of other combinations and sounds, and try to listen for them. With your eyes closed, do sounds seem closer or further away? When your eyes are opened, are sounds different than when they are closed?

Week 3: Scent

How many different scents can you be aware of throughout the day? How do different smells change your mood? What memories are stimulated by different scents? Can you alter your emotions or energy by being aware of different smells, or consciously choosing a scent that reminds you of something? How does a strong odor affect your mood? And a faint scent? Do natural scents from the wilderness have a different feel to them than artificial scents like perfume or gasoline?

Week 4: Taste

Pay close attention to every taste throughout the day. One of the most accessible tastes is from eating and drinking. Try to taste each bite of food as though it were for the first time. Roll it on your tongue, chew it slowly, savor the flavor and see how it stimulates emotions, memories and energy levels. Try to taste the individual flavors—the saltiness or sweetness, the taste of any herbs or seasonings, and so on. Do this with every taste, even the ones that you do not find pleasing. Be aware of how taste can influence you. Are you drawn towards certain tastes? What are they, and how do they change or alter your moods? How is imagining a taste different from actually tasting something? If you imagine tasting or smelling something, can it alter your mood? Try the same with actually eating or smelling. How is it different? Food and drink are a type of alchemy that we engage in daily, and which affects our minds and bodies. See what other types of taste experiments you can try.

Week 5: Touch

Be aware of all touch sensations. Begin with your fingers. Every time you engage with something physically, see how it feels to your hands. Is it smooth or rough? Firm to the touch, or softer? Cotton feels very different from a table top, while sandpaper will feel different from both. Try to become aware of these differences as you touch the world. Expand this to the rest of your body, and see how much you can feel. Do you feel the clothes on your body? Can you feel your hair? Or your skin? What do your bones feel like? Or the blood pumping through your veins? What does the wind feel like? Or sunlight? Think of other combinations of touch to explore, and strive to be aware of them.

In addition to the week-long sensory explorations, incorporate the following practices during the day. All of these help to remind us to be present and open to impressions and influences from more subtle realms.

Are You Awake?

Throughout these practices, and in general throughout your days, stop and occasionally ask yourself, "Am I dreaming?" Think about the apparent differences between waking and dreaming. When you are in a dream, it seems just as "real" as so-called waking consciousness. How can you really be sure that you are awake? There will be more on this later in Chapter 15, "Dream Magic", but for now start to open up to the practice of checking yourself to see what state you are in.

Are you awake? Or are you dreaming, right now?

Shadow Watching

Throughout the day, pay attention to shadows. We often take it for granted that shadows are present during the day. Seek them out intentionally, and see how they present themselves in different places and hours. Notice them in relation to the position of the sun and the seasons. See how shadows tend to lengthen in Autumn as compared to Summer; yet, throughout, they are present.

Towards evening, as the Sun is setting, notice how shadows start to encroach more in every situation. If you can walk through the wilderness or nature, maybe a forest trail or a park, see how the shadows work with the sunlight, projecting into the peripheries of your visual field as well as right in the center. What sort of shadows do trees make? Or buildings? What shadows do clouds make across the landscape? The shadows of branches and leaves can often make incredible, detailed images. What sort of colors do you see in the shadows? Where is your own shadow? What does it do during the day? How is it different in the morning as compared to the afternoon? And in the evening?

When you are indoors, notice how shadows are always present. Light coming in through windows casts its own sort of shadows, whereas electric lights may reveal others. Keep your vision wide, and see what shadows are in the periphery of your vision.

Notice how even on the brightest of days or in a well-lit room, there is always a shadow presence nearby. Stay aware of this ever-present darkness, and welcome it into your days.

Signs and Omens

Any time you see a woman dressed in red clothing, silently acknowledge the Yoginis. While it is true that, on a certain level, everything is an expression of the divine feminine power that is *shakti,* women and the color red are symbolically powerful reminders of this ever-present radiant life force.

When you see a black crow, cat or dog, silently acknowledge the Yoginis. Extend this further, to any black animal, seeing it as an envoy of the Yoginis.

The more you look for these living symbols in the world, the more they will tend to present themselves to awareness.

14. Night Magic

Night is the traditional time of witchcraft and sorcery. The sun has set, and the world has descended into shadows and darkness underneath the distant stars. With this comes a shift in the senses, as they are more heightened and sensitive to the world around them, both seen and unseen. The veils between worlds have fallen, the shadows take on lives of their own, and the night is watching.

Most active sorcery with Yoginis will take place during these hours of darkness. This is the time to evoke their presence, to do spellcraft with their aid, and to celebrate and honor them with offerings.

With this work, we bring in elements of witchcraft and sorcery to work with the Yoginis.

Moon Phases

Sorcery and witchcraft are deeply associated with the Moon. The Moon is the mistress of the night, and when you are cavorting in the circle with the Yoginis, the phases of the Moon mark out the Yogini calendar.

As a general rule, the waxing moon (bright lunar fortnight) is best for works that are positive in nature. This is a time of increase and light, where it is more effective to perform spells of creation. Healing, acquisition of wealth or other material gains, and learning, are all beneficially impacted during the waxing moon. The dark lunar fortnight is associated with decrease, solitude, meditation, destruction. This is the time of cutting through illusions, or destructive magic, curses, restriction and binding. This schema is an oversimplification, but one that is useful and practical for most situations.

The Lunar phases are classified into two groups of Goddess, the *Nityas* (Eternities). The *Nityas* are associated with the Great Goddess in her forms of *Kali* and *Lalita*.

To the waning moon is attributed the dark phase of the Goddess in her form as *Kali*, and her 15 *Nityas*:

1. Kali
2. Kapalini
3. Kulla
4. Kurukulla
5. Virodhini
6. Viprachitta
7. Ugra
8. Ugraprabha
9. Dipa
10. Nila
11. Ghana
12. Balaka
13. Matra
14. Mudra
15. Mita

The waxing, or bright phase of the moon is associated with the Goddess in her form as *Mahatripurasundari*, also called *Lalita*:

1. Kamesvari
2. Bhagamalini
3. Nityaklinna
4. Bherunda
5. Vhanivasini
6. Mahavajresvari
7. Duti
8. Tvarita
9. Kulasundari
10. Nitya
11. Nilapataka
12. Vijaya
13. Sarvamangala
14. Jvalamalini
15. Citra

The *Nitya* goddesses are formidable in their own right, each having her own visualization, rituals, preferred offerings, and *mantras* to work with them directly. As this would be another book entirely, it's out of scope for this work, but it's good to be aware of them and their influence. You will also notice that a group of the Yoginis given in this book are related to the *Nityas* by Tribe.

As a beginning practice, and to become more sensitized to their influence, pay attention to the phases of the Moon. Spend time Moon gazing, just letting the glow of the moon in her different phases shine on you for a few minutes. Call out to the *Nitya* that is predominant in the current phase with a prayer, for example:

> *Om! Hail Goddess Kamesvari!*
> *May your influence cover me,*
> *and empower me with your vitality!*
> *Svaha!*

Shadow Temple

As an adjunct to your Shadow Circle, which may be out in the open underneath the night sky, or indoors with an altar, a subtle *mirror* of the physical temple is also constructed with visualization—this is the Shadow Temple.

The Shadow Temple is where all of your sorcery will be conducted in the astral or dream realms. While outwardly you may be casting a circle with an athame, simultaneously with the imagination you will be building up your Shadow Temple and conducting rituals there.

The design of the temple is completely open to you. It can be simple or elaborate. It may be a visualized version of what you have in the physical realm. In this way, eyes open or closed, you will essentially "see" the same thing. Or you might treat it more like a VR (virtual reality), where the Shadow Temple is more elaborate than the physical circle.[19] You could design it along the lines of the Yogini temples of India, with a circular main structure holding spaces for the Yoginis, and an open roof exposed to the depths of the night sky. A sacred grove of trees would be an excellent Shadow Temple, especially if you do not have easy access to the wilderness. In this way, you carry the wilderness with you at all times.

For many years I worked with a temple that was constructed of the *Yantra* of the Goddess Kali on the floor, with four pillars at the quarters that had blazing torches on them. In the center was a small altar which held all of the tools, with ghostly clouds of incense slowly curling up into the darkness. The temple was protected in the distance by mountains, and the sky was the only ceiling—rich, deep and dark, with luminous stars overhead. I can still feel the coolness of the smooth stones underneath my feet, the faint warmth from the torches, and the scent of the jasmine incense.

You will return to the temple repeatedly, and over time it will begin to take on a life and energy of its own. Take time to visualize it in detail and build it up solidly in the imagination. You want to get to the point where you can instantly see the temple, as though you open your eyes on the astral and are looking right at it, experiencing directly with your subtle senses.

To aid with this, try doing your rituals in this temple. While you act out the movements physically, see yourself doing all of the movements and actions in the Shadow Temple.

Sigils

A technique that I have found to work exceptionally well with these goddesses is sigils. Communicating with them by means of these enchanted and empowered lineal figures seems to open up a bidirectional gateway in consciousness, linking the mind and energy of the

---

[19] Unlike technological VR, which currently looks far more primitive than the world, with the Shadow Temple you would build a visualization that is far more detailed and rich than what appears in the "real" world.

body with the Yoginis in a direct way. It opens a doorway through which the Yoginis may come and go easily between dimensions, and provides for direct and clear communication.

The analogy may be seen in the tantrik *yantras,* lineal figures which are embodiments of the Goddess herself. With sigils, we are creating a type of *yantra* dynamically as the situation and environment requires, whether to work with a specific Yogini, or to highlight a request. Where a *yantra* is encoded in such texts as the *Saundarya Lahiri* to achieve different aims (such as a *yantra* for "acquiring wealth"), with the usage of sigils we are able to fine-tune the connection, directing the spell with precision. Sigils are extremely versatile, and are applicable to any event or desire.

The practice of sigil magic is most notably exemplified by the artist and occultist Austin Osman Spare. Born in London in 1886, Spare was a natural witch with an uncanny ability to illustrate his visions and visitations with the ethereal realms and beings in great detail. His talent to reify visions of ghosts, demons and otherworldly phantasms into visual images is extraordinary, each drawing or painting a gateway into the Abyss. His technique for sigil magic is seemingly simple, and yet is perhaps one of the most potent tools of sorcery. "Dreams shall flesh," as he writes in his book, *The Grimoire of Zos.*

Spare's technique is simple enough. First, think of a desire that you have and want to make manifest. Write this out in a simple sentence. Remember, keep this *simple.* If you have a complex desire, split it up into smaller tasks. Instead of trying to encode *"I have a high paying job and am using the extra money to take a trip to Lisbon,"* break this up into smaller parts. *"I have a high paying job"* will be one sigil, and *"I am taking a trip to Lisbon"* is another. Also, this works best to have your desire written out in the present tense. *"I **have** a high paying job"* rather than *"I **want** a high paying job."* This signifies to the mind that whatever is desired *has already happened—it is already manifest.*

Now that you have the desire written out in a simple sentence, cross out any vowels and duplicate letters, so that only one instance of each letter remains. "I have a high paying job" becomes IHVGPYN.

Next, here is where your creativity and art come in. This jumble of letters—which bears no resemblance to the original intent—is now rendered into a glyph or image. Aim for simplicity of design, and something that is attractive to you. It is helpful if it is also easy to visualize, although this can be worked around by having the sigil with you during the next part of the work.

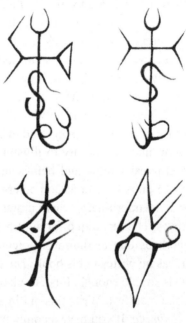

Sigils
(by Kat Lunoe)

The final image should have no resemblance to the original intent. While I prefer to stay away from theory too much in this book, focusing more on the great *mystery* of experience, it is worth noting that a large part of the *shakti* or power of sigils seems to be in their ability to bypass the conscious, rational mind by speaking to the subconscious directly in the language of symbols. The desire is encoded into a glyph which bears no resemblance at all to the original thought, so that the rational mind cannot make sense of the image. When the rational mind is temporarily subjugated or stunned by the imagery, it seems to allow the encoded message to be planted deep into the creative darkness.

The next part of the practice is to empower the sigil, seeding it into the subconscious mind and energizing it. Part of this is already happening while you are drawing the image. Focusing on the lines as they are being drawn is another meditative act. To truly seal the intent, the original meaning of the symbol needs to be forgotten. There are a variety of techniques to do this. If you have a strong meditation practice, you can utilize the power of concentration on the figure itself, without the mind translating and repeating the meaning behind it. This can be exceedingly difficult, but not impossible. Or, during periods of heightened energetic enthusiasm, the meaning of the sigil may be forgotten. So, for example, you might engage in an ecstatic dance while staring at the image, allowing all thoughts to be suspended, the body energized by dance and music, while thoughts are suspended and awareness is only on the image of the sigil. Another highly energetic activity is sex, which already has transformative and gnostic effects. Visualize the sigil while having sex; at the moment of orgasm the release of energy with the temporary loss of all boundaries will send the sigil deep into the subconscious.

A technique developed by Spare, mentioned by Kenneth Grant in his book, *The Magical Revival*, is to create several sigils ahead of time, all for more generic desires that you would generally want to manifest—good health, money, intelligence and so on. Along with these, also create more specific sigils for the one-off situations that you want to work with. For example, I might create generic sigils for optimum health, ideal weight, charisma. Then, I create a sigil for a more specific situation, such as getting a new car. Spare's technique was to write each of the symbols down on a card, mix them up and set them aside for a few days before working with them. At that point you would have no idea which symbol corresponded with which desire.

An adaptation of this, once you have a few sigils created, is to consecrate them all at the same time, with no conscious idea of which desire is encoded. This collection of sigils is then given as an offering to the Yoginis.

In acts of communion or communication, sigils might arise spontaneously in consciousness—a message from the Yoginis, or a set of instructions that works on reprogramming aspects of your mind. This is again meeting at the Crossroads, the meeting ground between the rational and irrational, where dream and objective reality are not so distinct, and everything is not as it may seem.

Yogini Sigils

A special case of the above sigil technique is to create a unique sigil for each of the Yoginis by using their names to generate the image. Each of the Yoginis will then have a special figure that is completely unique to both you and the Yogini. If you are using the *Yogini Yantra*, you can write one symbol on each of the petals to further empower the *Yantra*, having an instant communication device. Similarly, the images can be put onto the Yogini Stones.

Yogini Sigil
(by Kat Lunoe)

Make these as simple and esthetically pleasing to your own sense as you can. Unlike sigils used for spellcasting, where it is essential to forget the original desire encoded into the symbol, with Yogini Sigils you are creating a talismanic device that is keyed to both you and the Yogini, and which can be used to immediately connect. It will become a sign that you will both recognize and use in communications.

Having all of the Yogini's names in the form of sigils on the *yantra* will make the device become an attractor, with an almost magnetic pull to it. Like bees to honey, this will enhance all aspects of Yogini magic, becoming a focus through which communication between you and the goddesses is enhanced.

This also opens the *yantra* as a type of oracular device. If you have a problem or issue that you want to address with a Yogini, but are not certain which one would be best to help, this works well. Have the Yogini *yantra* before you, and after going through the circle openings and the *chakra* activation exercises, think of the problem that you have, and ask to have guidance from the Yoginis. With eyes closed, let your finger fall on the *Yantra*. Whichever petal your finger fell on is the Yogini that you will then evoke to work with.

You can also paint or etch the sigil on the Yogini stones if the material allows. Similar to the process with the *yantra,* hold your question in mind and reach for the stones with eyes closed. The one that you select is the Yogini that is most appropriate for at the time for the issue you are working with.

You can also make individual talismans for a Yogini. You might have one that you are working with more closely, or have made an agreement to honor with a special, permanent talisman. Perhaps you need a portable one to carry with you, and could make one on a small piece of parchment paper. You might have the sigil fashioned into some jewelry—a pendant or a necklace, or a design for a tattoo. These are just a few ways to have the Yogini's influence with you at all times.

Shadow Goddess

To deepen the practice of sigils, work with the *chaya devi* or shadow goddess. This technique has been given in detail in Kenneth Grant's *Cults of the Shadow,* and is elaborated here to work with the Yoginis. This is a powerful method for charging sigils, and a means of communing with the Yoginis in a deep and intimate exchange of energy.

Yogini Sigil
(by Kat Lunoe)

In this practice, the Yogini is visualized as clearly as possible. Take time to clearly see her appearance in every detail: the style of dress and ornamentation, her hair, her fragrance, the glow of her eyes, the implements she is holding. The more detail you can put into her visualization, the more the Yogini will be able to use this mental image as a living talisman that she will be able to enliven with her own energy when evoked. Here is where your meditation practice will again come into great use: the more you are able to concentrate on building up the image in detail—leaving out distracting thoughts or mind-wandering—the more you will add to the buildup and flow of energy.

Upon the Yogini's forehead, at the position of the third eye (in the middle of the brows), visualize the Sigil that you will be working with in luminous, crimson-red light. The effect can become extremely hypnotic as you see the face of the Yogini directly before you, looking into her eyes, with the sigil emblazoned on her forehead, radiating between you.

Now, raise the energy level in your own body by performing the **Chakra Activation** and **Circulation** exercises (see Chapter 6, "Wheels of Starlight"). While doing so, see the Yogini simultaneously activating her *chakras* and circulating the serpentine light in her body.

The next sequence of actions will be a synchronized breathing with the Yogini, while visualizing energy moving with the *breath* via the *eyes*. While humans generally are not capable of breathing through their eyes, in this tantrik visualization there are no such physical limits. Feel and see lightwaves of energy, undulating and flowing from the eyes with the breath.

Hold eye contact, and synchronize your breathing with the Yogini. As she circulates the serpentine light in her body, she breathes it out towards you from her right eye. Inhale, bringing her essence in the form of serpentine lightwaves into your body with the breath through your left eye. Feel the warm currents of light flow down through you on the left side, merging with the energy of your body and *chakras,* enlivening the senses.

As you exhale, your breath commingles with the breath of the Yogini and moves up the right side of your body. See and feel your mixed essences flowing towards the Yogini from your right eye, who breathes it in with her left, again mixing your breath and energy with her own.

Continue this cycle of breathing in and out one another's flowing, ophidian, light rays and breath, intermingling together energetically. You both become intertwined in the circulating waves of light and breath, continuously flowing back and forth, essences intermingled.

All the while, maintain gentle eye contact with the Yogini, the Sigil's radiance glowing luminously on the Yogini's forehead, pulsating and vibrating.

The physical sensations during this exercise can build up tremendously. Think of the slow, passionate, long build up during sex. Resist the urge to "ground" these feelings and sensations in any way. Instead, let it continue to build with pleasurable tension as the body and mind are bathed in this warm, honeylike radiance, and the desire *(kama)* continues to build.

It is during this communion that your desired intent—encoded into the sigil—is transmitted to the Yogini. As the energy of the exchange increases, your body and that of the Yogini are entwined in lattices of circulating, pulsating currents of breath and flowing light vortices. Again and again, resist the urge to release; let the tension and longing build until it becomes unbearable. Finally, when you can no longer hold back, release into ecstasy. As you fade into Bliss, let the last vision be that of the glowing Sigil on the Yogini's forehead.

Couple and Group Work

This practice can be adapted for a couple, or a group with multiple couples. Taken to the extreme, there could conceivably be 64 people, each couple working with a Yogini.[20]

In this ritual, the couple(s) sit facing each other. Rather than building up the image of the Shadow Goddess, your partner should be seen as the Yogini herself. One member of the pair may elect to be the host for the Yogini, and has the Sigil traced on their forehead with red *sindhoor* or face makeup (black eyeliner, for example, or any color that seems to resonate with the Yogini that is going to be invoked). There are variations on this. For example, both members of the couple may act as host for the same Yogini, each having the sigil on their forehead; or alternatively, each may have a different Yogini sigil on their forehead, so that different Yoginis are interacting with each other through the participants.

Proceed as with solitary workings: open the circle and then have everyone perform the *Chakra* exercises to build up and circulate energy. Then proceed to the practice proper, looking into the eyes of your partner and synchronizing breaths. Then follow the same circulation of breath and energy as with solitary workings, with the breath flowing out from the right eye, and being inhaled with the left eye. All the while the energy is intermingling, forming a latticework of opalescent and crimson scintillating radiance between the participants.

Resist any physical touch during this ritual. The visualization and synchronization of breath will build up a veritable volcano of power within the participants. The natural reaction to these sensations is to immediately seek to fulfill the desire. Let your *mantra* be "Look, but

---

[20] Covens often have a maximum capacity of 13 people, as anything more becomes unwieldy. If anyone manages to organize a Yogini Circle of sixty-four people, please write to me and let me know how it went!

don't touch!" This is not some moral injunction or mysticism; rather, this is a very practical exercise. The sheer force of desire, the huge buildup of libido, will have a tremendous effect on your mind. Try with all of your intent to resist any physical touching, and allow the tension and libido—the movement of *kriya*—to continuously build up, with nowhere to escape to. Let the longing and desire continue to build with aching intensity. With the energy so confined, and no direct physical release, it will be channelled into your tantrik ritual, charging the sigil and sharing the bliss with the Yoginis. A non-physical explosion in consciousness that reverberates throughout every cell of your body, flooding the body with bliss. What may under normal circumstances be a few seconds of orgasmic pleasure can instead be minutes or even hours of continuous waves of the most intense, illusion-shattering, non-dual Bliss.

Afterwards, if you choose, you can ground the energy physically and offer it up to the Yoginis. Share the offerings with each other, and savor the sensual aspect of the encounters. Really pay attention to every taste, scent and touch; be fully aware of every experience as it is happening. Dedicate all of this to the Yoginis, giving thanks and gratitude for sharing their energy with you.

Mahamaya

Mahamaya
(by Kat Lunoe)

One Yogini that bears special mention is *Mahamaya*. Her name means "Great Illusion". As with all of her sisters, she is a shapeshifter, capable of appearing in any form she desires. As the great sorceress of illusion, she is skilled in deluding the senses and producing incredible mirages. Of all the Yoginis, she is has the most fluid form, ever-changing and transforming shapes and colors across the spectrum of human, theriomorphic and otherworldly appearances.

Mahamaya comes from a powerful lineage, the confluence of the Goddess in her forms of Kali and Lalita Tripurasundari, she is none other than Kamakhya, the "renowned goddess of desire" associated with the *shakti pitha* in Kamarupa, Assam.

As all experience is a magical display of consciousness, she is an enchantress of the world and the senses, capable of manifesting anything in the fluid energetic matrix that we think of as "reality." Under her influence, one can easily be caught up in dreams, fantasies and other phantoms of the mind for hours, days, weeks on end. She will keep the unwary ensnared in her fantasies and illusions. With her as your ally, the *sadhaka* becomes capable of cutting through the illusory nature of reality, and experiencing the pure light of consciousness itself. One of her many boons is the ability to mold the dream-stuff of consciousness into physical forms. This is the *siddhi* of magic and sorcery in its purest sense: the power to restructure the universe according to one's desires, to make the "unreal real."

Mahamaya may first appear as a lithe, female silhouette that seeps out of the shimmering shadows. As the image takes on substance, her long black hair flows freely past her shoulders. She wears a black *lehenga* and a small black blouse. Her skin is darkness itself, an almost luminescent, inky blackness. Her face is stunningly beautiful, enrapturing the mind and destroying all thoughts. In the mind of the prepared *sadhaka,* this can be liberating and lead to experiences of non-dual awakening. More likely, the practitioner approaching her will become dull-witted while experiencing her presence, the mind stunned into submission and enraptured by her illusions.

With diligent meditation practice, the mind can become trained enough to withstand her charms, at least for brief periods of time. It is then that she may be approached as a Shadow Goddess, and with offerings and supplications she may be willing to use her charms *for* the practitioner rather than *on* the practitioner. She may be willing to work with you if approached respectfully and devotedly.

As a Shadow Goddess, her dark appearance sinks even further into the mysteries of illusion . Her face melts into the shadows, and where before was incredible beauty, vibrates and throbs a void of pure darkness. Upon this black hole cast your Sigils, where they glow eerily in the void, pulsating slowly with ancient starlight.

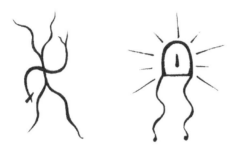

Yogini Sigils
(by Kat Lunoe)

15. Dream Magic

Just about every culture and tradition has some kind of relationship with dreams. The ancient Egyptians believed that dreams were messages from the realm of the Gods, and the place of shades, and the stars, where the dead also continued to exist. It may be that some of their rituals were intended to produce more magical dreams for spiritual journeys and sorcery. Dreams played large roles in ancient Sumerian, Greek, and Roman cultures, and their symbols and interpretation were regarded as omens and communications from the Gods. The Ottoman empire used passages in the Quran to help with dream interpretation. The Christian Bible is filled with prophecies that came from dreams. Shamanism crosses many cultures; with its many approaches to journeying in the spirit realm, it has a wide swath of dream practices. Many indigenous people around the world have placed heavy emphasis on dream journeys and symbolism. Australian Aborigines believed that the universe was part of a great dreaming that brought it into existence, and used dreams for symbol interpretation and dream journeying. Native American traditions are so deeply embedded with dream imagery and journeying that they have Dream Catchers, woven geometric images designed to help capture dreams in flight. The Tibetans have deeply rooted systems of tantrism that work with dream yogas; many of these systems have even been received in dreams from Yoginis. Many of the Hindu Gods and Goddesses have made themselves known in dreams, resulting in the founding of temples, or the initiation of entire traditions. Only the "modern" and "civilized" societies that have embraced a materialistic worldview seem to downplay the importance of dreams, relegating them at most to the realm of psychology, with little thought about deeper implications.

Whether by sign or symbol, prophetic or inspirational, dreams have woven a rich tapestry throughout human experience. They underlie our days, a quiet backdrop of faint memory that persists in the background throughout life, often unnoticed or forgotten during the day's activities. In aboriginal cultures dreams often dictate the actions of the day, giving guidance and omens for a good hunt or crop, or for healing sickness, avoiding disaster, good marriage, or child bearing—in short, every aspect of waking life finds its guidance in the dream world. Contrast this with Western societies, where culturally it seems more of a background discussion, an afterthought that may occasionally come up at a dinner party as a curiosity.

Sometimes dreams demand attention, welling up in consciousness, unexpected, wild manifestations that might change the course of history (such as Constantine's vision of the Cross). More often they are a deep, unexplored ocean of imagery and sounds, a backdrop to waking experience, an echo or faint image, or an endless gallery of ghostly images, always absorbing, reflecting, manifesting change in our consciousness in unfathomable ways. The dreaming is a continuous process, and we are the results of such dreams. Ignoring their significance does not remove their power; unexplored dreams are just as effective at ruling over waking consciousness, whether we have the wisdom to pay attention to them, or discard them unexamined. They silently, quietly, underlie our days, while openly ruling the night.

It is in the realm of sleep that our relationship with the Yoginis deepens and matures into a wild, creative exploration of vast landscapes, strange wilderness locations, deep dark oceans, jungles filled with strange creatures, interstellar civilizations, cyclopean ruins, and more. The plasticity of the dream world, and its constant vibrating between day consciousness and astral realms, makes it an ideal meeting ground to cavort with the Yoginis. Once again, we find ourselves deep inside the Crossroads.

When you enter the dream world with the Yoginis, you are entering into a plane where the laws of physics are turned upside down, or do not even apply. It is a realm openly ruled by consciousness, with its demonstrable creative capacity to modify itself into any shape, color, experience. In the dream world you can fly into the sky with the Yoginis, and attend their nocturnal Witch's Circle underneath the full moon. In this realm symbols are alive, and the language of symbolism underlies everything. Not a single speck of dust is without meaning, as this is the dimension of living symbols.

Dream Magic is the culmination of everything you have been practicing with Day and Night Magic. In the realm of dreams, all barriers are removed. Working in the dream state is often where communications from the Yoginis take place. This could take the form of signs and symbols, omens of personal significance, or direct communications. You may receive new *mantras,* or be empowered to work with existing ones that previously seemed elusive or closed. You may meet with people that you have not met before, or who have already died in the material world. Likely your creativity will increase with dreamwork, which impacts the waking world with newfound inspiration and endeavors.

Working with the Yoginis tends to increase the depth of your dreams automatically. Working with the material feeds creativity, which bleeds over into the dream states. When you start to seed your dream states with intent, the potential to expand in this area increases dramatically. When you can consciously work with your dream states, with lucid dreaming, then there truly is no limit to the vistas and cosmic explorations that can be done. This type of lucid dreaming is the highest dream yoga.

Keep a journal near your bed so you can record your dreams. Trying to write with pen and paper after just waking from a dream may seem daunting at first, but really does get easier over time. Still, some people may prefer to record the dream audibly, which works well, too. Most smart phones have some voice recording ability that works well for this.

Dream Seeding

These seeding exercises will help to program your mind for more vivid, luminous dream states. The communications that you receive in these states can be some of the most profound and inspiring. As you progress with them, you may achieve lucidity, the state of being aware that you are dreaming, while still dreaming. With lucidity you will be able to work with the Yoginis in a realm devoid of the restrictions of the material, day consciousness. Even without lucidity, these practices will help to enhance your dreams, making them more detailed, more vivid, and more significant to your work with Yogini Magic.

For all of these exercises, you may find that lighting a single candle in your bedroom helps to keep you just on the threshold of deep sleep, without going too deep. In this way, having one foot still in the waking world and the other in sleep, you may find it easier to slip into lucidity. Experiment with and without a candle to see what sort of effect it has on your dreams.

The practices of meditation (Chapter 4, "The Circle of Awareness") and *chakra* energy work (Chapter 6, "Wheels of Starlight") done regularly during the day and before sleep will help to prepare the mind and body for these enhanced nocturnal adventures. Regularly working with the Yoginis with **Opening the Circle** (Chapter 11) and the **Yogini Sadhana** (Chapter 12, "The Feast of the Yoginis") will further seal the connections among the waking mind, the dreaming state, and the realm of the Yoginis.

It can take some time and persistence to work with dream states, so don't get discouraged if you do not have immediate results. In addition to the above, continue with the practices of the Day and Night, and do the seeding exercises nightly before sleep.

Write down your dreams when you awake from them. This act of immediate recollection is important to the practice, as the details of dreams tend to fade quickly when the mind shifts into the waking state. If not carefully tended to upon awakening, the most profound, detailed experience that seemed to have lasted for hours, will rapidly disintegrate into a faint afterthought. Working with dream states may take time and patience, but the rewards far outweigh the work!

Try working with one exercise for a week before moving on to the next. However, if you find that a particular approach works better than another, you might stick with it longer or incorporate it into your regular practice.

Exercise 1

Before going to sleep, spend a few moments gazing at your *Yogini Yantra*. State the intent that you want to meet with the Yoginis in your dreams tonight. Hold this thought as you fall asleep.

Exercise 2

Lying in bed before falling asleep, state the intent that you want to meet the Yoginis in your dreams tonight. Imagine that at your throat is a gently glowing red sphere of light, about the size of a small marble or pearl. Gently hold this image as you fall asleep.

Exercise 3

With this exercise, you will focus on one Yogini. As you lie in bed before falling sleep, state the intent that you want to meet the specific Yogini in your dreams tonight. Say her name, and visualize her sigil on your forehead, in a sphere of gently glowing, red light. Gently repeat her name as a *mantra* as you maintain the visualization and fall asleep.

Exercise 4

Before going to sleep, select one of the Yogini Stones. Hold it in your hands, carefully feeling the sensations that arise. Is it cold to the touch? Warm? Is the stone smooth or does it have a rough surface? Gently run your fingers over the stone, connecting with all the sensations. As you fall asleep, see if you can still feel the sensations of touching the stone, while stating the intent to meet with the Yoginis in your dreams tonight.

Exercise 5

Spend a few moments gazing at the *Yogini Yantra*. State the intent that you want to meet with the Yoginis in your dreams tonight. As you lie in bed, gently repeat the *mantra* **AIM KLIM SAUH** as you fall asleep. The *Vamakesvaratantra,* a work of Sri Vidya, states that this *mantra* causes the Yoginis to appear.

Exercise 6

As you lie in bed, state the intent that you want to meet with the Yoginis in your dreams. Imagine the full moon in the night sky, bright and luminous, majestically shining in the darkness. Maintain this image as you fall asleep.

Exercise 7

Before falling asleep, state the intent that you want to meet with the Yoginis in your dreams tonight. Visualize a sphere of pure, crystalline, white light above your head, about the size of a soccer ball. It pulses and glows, rotating clockwise. See gentle, honey-like tendrils of light drip down onto your head and slowly, warmly cover your entire body. Rest in this warmth, with the sphere of light rotating above your head as you fall asleep.

Exercise 8

As you lay in bed, state the intent that you want to meet with a specific Yogini in your dreams tonight. Visualize the bright full moon, and the sigil of the Yogini you wish to meet glowing on the face of the moon, as you fall asleep.

Exercise 9

Before going to sleep, gaze at the *Yogini Yantra* for 5 minutes. Keep the eyes relaxed on the *yantra,* without strain. As you lie down to sleep, visualize the *yantra* in space in front of you. Fall asleep seeing the *yantra* as you state the intent to meet with the Yoginis tonight.

Exercise 10

While lying in bed, state the intent to meet with the Yoginis tonight as you dream. Then, mentally, slowly recite the *mantra* **HRIM SHRIM KRIM PARAMESHVARI SVAHA** as you fall asleep. This *mantra* is associated with the Great Goddess.

Exercise 11

This is an advanced practice, as it can also stir up a lot of energy that may not be conducive at first to entering into the lands of sleep and dreams. With some experience, however, it will become a gateway to extremely vivid dreams. The practice is to engage with the Shadow Goddess working (Chapter 14, "Night Magic"), while lying in bed before sleep. Take some time to build up the image of the Yogini, and then go through the practice while lying in bed. As the honey-like, serpentine waves of light encircles and envelopes you, focus on the eyes of the Yogini smoldering in the darkness as you fade into sleep.

As an enhancement to all of the preceding exercises, you can engage with any of them in your Shadow Temple. As you lie in bed, visualize yourself as standing in your temple, and do the seeding exercises as you fall asleep.

The Empire of Dreams

The seeding exercises, if worked with persistently, can enhance awareness during dreams. Rather than being a passive observer, you will find that dreams become another level of awareness, just as vivid and "real" as waking states. Entering into dreams with awareness opens the door to a vast, new kingdom to explore.

In a typical night, we cycle through different levels of sleep about every 90 minutes, with periods of deep, dreamless sleep and dreaming

(REM) sleep going through phases over the course of the night.[21] It's common to briefly wake up during the transition from these periods. If you do happen to wake up at any point during the night, start with the seeding exercise again as you fall back to sleep. If you have a single candle lit in the room, the light will help you to wake up enough to remember to perform the seeding exercise again.

To further enchant this process, so that the seeds we are planting can grow, make the act of going to sleep a ritual. As you light the candle, make a silent aspiration to the Yoginis, offering them this light and its warmth as an offering. Give some of your own energy, rubbing your hands together and then placing them palm outwards towards the candle, adding your energy to its heat. Offer all of this to the Yoginis.

The realm of dreams is one of the most magical dimensions we can work in. With some persistence and practice, you will remember more of your dreams. The detail of the memories will also increase, and you will be amazed as you start to be consciously aware of your vivid, detailed dream adventures.

Throughout history and across many cultures, dream encounters have brought forth new visions, creative explorations, solutions to problems, and more. Two examples close to my own heart: Austin Osman Spare worked with dreams, and his art shows fantastic, magical landscapes and denizens of other realms that he encountered. The lifelike countenances of the ethereal spirits he drew seem to come to life right on the page. The other is H.P. Lovecraft, the prolific writer of weird fiction. His vivid, lifelike dreams would span galaxies, and the entire duration of ancient civilizations and cosmic entities.

In my own experience, dreamwork has become an essential aspect of all other practices, serving as a foundation for the rest. In fact, much of this book was the result of dream magic, working with the Yoginis for over a decade. It is in dreams that I have received new *mantras* directly from the Yoginis, *mantras* which have proven to be of great significance in my personal work. I have also received transmissions

---

[21] See, for example, www.ncbi.nlm.nih.gov/books/NBK526132

of existing *mantras,* empowering them and breathing life into them. It is from dream encounters that the instruction on Yogini Stones was transmitted, as well as the construction of Yogini Sigils. Many of the descriptions of the Yoginis in Chapter 8, "The Sixty-Four Yoginis" came from dream encounters.

The sense practices of Day Magic will enhance your overall awareness of the body and senses, and what sort of effects they have on your emotions, moods, memories and energy levels. The practice of checking throughout the day to see if you are awake or dreaming, and the overall practice of enchanting your life, will feed into your dream life.

The many practices of Night Magic will continuously build up the imagination and your ability to visualize. The constant awareness of the lunar phases and the *Nityas,* the practice of building up and working with the Shadow Temple, developing sigils for spell crafting—all of this work will enhance your sorcery, and feed deeply into your dreams. Working with the Shadow Goddess and the Yogini Sigils is the gateway to the dimension of dreams, crossing the border between wake and sleep, with the unification of Awareness. All of these practices have been building up towards the work of Dream Magic.

As you add the seeding techniques and the ritualization of the sleep process, you may break into lucid dreaming. This is a level of awareness where the dreamer knows that they are dreaming. In such a state you are able to willfully guide the dream, interacting with the Yoginis directly and consciously. This can enhance your practice a million times over, as you are now able to interact with the Yoginis consciously at all times. Rather than passively dreaming, you become an active dreamer.

The realm of sleep is the gateway to the depth of the universe, and beyond. Dive in, and go deep.

16. Offerings

[...] in a lonely and desolated place, decorated with garlands of flowers, fragranced with burning incense, one should practice the sadhana by offering fish, meat and wine, eating a variety of delicious foods and enjoying the wine with the Shakti[...]

— *Kaulajnananirnaya*, Chapter 8

I arrive at the secluded oak grove a little before sunset. The large trees with their crooked, bent and knobbled limbs each have a character, a personality of their own. Their dark, grey trunks reach up to the sky in crooked paths, like dried, skeletal limbs of some ancient giants, making a dark canopy covering the sky that always adds to the shadows of this place. Even during the day, or in the midst of summer, this place is quiet and dark, otherworldly. But it is Autumn now, and the mysterious power of the place is enlivened with a quiet urgency, as though the trees contain some secret. The breeze blowing through the branches sounds like whispers, the great oaks holding court in some primeval celebration.

Some of the trees in the deeper parts of this forest are over 300 years old. They have been here longer than the country I live in has existed. The land feels sacred here. I am not the first to notice this, of course, and there used to be Native American tribes in these lands. They would take the acorns from the oaks to make their food. They lived with the land and treated it with respect and honor, taking only what they needed and sharing this place with the other natives— coyotes, mountain lions, deer, hawks, owls, snakes. This oak grove is the hub of an entire civilization that lives underneath the radar of the human world, a population that lives largely unseen, and yet they roam the land and skies, keeping a wary distance and outlook on us.

As I ascend the hill and come to a clearing, the large bright autumn moon shines through low on the horizon in the east, and in the west the last ruddy glow of the sun sinks below the horizon. The earth is enveloped in shadows beneath the glowing, luminous moon.

I sit down in the open space, remove a Yogini Stone, and hold it briefly to my heart before placing it on the earth before me. With quiet expectation, I look towards the moon and call to the Yoginis. I say a silent prayer, and place some berries and nuts before the stone. I hold a bottle of fresh water aloft to the sky, and then pour some onto the earth. I rub my palms together, and project my energy out into the night sky, offering all to the Empresses of the Night.

The spirits of a place are around us always—silent, (usually) invisible inhabitants that inhabit the forests and groves, the open fields, the rivers and mountains, the open deserts. You might sense them as fleeting shadows out of the corner of your eye, a swiftly moving presence that is gone when you turn to look. Maybe a gust of wind that sends chills down your spine. A voice calling your name, seemingly from nowhere, dreamlike yet vivid, an echo in consciousness that is only heard subtly. Listen too closely or with the rational mind, and it is quickly lost, giving way to the cacophony of sound that is your own thoughts. What—from the perspective of the rational mind—looks like a coyote on a hill, your inner eye sees as an encounter with a spirit or guardian of the place. Even encounters with people, in both dreams and waking states, can be encounters with spirits that are establishing communication; or more often, silently observing, watching over a hill or forest, almost every tree populated with its own local spirits.

The practice of giving offerings to the spirit world goes back into the mists of time. If you grew up in a Western country, it may seem like a bizarre practice. I know it was for me when I first started encountering it as a child. I remember being 12 years old and wondering why the Taiwanese restaurant had a statue of Buddha in the corner, with fresh fruit on a plate in front of it, along with incense and a candle. Or, a few years later when I stumbled into an Indian-owned shop that had a large statue of Ganesha, the elephant-headed god popular among students studying for their exams and tantrikas celebrating their rites. In addition to a small candle, thick incense sticks and a plate of fruit, people had tucked dollar bills into every corner of his twisted trunk, and a pile of coins lay around his dancing feet.

At the time I had a vague idea that this was some sort of magical act, but it was just as mysterious and on par with tossing coins into the fountain at the local library and making a wish. Needless to say, I did not get a lot of exposure to these practices as a child!

In the tombs of ancient Egypt there are extensive depictions of the deceased being presented with food and drink, along with clothing, animals and personal attendants. Throughout India and Nepal the streets are richly populated with shrines, roadside altars, and make-shift, sacred spots around trees and rivers. With few exceptions these are all attended to daily with offerings of food, drink, candles and incense. Up in the mountains, the Himalayas are dotted with shrines made from natural outcroppings of rock, and the temples *(gompas)* are populated with Buddhist monks giving their offerings of oil lamps and *tormas,* a sort of grain cake that replaces meat offerings. Japan is richly populated with shrines dedicated to the *kami* or local spirits, who take their own offerings regularly. Throughout the world and across many cultures and traditions, the practice of giving food and drink to the spirits, and often ancestors, is a common practice.

The sharing of food is one of the most fundamental bonds that we have. Whether sharing with friends or strangers, to break bread together is an ancient, connective thread through time that brings people together. Whether a formal multi-course meal, or sitting on the street corner sharing a snack with a friend, this act is a ritual of sharing space and inviting intimacy and the exchange of energy.

We also carry this over into sharing food and feeding our domestic animals. Across species, we share food in time and space. You probably do not eat your dog's food, or give your cat a plate of spaghetti, but many people living with animals find that they will all eat around the same time, sitting down to a meal while the dog eats theirs— human and dog (or cat… cow… horse…) all eating at similar times. During these meals, no matter how simple, there is a sacredness and a tangible bond. In my own case, my dog always wants to eat at the same time as the rest of the household. There is a naturalness to it, a sort of energetic bond that develops. Even in the wild, coyotes tend to share their findings with their tribe, in a natural energetic connectivity to each other and the land as they feast.

This exchange of energy provides some clues to the practice of giving offerings to establish a strong bond and deep relationship with the Yoginis. Offerings are a vital component of this relationship. As when you have a guest over and is it natural to offer them something to drink—maybe a glass of water—this simple act of welcoming is applied to the spiritual realms. Even more so, when you have the presence of these mighty Goddesses before you, it's a good idea to have something to give them in exchange for simply acknowledging your existence. If you are approaching them to ask for something, or you hope to develop a deeper relationship, you do not want to show up empty-handed, so to speak. It's good to remember that in the Hindu tantras the Yoginis are portrayed as fierce, blood-drinking and flesh-eating supernatural witches. Best not to become too lackadaisical when encountering them.

As you come into accord with a particular Yogini, she will make her preferences known. One might favor an offering of sweet rice, while another will only take wine and cooked lamb. Stay awake and aware; be attentive to what they might ask for. It's just as vital to the connection to ensure that you are giving them what they prefer, as it is to be careful you are not giving them anything they find offensive, inciting their scorn... or worse, their wrath.

To enter into this type of relationship with the Yoginis is deeply rewarding. Develop it slowly and lovingly. There are some offerings that are typically accepted by all, which is a good place to start before widening the offerings to more specific items that might have specialized purposes—or come with an even deeper commitment.

Fresh water is a good choice. Water is receptive, lunar energy that is both a life-nurturing substance, as well as being helpful to increase psychic openness and awakening. It is used to purify, cleanse and refresh, making it an ideal drink to offer.

Rice, cooked or uncooked, is a good food choice. Rice and water (or in the West, bread and water) are basic staples in most households, eaten at almost all meals. Giving what you consider a basic meal is an act of generosity and an invitation; it is a call to bring the guest in, to sit together for a time in the same space, and commune.

Nuts and berries are also good, generally nutritious and non-offensive first offerings. Fruits are common: bananas, apples, oranges, grapes, figs and so on are all good.

Besides plain water, good choices include tea, coffee or water scented with the essence of rose or fruits.

Sweets can be given, and are generally very well-received. Some chocolate, small cookies, or rice pudding. Once I even offered a slice of chocolate cake (*Devil's Food,* naturally).

In the Hindu tantras, one offering that is almost universally given is wine (which can be a code word for any alcoholic drink). In practice I have found wine to be too rich for offerings unless only one glass is used, but your experience may differ. Beer and whiskey have been used effectively in my own experience. Many of the Yoginis are fond of drunkenness or intoxication, and will drink you under the table (or the circle of stones).

Alcohol is one of the main elements from the *Vira Sadhana* or "Hero's Ritual". With tantra, it is said that those things which may be your downfall are the same items which can lift you up—if you can successfully navigate the razor's edge and not fall off the precipice of pure hedonism.

The *panchamakara* ("Five M's" offering), so called because each of the five elements begins with the letter "M" in Sanskrit: *madhya* (wine), *mamsa* (meat), *matsya* (fish), *mudra* (parched grain) and *maithuna* (sexual congress) is an example of using those items that may be abused in order to rise above the purely animalistic aspects and attain spiritual awakening. The "Five M's" are a controversial subject, with many layers of interpretation and execution. The elements may coalesce between the layers and meanings, rendering them as living symbols and practical alchemical practices that work upon consciousness in direct and unexpected ways.

The "Five M's" offerings are *rahasyapuja,* meaning "secret ritual". It's not enough that they are a complicated subject in themselves with various layers of meaning depending on one's approach and understanding, from the gross to the more subtle. Compounding this, their interpretations have been intentionally obfuscated by authors of the tantras through the use of *shadow language*. This is a special type of coded language used in tantric texts which may say one thing, but mean something else entirely. This has led the different schools and individual teachers of the tantric lineages to each give their own take on the elements and their execution. The very number of five offerings is somewhat controversial, likely a later adaptation of what was in its earliest form only two elements: wine and meat.

Sir John Woodroffe notes in his classic *Shiva and Shakta* that the five elements have at least three layers of meaning, depending on whether they are being viewed from a coarse/dense/beastly point of view *(tamasic/pasu),* the transformative/heroic warrior view *(rajas/vira),* or the refined/subtle/divine view *(sattvic/divya).* In this way meat may be substituted with ginger, or it may be seen as the body of the *sadhaka* which is offered up. Wine might be replaced with water, or it could be viewed as the intoxicating *amrita* that is produced with the ascent of the *kundalini*. The union of *maithuna* transforms from physical copulation to visualized union; or it may stand for the ecstatic bliss that enraptures the awakened consciousness in non-dual realization.

The *Kaulajnananirnaya* discusses the "five nectars" *(panchamrita),* as the "secret of all secrets", and says that the Yoginis will always grant *siddhis* to those that offer the sacred ambrosias which consist of: excrement, semen, blood, bone marrow, and urine. Also, special rites were offered with beef, ghee, blood, milk and curd.

These "five jewels" or "ambrosias" were also used by some of the *Kaulas* as an alternative initiation rite. The *guru* would prepare a skull cup with alcohol and the five jewels, muttering *mantras* over the entire portion and then presenting it to the candidate. These five ambrosias were: semen, menstrual blood, urine, excrement and phlegm. If the candidate unhesitatingly took the cup and drank it, this was considered proof of their attainment and their realization of the "one taste" of non-dual consciousness. The ceremony was also accompanied with copious amounts of alcohol, ecstatic dance, laughing, poetic recitations, weeping and other spontaneous activities).[22]

A consistent offering that appears throughout different sources is alcohol with menstrual blood and semen. This nectar was collected during sexual intercourse during menstruation, and combined with the alcohol in a skull cup to be consumed by the participants.

The "secret of secrets" is said to be to offer, without fear, and from the position of non-duality, all offerings. One should drink as much liquor as desired, along with cooked meat. If these offerings are given without the correct mindset, one is considered an animal and unworthy of the Yoginis.

I encourage you to think carefully about the Five M's and the Five Nectars. Rather than just blindly trying to follow something that appears transgressive and edgy, look closer into what these elements may mean to you. Originally many of these were taboo items, the epitome of what was considered unclean in a strict Indian Brahman society. As a decidedly antinomian practice, touching and offering what was considered unclean and turning it into nectar was a powerfully transformative act that had the potential to shatter ego and personality blocks. What was transformative in that specific context may just be provocative or ineffective in a very different one.

Look at your own conditions carefully, and analyze what blocks in your personality may be keeping you from knowing freedom. For example, depending on your upbringing and the culture and society you find yourself in, it may be more transformative to eat vegan food and give up alcohol rather than offer up cooked meats and single-malt whiskey. Contemplate honestly what your fear, and what holds you back. What repulses you, such that without even having to think about it your body tenses up? What are your weaknesses? What is it about some people that annoys you or promotes your biases? The more

---

22 For more on this, see Alexis Sanderson's *A Commentary on* the *Opening Verses of the Tantrasara*. New Delhi: D.K. Printworld, 2005.

honestly you can approach your self and examine your own obstacles, the more transformative your offerings will be. Ultimately, what you are giving to the Yoginis is your essence, your energy—and they will return it to you enhanced a thousand times, purified and energized.

In the tantrik schools of Buddhism such as *Vajrayana,* the offerings have been reinterpreted into the *ganachakra.* Given to the wrathful forms of Yoginis and protector deities who were accustomed to meat and alcoholic offerings, the Buddhist saint Padmasambhava transformed the offerings into the *ahimsa* (non-violent) form by turning meat sacrifice into *torma,* cakes made of grains and sugar that are shaped into various symbolic forms and elaborately painted, thus negating the need for animal sacrifice while still fulfilling the appetites of the fierce Goddesses.

In my own case, I have utilized meat and alcohol predominantly for regular offerings while performing *sadhana.* When out in the wild, the offerings have mostly been small fruits, nuts and some fresh water. One offering that I always give is my energy; for example, I rub the palms of my hands together rapidly until they are warm, and then hold my arms outstretched towards the altar (or the sky) and project the energy out towards the Yoginis.

It should be apparent that the practice of giving offerings should be done mindfully, and with care. As I mentioned at the beginning, the sharing of food and drink is one of the most intimate acts which leads to a sharing of energy between beings—a communion—with mutual exchanges.

The food and drink that we prepare has our own essence in it. Your thoughts, hopes, aspirations, dreams, intuitions—all of this and more goes into food preparation. You can feel the difference between a meal cooked by a loved one versus a fast food item picked up on the way to work. These differences run far deeper than just the ingredients, as there is a subtle essence that is conveyed in food.

When you give offerings to the Yoginis, they in turn may confer their blessings, boons, magical support and aide. We each become accustomed to one another, and a sense of accord may be established. This is very much the forging of one's own Yogini *kula* (tribe).

Consistency is an important component of these relationships. If you commit to giving a weekly offering, keep that commitment. This is how trust is built, as well as being an important practice to build a powerful Will *(Iccha Shakti)*. If you make a commitment but then keep changing it, that is not going to win you a lot of trust or a strong will. The Yogini(s) expect you to keep your word. Why else would she be even passively interested in helping you or maintaining any sort of bond?

This becomes amplified if you are working with the tantrik offerings, such as meat and alcohol, or sex, or the "Five M's". This becomes a blood commitment that must be maintained once it is established. The Yoginis are incredibly giving magical beings that will gladly lend their energy and wisdom to your practice—but you do not want to cross them. The consequences could be like throwing yourself into the den of a lioness—and the lioness is hungry, having not received what she is accustomed to.

There are situations where you may feel called to make an additional offering, or one that is exceptional. Maybe you have a commitment on a daily basis to give fruit, candle and incense. Then you have a big project or challenge that you need support with, something that could use an additional push. You decide to do a one-time offering of lamb, and some drinks of whiskey, along with the usual offering. So long as you have clarity of this intent and communicate it clearly, this should be received and accepted. *"Oh mighty sorceress Mohini, I am offering you this special preparation of lamb and spirits. Please help me to achieve my goal!"* Such clarity of intent will help you to define the parameters clearly, avoiding any misunderstanding.

Another approach is to implore the Yogini for something, saying that if she helps you with this or if the goal is achieved, you will honor her with a special offering, and spread the word about her or the power of the Yoginis. This might be helpful with a larger project. Similarly, promising to give a special offering for a set period of time, such as a span of a few weeks or months, can also work wonders.

Other possibilities are to set up a permanent shrine for a specific Yogini, or have the *Yogini Yantra* engraved in metal and have that set up permanently. Taking this further, you might dedicate a work of art that you have created or had commissioned specially for the Yogini.

Each of the Yoginis has her own personality, and there are countless numbers of them. With this in mind, you have to approach each one with fresh eyes and come into a living relationship with her, seeing what she prefers. As with any relationship, it is a learning process and should be treated delicately, and with an open heart.

The offering of sex is important to consider. The exchange of sexual energy, even more than food, is intensely intimate. The bliss of orgasm is close to the bliss of cosmic consciousness—the *ananda* or sublime bliss of realization of the divine. *Ananda* is beyond concepts, pure non-dual awakening, the dissolution of self and other. The bliss that is possible with orgasm can be a gateway to *ananda,* and this is one of the reasons you will see tantrik depictions of deities in "blissful union."

Solitary sexual acts are a powerful offering. The dedicating and giving of orgasm to a Yogini, inviting them into your body to experience the bliss, is a welcome, highly sacred offering.

If you have a willing partner, sexual offerings are a powerful means of communion. It also opens the door to such techniques as sexual sorcery, and incorporating it into working with the Yoginis (some of who are adepts at this particular type of magic).

Should you feel drawn to explore this type of working with another person, first and foremost it is essential to have complete consent. Do not try to lure people into having sex with you because you are so "mysterious and magical" and are working with Yoginis! This is more of a pathetic excuse to try to get your rocks off, rather than any real magic. These goddesses that you are communing with will see your intent clearly, and they will joyously reject false offerings, or offerings made form the wrong intentions. The sword you hoped to send to a difficult situation may end up psychically crippling you instead. Always act with integrity and clarity, with yourself and with your partner(s).

As an offering, sex invites the Yoginis to take possession of your body, so that the Yogini may experience the *ananda* through all of your senses. This is a deeply intimate communion. Also, working with the Yoginis should not suspend common sense. The Yogini is not going to prevent the transmission of STDs. Being possessed by a Yogini is not going to prevent pregnancy. Do not engage in stupidity on behalf of these goddesses. Not only will you make yourself and partner miserable, but your ties with the Yoginis would likely be ruined, and you will find that whatever you were attempting to enchant, whatever sorcery you had hoped the Yogini would do, turns into a negative current of ill omens and of life falling to pieces. Just don't do it. Respect towards the Yogini also means respect towards your partner(s). If this is not maintained, the Yoginis will see right through the lies and tear you to pieces—not the kind of fresh meat you want to be.

It should also be apparent that whether solitary, with a partner, or a group, if rites are performed outside they need to be carefully thought out ahead of time. If you are working with a Yogini outside in a place where people might stumble upon you in the middle of the act, it probably will not end well for anyone involved. Working with the Yoginis does not mean you won't get fined or go to jail. Many pagan groups are well-versed in seeking out good locales for their nocturnal rites, away from prying eyes. In short, Yogini magic is not an excuse to leave common sense at the door. Come to the crossroads fully informed and aware of the mundane, so you can effectively focus on the magic without distraction.

Offerings are an integral part of building and maintaining a relationship with these shadow goddesses of the night. You are embarking on one of the most significant and rewarding relationships, going deeply into the dark forests and wilderness of the sensory world. The Bliss obtained in giving offerings will lead to realms of non-dual realization and Awakening.

17. The Black Void That is the Womb of All

I sit down on the old, moss-covered tree trunk. One side of it is decomposing slowly back into the dark earth, a fallen companion to the Oaks that cluster around it. Closing my eyes, I take in a full, deep breath. The chill of the autumn breeze fills my lungs, causing a slight shiver. The scent of the forest—moss and leaves and dew intermingled with acorns and pine—wafts over the space. As I exhale, my breath flows out in a ghostly, faint cloud that quickly rises up, vanishing among the dark, crooked boughs of the trees that surround me. I breathe in again, feeling as though the Oaks have crept in a little closer, curious about my intentions, bending slightly with creaking limbs. They start whispering in ancient tongues to one another, the breeze blowing through their branches causing the rustling of the leaves to pick up, the sound expanding across the sky.

The Shadow Temple rises up, superimposed against the forest. Its own strangely alive oaks and pine trees have an ethereal glow, as though composed of luminous starlight that has crossed oceans of space to form into the branches, pine needles, twisted trunks. Their sap flows slowly within the almost translucent forest, an eerie golden elixir, the blood of the forest. The temple shimmers amidst the other forest that is cool and dark and quiet now, an interweaving of colors pulsating, throbbing slowly in the night.

I take out a Yogini Stone from the pouch, and feel its smooth, cool surface with my hands. I trace over the sigil slowly, gently with my right index finger, feeling the slightly upraised texture of the symbol. Quietly I whisper her name, seeing her sigil light up in an eerie red glow of luminescence with my mind's eye.

I open my eyes and see the sigil in the air before me, a faint glow against the great branches and gnarled trunks of the Oak trees. It throbs slowly in the forest, a pulsing glow in contrast to the dark greens and browns of the trees. The spectral hues of the shadow trees have grown brighter now, like seeing through a thick haze of colored air that weaves serpent-like around the center.

I take out the rest of the stones, and place them in a circle around where I am sitting on the old decaying log. It feels as though the forest is watching, getting quieter. As the wind in the branches slows down, the rustling stops. Through a clearing in the branches, the stars glisten, pale sentries that have existed long before the first faint tremblings of life on this planet, and have continued on, seeing entire civilizations come and go. Off to the left, the gibbous moon's weird glow shines through, casting her own shadows and strange reflections through the trees.

I welcome the guardians of the eight directions of space, arising out of the swirling colors, pools of bright ink coagulate into female shadows with long, flowing hair. Before me arises Brahmi, proud and glowing in a golden light; behind me Maheshwari dripping deep, blue colors like the ocean; on my right hand, Narayani with crackling flames; and on my left, Chamunda creeps out from the dark gloom.

In the spaces in between the atmosphere ripples and melts, as shadows seep through dimensions, coalescing into dark forms, again, strange colors unwrapping from the strange shadowy darkness. I welcome Kaumari, Narasimhi, Aparajita, Varahi to the circle.

I stand in the circle, raise up my arms to the sky, and call the Great Sorceresses of the Night:

> *Om Sri Kali Nitya Siddhamata svaha! Eternal Dark Goddess Mother of the Sorcerers, please accept this offering of my body and senses!*
>
> *Om Sri Kapalini Nagalaksmi svaha! Skull Bearing Serpent Goddess of Wealth and Prosperity, please accept this offering of my body and senses!*
>
> *Om Sri Kula Devi Svarnadeha svaha! Illumined Tribal Goddess of Lustrous Golden Body, please accept this offering of my body and senses!*

Om Sri Kurakula Rasanatha svaha! Mistress of Sorcery Offering a Skull-Cup of Nectar, please accept this offering of my body and senses!

Om Sri Virodhini Vilasini svaha! Charming Mistress Who Dispels Opposition, please accept this offering of my body and senses!

Om Sri Vipracitta Raktapriya svaha! Wise Goddess Who Loves Passion, please accept this offering of my body and senses!

Om Sri Ugra Rakta Bhoga Rupa svaha! Goddess of Terrifying Form Who Enjoys Blood, please accept this offering of my body and senses!

Om Sri Ugraprabha Sukranatha svaha! Wrathful Resplendent Goddess, please accept this offering of my body and senses!

Om Sri Dipa Mukti Rakta Deha svaha! Whose Passionate Body is the Lamp of Liberation, please accept this offering of my body and senses!

Om Sri Nila Bhukti Rakta Sparsa svaha! Dusky Night Goddess Who Enjoys Passionate Touch, please accept this offering of my body and senses!

Om Sri Ghana Maha Jagadambha svaha! Auspicious Dark Goddess, Great Mother of the World, please accept this offering of my body and senses!

Om Sri Balaka Kama Sevita svaha! Youthful Lady Served Through Desire, please accept this offering of my body and senses!

Om Sri Matra Devi Atmavidya svaha! Mother Goddess Who Reveals Highest Truth, please accept this offering of my body and senses!

Om Sri Mudra Purna Rajatkripa svaha! She Who is the Seal of Graceful Governance, please accept this offering of my body and senses!

Om Sri Mita Tantra Kaula Diksa svaha! Tantrik Initiatrix Who Establishes the Kaula Path, please accept this offering of my body and senses!

Om Sri Mahakali Siddhesvari svaha! Radiant Dark Queen of the Shaman Magicians, please accept this offering of my body and senses!

Om Sri Kamesvari Sarvasakti svaha! Empress of Sexual Desire and Power, please accept this offering of my body and senses!

Om Sri Bhadamalini Tarini svaha! Saviouress Whose Yoni is Flowering, please accept this offering of my body and senses!

Om Sri Nityaklinna Tantraprita svaha! Eternally Wet Goddess Who Takes Pleasure Through Tantra, please accept this offering of my body and senses!

Om Sri Bherunda Tattva Uttama svaha! Terrible Goddess of Excellent Essence, please accept this offering of my body and senses!

Om Sri Vahnivasini Sasini svaha! Fiery Mistress of the Crescent Moon, please accept this offering of my body and senses!

Om Sri Mahavajresvari Rakta Devi svaha! Great Thunderbolt Goddess of Passion, please accept this offering of my body and senses!

Om Sri Sivaduti Adi Sakti svaha! Highest Feminine Power, Messenger of Awareness, please accept this offering of my body and senses!

Om Sri Tvarita Urdhvaretada svaha! Witch Queen Who Swiftly Raises Energy Upwards in Ecstasy, please accept this offering of my body and senses!

Om Sri Kulasundari Kamini svaha! Most Beautiful Voluptuous Tribal Goddess, please accept this offering of my body and senses!

Om Sri Nitya Jnana Svarupini svaha! Eternal Goddess Whose Form is Gnosis, please accept this offering of my body and senses!

Om Sri Nilapataka Siddhida svaha! Auspicious Sapphire Goddess of Perfection, please accept this offering of my body and senses!

Om Sri Vijaya Devi Vasuda svaha! Victorious Goddess Who is Giver of Wealth, please accept this offering of my body and senses!

Om Sri Sarvamangala Tantada svaha! All-Auspicious Giver of Tantra, please accept this offering of my body and senses!

Om Sri Jvalamalini Nagini svaha! Snake Goddess Wearing a Garland of Flames, please accept this offering of my body and senses!

Om Sri Chitra Devi Raktapuja svaha! Prismatic Goddess Whose Worship is Passion, please accept this offering of my body and senses!

Om Sri Lalita Kanya Sukrada svaha! Playful Maiden Who Gives Semen, please accept this offering of my body and senses!

Om Sri Dakini Madasalini svaha! Resplendent Sorceress Shining with Bliss, please accept this offering of my body and senses!

Om Sri Rakini Paparasini svaha! Sensuous Enchantress of Witchcraft Who Destroys Sin, please accept this offering of my body and senses!

Om Sri Lakini Sarvatantresi svaha! Desirable Enchantress of All Tantras, please accept this offering of my body and senses!

Om Sri Kakini Naganartiki svaha! Wanton Enchantress of Serpentine Dance, please accept this offering of my body and senses!

Om Sri Sakini Mitrarupini svaha! Alluring Enchantress in Friendly Form, please accept this offering of my body and senses!

Om Sri Hakini Manoharini svaha! Sorceress Who Bewitches the Mind, please accept this offering of my body and senses!

Om Sri Tara Yoga Rakta Purna svaha! She Who is Accomplished at Liberation Through Unification of Passion, please accept this offering of my body and senses!

Om Sri Sodashi Latika Devi svaha! Slender Creeper Goddess of Sixteen Desires, please accept this offering of my body and senses!

Om Sri Bhuvanesvari Mantrini svaha! Queen of the World Who Gives Mantra, please accept this offering of my body and senses!

Om Sri Chinnamasta Yonivega svaha! Wanton Enchantress with Wet Yoni, please accept this offering of my body and senses!

Om Sri Bhairavi Satya Sukrini svaha! Terrifying Sorceress Whose Truth is Fertile, please accept this offering of my body and senses!

Om Sri Dhumavati Kundalini svaha! Dark Smoky Goddess of Serpentine Fire, please accept this offering of my body and senses!

Om Sri Bagalamukhi Guru Murti svaha! Intoxicating Beauty in the Form of Teacher, please accept this offering of my body and senses!

Om Sri Matangi Kanta Yuvati svaha! Youthful Beauty Enhanced by Love, please accept this offering of my body and senses!

Om Sri Kamala Sukla Samsthita svaha! Sorceress Arising as Radiance from the Lotus, please accept this offering of my body and senses!

Om Sri Prakriti Brahmendri Devi svaha! Nature Goddess of Supreme Reality, please accept this offering of my body and senses!

Om Sri Gayatri Nitya Citrini svaha! Brightly Ornamented Goddess of the Eternal Sacred Song, please accept this offering of my body and senses!

Om Sri Mohini Matta Yogini Svaha! Intoxicating Desirable Sorceress, please accept this offering of my body and senses!

Om Sri Sarasvati Svarga Devi svaha! Eloquent Goddess of Heavenly Bliss, please accept this offering of my body and senses!

Om Sri Annapurni Siva Samgi svaha! Auspicious Goddess Who Nourishes All Beings, please accept this offering of my body and senses!

Om Sri Narasimhi Vama Devi svaha! Warrior Goddess of Tantrik Magic, please accept this offering of my body and senses!

Om Sri Ganga Yoni Svarupini svaha! Sorceress of Beautiful Flowing Form, please accept this offering of my body and senses!

Om Sri Aparajita Samaptidha svaha! Enchantress Bestowing Unconquerable Perfection, please accept this offering of my body and senses!

Om Sri Chamunda Pari Anganatha svaha! Slayer and Ruler of Imbalance, please accept this offering of my body and senses!

Om Sri Varahi Satyekakini svaha! Wild Enchantress of Truth, please accept this offering of my body and senses!

Om Sri Kaumari Kriya Saktini svaha! Young Goddess of Powerful Action, please accept this offering of my body and senses!

Om Sri Indrani Mukti Niyantrini svaha! Lady of Heaven Who Gives Liberation Through Restraint, please accept this offering of my body and senses!

Om Sri Brahmani Ananda Murti svaha! Creative Enchantress Who is the Embodiment of Bliss, please accept this offering of my body and senses!
Om Sri Vaisnavi Satya Rupini svaha! Goddess of Preservation Whose Form is Truth, please accept this offering of my body and senses!
Om Sri Mahesvari Parasakti svaha! Enchantress of the Highest Power, please accept this offering of my body and senses!
Om Sri Lakshmi Manoramayoni svaha! Goddess of Fortune Whose Yoni Charms the Mind, please accept this offering of my body and senses!
Om Sri Durga Satchitananda svaha! Invincible Warrior of Truth, Consciousness and Bliss, please accept this offering of my body and senses!

Scintillating ophidian waves and undulating tendrils of darkness melt and shimmer in every direction, while the wind blows through the canopy of oak trees, causing branches to creak and moan. Intermixed with the Shadow Temple that flashes a nocturnal radiance, starlight dripping through dimensions and swirling through the forest like ghostly snakes that hiss as they coil and uncoil across the grove.

I wave fire and incense three times, and sprinkle water in circles. I rub my hands together making heat, and offer it out into the slowly swirling shadows, inviting the great circle of Sky Witches to feast and enjoy through me.

Like a multitude of weird rainbows in the darkness, prismatic hints of color flow and dance around me. Glistening diamond shadows appear and disappear rapidly in the air that quivers and vibrates around me. The night sky is like a wet palette of shades, melting into diaphanous, dancing shapes out of the corner of my eyes. In the trees and the wind, I can hear the faint sounds of anklets jingling and laughter, whispers and chants. The glowing Moon herself seems to be holding court over the proceedings, milky whiteness flowing in between spaces and breaths.

The dance of the Yoginis, the Witches' Sabbath, arising from the darkness of nothingness. Swaying forms and shapes that keep changing, sometimes a glimpse of beauty, quickly shifting into a grotesque animal figure, and then again dripping into a flowing stream of colors and the scent of wild flowers. A skeleton-like phantom, her white fangs shining, then melting into a voluptuous goddess, radiantly smiling, then gone again, a rainbow shadow flashing living blackness.

Sky Dwellers, arising seemingly from the emptiness of space. The black void at the center of all experience. The nothingness that is the manifold variety of all experience. Every sight, every scent, every form, every sound, every touch, in dream and in wakefulness, in shadows and in light, a constant iridescent radiance of the night, a contradiction of every thought, an opening of the void in the center of all creation and nonexistence that comes forth ceaselessly, wave after wave, an eternal cosmic storm of creation that brings with it the illusion of space and time, countless life and death in an eternal cycle. From this sublime, radiant darkness, this void, all of creation ever goes forth. From the darkness of the Void we come, and to the darkness of the Void, we return.

They have been here since before humans started crawling and walking on the earth. They have seen civilizations rise and fall across the globe. All of our human concerns, ambitions, power plays, they have been witness to. Every war, cataclysm, injustice, the Yoginis have watched, and sometimes participated in. More often on the periphery, the borders of day consciousness, they have danced and celebrated their rites, occasionally making their presence known to the primitive animals that were beginning to experience higher levels of consciousness. Some have guided, helping kingdoms to rise and destroying others. Always protectors of the natural world, they have watched as cities raised up, destroying the landscape. Long after humans have died out, they will still be here, ancient and powerful intelligences, beings that defy simple definition, shapeshifting feminine powers that permeate time and space.

Sky Dancers, Queens of the Night, we welcome you!

The Goddess Kali
(Photo courtesy of
commons.wikimedia.org/wiki/File:Calcutta_Art_Studio_-_Goddess_Kali_-
_1883.jpg)

Her divine form, like a black storm cloud
  illumined by the sun,
she stands unveiled,
  her long hair falling free like monsoon rain.
Be lost in awe of her, O mind,
for you will never comprehend her.

— *Ramprasad Sen*[23]

---

[23] *Mother of the Universe: Visions of the Goddess and Tantric Hymns of Enlightenment,* translated by Lex Hinton.

Appendices

Appendix 1: Additional Yogini Lists

I give a few Yogini name lists here for exploration, with no commentary. As your practice deepens, you can use these as a launchpad to explore more, and venture into realms that are entirely unique to your experience.

As you work with these Goddesses, try to experience them fully and in detail. As you become sensitized to their energy, you will receive visual and other impressions. If you are artistically inclined, you might make images of the Yoginis, guided by your intuitions as you feel their names in your heart and come into accord with them. You might make unique collections of Yogini Stones that are attuned to them, with their own sigils and colors. This can also be done with the Yogini *Yantra* based on your experience with them, applying colors to the petals that resonate with the Yoginis.

As always, approach them with respect. Give them time to feel your unique energy. Approach with offerings and openness, and see where the Circle brings you.[24]

Yoginis of Kaulajnananirnaya

1. Jaya
2. Vijaya
3. Jayanthi
4. Aparajitha
5. Divya
6. Maha
7. Siddha
8. Ganeshwara
9. Predasini
10. Dakini
11. Kamala
12. Kaalaratri
13. Nisasari
14. Dankarini
15. Raudri
16. Hoomkarini

---

[24] While I do not cover it in this book, there is an entire cosmos of Yoginis associated with *Sri Vidya*. See *Fractals of Reality, Living the Sricakra* by Kavitha Chinnaiyan, MD for an excellent overview.

17. Urdvakesini
18. Virupakshi
19. Suklangi
20. Narabhojini
21. Patkari
22. Virabadhara
23. Doomangi
24. Kalakapriya
25. Korarakthakshi
26. Viswarupa
27. Abhayankari
28. Virakowmari
29. Chandika
30. Varahi
31. Mundadarini
32. Rakshasi
33. Bhairavi
34. Dwangshini
35. Doomrangi
36. Predavahini
37. Katwangi
38. Dirgalamboshti
39. Maalini
40. Matthayogini

41. Kalini
42. Chakrini
43. Kangali
44. Bhuvaneswari
45. Chataki
46. Mahamari
47. Yamadhuti
48. Karalini
49. Kesini
50. Marthini
51. Ramajanga
52. Nivarini
53. Visalini
54. Karrmuki
55. Loli
56. Adomuki
57. Mundakradarini
58. Vyakrini
59. Kangkshini
60. Predarupini
61. Durjati
62. Kori
63. Karali
64. Vishalambini

Yoginis of Odisha

1. Maya
2. Tara
3. Narmada
4. Yamuna
5. Shanti
6. Vriddhi

7. Gauri
8. Aindri
9. Tripura
10. Ranavira
11. Ushtrarudha
12. Vaishnavi.

13. Kalaratri
14. Vadyarupa
15. Charchika
16. Marjari
17. Chinnamastaka
18. Vrishabhanana
19. Jalakamini
20. Ghatavara
21. Vikarali
22. Sarasvati
23. Virupa
24. Kaveri
25. Bhalluka
26. Narasimhi
27. Viraja
28. Vikatanana
29. Mahalakshmi
30. Kaumari
31. Mahamaya
32. Usha
33. Karkari
34. Sarpasya
35. Yasha
36. Aghora
37. Bhadrakali
38. Matangi

39. Vindhyavalini
40. Abhaya
41. Maheshvari
42. Kamakshi
43. Kamayani
44. Ghatavari
45. Stuti
46. Kali
47. Uma
48. Narayani
49. Samudra
50. Brahmani
51. Jvalamukhi
52. Agneyi
53. Aditi
54. Chandrakanti
55. Vayuvega
56. Chamunda
57. Murati
58. Ganga
59. Dhumavati
60. Gandhari
61. Sarva Mangala
62. Ajita
63. Surya Putri
64. Vayu Vina

Yoginis of Hirappar

1. Bahurupa
2. Tara
3. Narmada
4. Yamuna

5. Shanti
6. Varuni
7. Kshemankari
8. Aindri

9. Varahi
10. Ranveera
11. Vanara-Mukhi
12. Vaishnavi
13. Kalaratri
14. Vaidyaroopa
15. Charchika
16. Betali
17. Chinnamastika
18. Vrishabahana
19. Jwala Kamini
20. Ghatavara
21. Karakali
22. Saraswati
23. Birupa
24. Kauveri
25. Bhaluka
26. Narasimhi
27. Biraja
28. Vikatanna
29. Mahalakshmi
30. Kaumari
31. Maha Maya
32. Rati
33. Karkari
34. Sarpashya
35. Yakshini
36. Vinayaki

37. Vindya Balini
38. Veera Kumari
39. Maheshwari
40. Ambika
41. Kamiyani
42. Ghatabari
43. Stutee
44. Kali
45. Uma
46. Narayani
47. Samudraa
48. Brahmani
49. Jwala Mukhi
50. Agneyei
51. Aditi
52. Chandrakanti
53. Vayubega
54. Chamunda
55. Murati
56. Ganga
57. Dhumavati
58. Gandhari
59. Sarva Mangala
60. Ajita
61. Surya Putri
62. Vayu Veena
63. Aghora
64. Bhadrakali

Appendix II: Recipes for Offerings

In addition to the chapter on Offerings, I provide here a few simple recipes for some of the special foods that might be given within the Yogini Circle, or while visiting Crossroads and other ritual or significant places and times. These are also a good alternative when the more strictly tantrik offerings of meat and alcohol are not given. All of these offerings have been received well by the Yoginis.

Many of these more simple food preparations are sweet, to emphasize the softer aspects of the Yoginis. This is no way belies their intense and powerful natures; rather, you can think of it as an attempt to appease them in a way that will encourage an exchange of energy that is akin to feeding a child or a loved one, gaining their trust and benevolence. In the tantras it is said that the Yoginis may be approached in multiple ways: like a sister, a daughter, a wife, a mother, or a lover. Each relationship is different, and will have differing energetic and other implications. Approach with a fierce nature, and receive fierceness from them (or quiet disdain!) Approach with gentleness and sweetness, and they may reciprocate in kind.[25]

Any offering should be considered carefully, using both the heart and intuition. When food is given that has been made by your own hands, it will increase your own energy in the food, which also enhances the gesture. In a very real sense, you are giving some of your self to the Yoginis. Some of us may not be very skilled in the kitchen and so may feel limited in what we can prepare as offerings. Hopefully a few of these simple recipes will help to fill that gap, and I encourage you to experiment with them and see how energetically it feels to offer food you have prepared. Contrast these with the more fiery offerings, and see how they are received.

---

[25] At the very least, you may save your head from becoming the main course in their dinner bowl.

Kheer (Rice Pudding)

2 1/2 cups of whole milk (adjust to your preferences, such as
    almond milk)
1/2 cup of uncooked rice
1/4 cup sugar[26]
1 tablespoon honey (optional)
1/2 tablespoon green cardamom
1/2 tablespoon almond slices (or pistachio)
1 tablespoon raisins

Put the milk and rice into a pan and heat on a medium low flame
until it begins to boil (careful not to boil over). Reduce heat to simmer.
Once the rice is cooked and has a creamy texture, add the sugar, stirring occasionally. When most of the moisture is absorbed into the rice
(about 15 minutes), add the almond, cardamom and raisins and stir
gently. Remove from heat, top with honey.

Meetha Dahi (Sweet Yogurt)

1/2 cup plain yogurt
1 cup whole milk
1/3 cup sugar (or more, adjusting for taste. *Jaggery* is traditional.
    Brown sugar is good alternative)
1/2 tablespoon cardamom powder

Put the milk into a pan and heat on a medium-low flame, stirring
frequently until the milk begins to boil. Continue to simmer, reducing
the milk. As parts of the milk dry and form solids on the side and
bottom of the pan, scrape those into the mix. When the milk is reduced
to about 1/3 or 1/2 of its original quantity, remove from heat and let it
cool for 5 minutes. Add the sugar, mixing well. Add the cardamom
powder and stir well. Add the yogurt and stir the entire mixture. Put

---

[26] Adjust for taste. Traditionally this is *jaggery,* made from sugar cane juice,
but any sugar will do. Brown sugar is a great alternative.

the mixture into a small cup (or cups), and set it in the refrigerator to cool and settle overnight.

Almond Cakes

1 cup flour
1/2 cup sugar
1/2 cup butter, slightly melted
1 egg
1/2 cup chopped almonds
1/2 tablespoon cardamom powder
1/4 teaspoon salt

In a large bowl add all of the ingredients. Mix well. Let the mixture sit in the refrigerator for a few hours until it has a doughy consistency. Preheat the oven to 350°F (175°C). Take a greased baking sheet, and pinch off small pieces of the dough mixture, laying down each small ball on the sheet. Flatten the balls out so that each is about the size of a small disk, about 1/4 inch (0.6 cm) thick. Bake for about 22 minutes. These can be made in batches and frozen for future use.

Toasted Cheerios[27]

1/2 cup of unsweetened Cheerios
1 tbsp. of cooking oil
1 tsp of black mustard seeds
3 curry leaves (optional)
1 pinch of turmeric
Salt to taste

---

[27] This recipe comes from Natasha. I used to offer plain Cheerios when I had no other suitable foods to give. One such time, Natasha looked at the plate of plain cheerios quizzically, and then took it into the kitchen. When she returned the Cheerios had been transformed into this fantastic enhanced dish. Ever since, it has been a favorite offering that is simple, yet deeply fulfilling.

Heat a pan with the cooking oil on a medium flame. As the oil heats, add the mustard seeds, the curry leaves, and the pinch of turmeric. Reduce the heat to low, and immediately add the cheerios and salt, pan roasting the mixture for 2 to 3 minutes while stirring frequently.

Dudh Kela (Banana & Milk)

This is a very simple offering that can be made quickly with a few simple ingredients.

1 cup whole milk
1 tsp. honey
1 banana

Warm the milk in a pan or microwave (don't boil it). Stir in the honey. Slice the banana, and add the slices into the mix.

Lassi

This drink can serve as an alternative to (for example) alcohol, or as an additional liquid offering alongside others.

1 cup plain yogurt
1 cup water
1/4 teaspoon cardamom powder
Pinch of salt

Mix all the ingredients and chill for an hour in the refrigerator. Add a little rose water for a different taste. You can also include a few pistachios for added flavor.

Select Bibliography

Chakravarty, H.N. *Tantrasara of Abhinavagupta.* Portland: Rudra Press, 2012.

Chinnaiyan, Kavitha, MD. *Fractals of Reality: Living the Sricakra.* Michigan: Sfaim Press, 2022.

Chinnaiyan, Kavitha, MD. *Glorious Alchemy: Living the Lalita Sahasranama, A Practical Manual of Srividya.* Salisbury: Sarum Press, 2020.

Chopra. Shambhava L. *Yogic Secrets of the Dark Goddess.* New Delhi: Wisdom Tree Publications, 2008.

Dehejia, Vidya. *Yogini Cult and Temples: A Tantric Tradition.* New Delhi: National Museum, 1986.

Devi Mahatmyam. English tr. by Swami Jagadiswarananda. Madras: Sri Ramakrishna Math, 1953.

Dupuche, John R. *Abhinavagupta: The Kula Ritual As Elaborated in Chapter 29 of the Tantraloka.* Delhi: Motilal Banarsidass Publishers, 2006.

Dupuis, Stella. *The Yogini Temples of India.* Varanasi: Pilgrims Publishing, 2008.

Dupuis, Stella. *Experiencing the Goddess: On the Trail of the Yoginis.* With contributions by Janet Chawla, Nilima Chitgopekar, Anamika Roy, Seema Kohli. New Delhi: Aryan Books International, 2019.

Fouchet, Max-Pol. *The Erotic Sculpture of India.* New York: Criterian Books, 1957.

Grant, Kenneth. *Cults of the Shadow.* London: Starfire Publishing Ltd., 2013.

Grant, Kenneth. *Images & Oracles of Austin Osman Spare.* London: Fulgar Limited, 2003.

Hine, Phil. *Yoginis: Sex, Death and Possession in Early Tantras.* London: The Original Falcon Press, 2022.

Kaimal, Padma. *Scattered Goddesses: Travels with the Yoginis.* Ann Arbor: Association for Asian Studies, 2012.

Kaulajnananirnaya: The Esoteric Teachings of Matsyendrapada (Matsyendranatha) Sadguru of the Yogini Kaula School in the Tantra Tradition. Edited & translated by Satkari Mukhopadhyaya in collaboration with Stella Dupuis. New Delhi: Adittya Prakashan, 2012.

Kularnava Tantra. Translated by Ram Kumar Rai. Varanasi: Prachya Prakashan, 2010.

Lal, Kunwar. *The Cult of Desire: An Interpretation of Erotic Sculpture in India.* New York: University Books, 1966.

Magee, Michael. *Tantra Magick.* Bombay: Taraporevala, 1992.

Magee, Michael. *Vamakesvarimatam.* Text with English translation of the Vamakesvara Tantra. Varanasi: Prachya Prakashan, 1986.

Magee, Michael. *Yaksini Magic.* London: Twisted Trunk Publications, 2019.

McDaniel, June. *The Madness of the Saints: Ecstatic Religion in Bengal.* Chicago: Chicago University Press, 1989.

McDaniel, June. *Offering Flowers, Feeding Skulls: Popular Goddess Worship in West Bengal.* New York: Oxford University Press, 2004.

Norbu, Namkhai. *The Cycle of Day and Night (An Essential Tibetan Text on the Practice of Dzogchen).* Translated and edited by John Reynolds. Barrytown: Station Hill Press, 1984.

Odier, Daniel. *Tantric Kali: Secret Practices and Rituals.* Rochester: Inner Traditions, 2016.

Power, John. *Nu Tantras of the Uttarakaulas.* Chelmsford: Phoenix Publications, 2001.

Power, John. *The Rainbow Bridge: The Shakta Tantrika of the Uttarakaulas.* Chelmsford: Phoenix Publications, 2020.

Ramos, Imma. *Tantra: Enlightenment to Revolution.* London: Thames & Hudson, 2020.

Rawson, Philip. *The Art of Tantra.* London: Thames & Hudson, 1973.

Roy, Anamika. *Sixty-Four Yoginis: Cult, Icons and Goddesses.* Delhi: Primus Books, 2015.

Satpathy, Sarbeswar. *Sakti Iconography in Tantric Mahavidyas.* Calcutta: Punthi Pustak, 1991.

Sen, Ramprasad. *Mother of the Universe: Visions of the Goddess and Tantric Hymns of Enlightenment.* Translated from the original Bengali by Lex Hinton. Wheaton: Quest Books, 1994.

Woodroffe, Sir John. *Sakti and Sakta.* Madras: Ganesh & Company, 1987.

Glossary

This glossary gives brief explanations of many of the key terms and Sanskrit words found throughout this book. In some cases, there may be a specific technical usage that is identified, so as not to confuse with what may be more well-known or common usage. For a comprehensive tantrik glossary see Mike Magee's excellent *Shiva Shakti Mandalam* site:

shivashakti.com/glossary

Abhaya – Fearlessness. The name of a traditional *mudra*.

Advaida – Non-dual, not divided. Tradition of Indian philosophy and spiritual practices for experiencing pure consciousness.

Ahimsa – Non-violence.

Ananda – Bliss.

Apanga – Sidelong glance. Many tantric texts describe how the *Devi*, with just a sidelong glance, may bestow boons or curses.

Asastriya – Not according to scripture.

Avesa – Possession by *mantra*. The act of possession by the Yogini via *mantra* recitation.

Bhairavi – Tantrik goddesses that have a fierce, warrior countenance.

Bhakti – Devotional love, usually directed towards a Goddess or God.

Bhava – Feeling. In *Bhakti, bhava* is almost similar to possession, when one is overcome with the feelings for, and of, the Goddess.

Bija – Seed. The *bija* is the seed of a *mantra,* usually a single syllable with no rational meaning. *Bija* is also the seed of all of creation, the beginning of the manifestation of the universe. Symbolized with the *bindi.*

259

Bindi – From *bindu* (point or seed), a *bindi* is a mark on the forehead usually made from sandalwood paste, but sometimes with *sindoor,* ash, or menstrual blood.

Brumisparsha – A *mudra* where the fingers of the left or right hand (depending on ritual intent) are extended touching the earth. Usually symbolizes blessings and fertility.

Chakra – Wheel. Subtle energy vortices that roughly correspond to anatomical regions in the human body, as well as to certain constellations and planets in space.

Crore – 10 million. Used to indicate cosmic proportions.

Dakini – Witch. Another name for name for Yogini.

Damaru — A type of small drum with two heads, most commonly associated with the God Shiva. Used in tantrik rituals and celebrations.

Devi—Goddess.

Digambara — "Sky clad," naked.

Dzogchen — (Tibetan) "Great Perfection", also called *Atiyoga;* (Sanskrit) "highest yoga". Tradition of Indian-Tibetan Buddhist teachings for discovering the nature of mind.

Gayatri – Hymn or song. Also the name of a Goddess and her famous *mantra.*

Ghanas – Tribe, troop, band, gang. The rowdy companions of Shiva, led by the elephant-headed god, *Ganapati* ("Leader of the Ganas").

Iccha – Will. One of the three primary *Shaktis.*

Japa – Recitation.

Jata – A way of wearing long hair tied above the head in a top knot.

Jivanmukti – Liberated while still living.

Jnana – Knowledge. One of the three primary *Shaktis.*

Kala – Emanation. In some traditions there are 16 *Kalas* that flow from the female body according to the phase of the Moon. These are used for producing elixirs and alchemical operations.

Kalika – The Great Goddess in her form as *Kali,* the Dark Empress of the Universe who rules over Time itself.

Kama – Desire, lust.

Kamandalu – Water pot.

Kavacha – Armor. Every Goddess has her own magical armor that the *sadhaka* can wear for protection by reciting the appropriate *mantras* and placing it on the body with *nyasa.*

Kaula— Tantrik *Shakta* cult founded by Matsyendranath, circa 10th century CE.

Khatvanga – Large staff with a human skull.

Kriya – Action. One of the three primary *Shaktis.*

Kula – Clan, Tribe, Circle. Also a "part", as in the body parts of the Goddess.

Kumari—Virgin. The living goddess of Nepal in the form of a chosen pre-menstrual girl. Also, a name of the Goddess.

Kundalini – The "coiled one." She is the Goddess in the form of the fire snake situated in the base of the spine. When dormant she rests in the *Muladhara* chakra at the base of spine, coiled 3 ½ times around herself. When she is awakened, she rises up the spine, activating the *chakras* with her movement.

Lalita – She who plays. The Great Goddess in her form as *Tripurasundari.*

Lehenga – A type of women's ankle-length skirt that rides on the hips.

Lila – Play. The dance of the Goddess in her playful form of *Lalita* weaves the magical illusion of the universe, *maya.*

Lingam – The male generative organ. Represented symbolically with a smoothed cylindrical stone that represents the phallus of the god Shiva. When shown with a *Yoni* it is the *Shiva Lingam.*

Mada – Intoxication.

Mala – Rosary. Used for counting recitation of *mantra.* Composed of various materials, each having an affinity to different aspects of divinity.

Mantra – Sacred sounds, words or phrases that have spiritual power. A *mantra* is the God or Goddess in the form of sound. Female *mantras* are called *Vidya.*

Maya – Illusion. The material universe is composed of *maya*, from the *lila* of the goddess.

Moksa – Liberation, Self-Realization.

Mudra – Ritual or magical gestures, usually made with the hands. *Sadhakas* use *mudras* in their rituals. The Yoginis often appear giving *mudras.*

Namavali – Name list.

Natha – Lord.

Nitya – Eternity. Goddesses associated with the phases of the Moon, with 15 goddesses of bright Lunar fortnight, and 15 goddesses of the dark fortnight.

Nyasa – Placing. The magical act of installing or awakening deities in parts of the practitioner's body.

Panchadatu – A magical metal composed of five alloys: mercury, silver, copper, zinc and iron.

Panchamakara – Five *(pancha) Makara* (the letter "M"). The tantric offerings of five elements.

Panchatattva – Five *(pancha)* Elements *(tattva).* In the context of Tantra, this refers to the offering of the "Five M's" *(panchamakara).*

Parampara – Lineage, tradition. The lines of succession or pedigree in a lineage.

Puja – Worship, usually external ritual.

Sadhana – Tantrik discipline performed by the *sadhaka* to achieve *siddhi* or *moksha*.

Sadhaka—Tantrik practitioner; tantrika.

Saktis – Powers of Siva personified as female.

Sastriya – According to scripture.

Sahaja – Free, easy, spontaneous. Also, orgasm.

Samavesa – Possession.

Sari – A traditional women's draped dress, consisting of a piece of silk or cotton that is 5–9 yards (4.5–8 meters) long, wrapped around the waist with the remainder over one shoulder or the head.

Shakta – The doctrine of power, energy and the Goddess.

Shakti – Female principle of spiritual energy, personified as the Goddess. Power in its most fundamental aspect.

Siddha – Adept. One who wields *siddhi*.

Siddhi—Magical power.

Sindoor – Vermillion paste, traditionally made from cinnabar, turmeric and lime. Modern cosmetic variants are made from flower petals and sandalwood paste. Married Hindu women wear it in the crease of their hair to show their status. Also used to mark *bindi* and *tilak* on the forehead in societal and initiatory traditions. Symbolic of menstrual blood, which is used in some tantrik rites.

Smashana – Cremation ground.

Svecchacara – The path of living life according to one's own Will. The natural, spontaneous state of the adept who has integrated the three primary Shaktis (*Iccha, Jnana,* and *Kriya*).

Suvasini – "Sweet smelling woman" or "beautiful fragrance." The tantric priestess. A Yogini.

264   **Gregory Peters**

Tilaka – A forehead mark made with ash, sandalwood paste, or other ingredients that indicates spiritual dedication. It may indicate being a member of a tribe or dedication to a particular Goddess.

Unmada – Madness. In this context, the divine madness that intoxicates consciousness.

Vajra – Lightning Bolt. A tantrik ritual tool.

Varada – A *mudra* of blessing and grating boons.

Vidya – Knowledge. In the context of tantra, this is the highest spiritual knowledge, the Goddess herself. Also female or Goddess *mantra* is called *vidya*.

Vidyadhari – Sorceress of the highest divine knowledge, a name of Yoginis.

Yogini – Witch-like tantrik goddesses that reign over magic, sorcery, enchantments and yoga. Also female adepts of yoga, embodiments of *Shakti,* each an emissary of the Great Goddess.

Yogini Kaula – The tantric lineage of the Yoginis. Semi-legendary cult that may have been established by Matsyendranath when he was in Kamakhya. More recent evidence seems to indicate that such a formalized lineage never existed, in which case the Yogini Kaula emanates directly from the Yoginis.

Yoni – Female sexual organ. Representative of the Great Goddess, Creation, Shakti. When shown symbolically it is often with the *Lingam,* creating and empowering the *Shiva Lingam.*

About the Author

(Photo by the Author)

Gregory Peters is an explorer of consciousness who has written about tantra, non-duality, and the intersection of East-West spiritual practice. He is an initiate of several tantric lineages, Dzogchen, and Western esoteric traditions.

His previous book was *The Magickal Union of East and West: The Spiritual Path to New Aeon Tantra.* Other works include collaboration on *The Rainbow Bridge: Shakta Tantra of the Uttarakaulas*; co-editor of the *Thoth Tarot*; *Astrology & Other Selected Writings of Phyllis Seckler*; *The Kabbalah, Magick, and Thelema: Selected Writings Volume II*; the privately published book *Stellar Tantra*; *Masonic Writings*; and several articles both online and in print.

Gregory was born in Stanford, California and lives in Northern California with his wife and family. Hiking, trekking and travel are some of his favorite activities. A devotee of the Goddess Kali, he enjoys traveling to sacred sites around the world, exploring spiritual practices from many cultures and traditions. Nature is his primal worship, with the crisp air of the Himalayas or the deep forests favored over temples built by hand. Nature and the night sky hold a deep wisdom for us, if only we are willing to open up and experience.

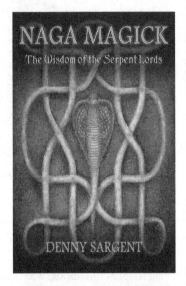

OTHER TITLES FROM FALCON PRESS

SEX MAGICK, TANTRA & TAROT
The Way of the Secret Lover
by Christopher S. Hyatt, Ph.D.

With Lon Milo DuQuette
Illustrated by David P. Wilson

A wealth of practical and passionate Tantric techniques utilizing the Archetypal images of the Tarot. Nothing is held back. All methods are explicit and clearly described.

"Each of us has a Guardian Angel — a companion and lover who waits just behind the images that flood our minds during sleep or reverie."

TANTRA WITHOUT TEARS
by Christopher S. Hyatt, Ph.D.

With S. Jason Black

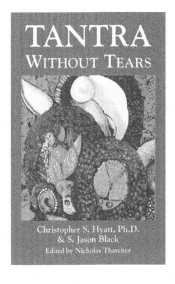

For the Westerner, this is the only book on Tantra you will ever need. A bold statement? Perhaps. However, the idea behind this book is simple. It is power. It is Kundalini, dressed in Western clothes. It describes experiences and techniques which allow you to glimpse beyond ordinary day-to-day reality, into the world of marvels — and horrors — of the Hindu and Tibetan Tantric traditions.

THE *Original* FALCON PRESS

Invites You to Visit Our Website:
http://originalfalcon.com

At our website you can:

- Browse the online catalog of all of our great titles
- Find out what's available and what's out of stock
- Get special discounts
- Order our titles through our secure online server
- Find products not available anywhere else including:
    - One of a kind and limited availability products
    - Special packages
    - Special pricing
- Get free gifts
- Join our email list for advance notice of New Releases and Special Offers
- Find out about book signings and author events
- Send email to our authors
- Read excerpts of many of our titles
- Find links to our authors' websites
- Discover links to other weird and wonderful sites
- And much, much more

Get online today at http://originalfalcon.com

Made in the USA
Coppell, TX
22 November 2024

40719569R00148